THE INTERPERSONAL, COGNITIVE, AND SOCIAL NATURE OF DEPRESSION

THE INTERPERSONAL, COGNITIVE, AND SOCIAL NATURE OF DEPRESSION

Edited by

Thomas E. Joiner
Jessica S. Brown
Janet Kistner
Florida State University

LAWRENCE ERLBAUM ASSOCIATES, PUBLISHERS
2006   Mahwah, New Jersey   London

Lawrence Erlbaum Associates, Inc., Publishers
10 Industrial Avenue
Mahwah, New Jersey 07430
www.erlbaum.com

Cover design by Tomai Maridou

CIP information for this volume may be obtained by contacting the Library of Congress.

    p. cm.

Includes bibliographical references and index.
ISBN 0-8058-5236-0 (cloth : alk. paper)
ISBN 0-8058-5874-1 (pbk. : alk. paper)

Books published by Lawrence Erlbaum Associates are printed on acid-free paper, and their bindings are chosen for strength and durability.

Printed in the United States of America
10 9 8 7 6 5 4 3 2 1

In honor of Jack Hokanson

Contents

Contributors

Lyn Y. Abramson, Ph.D. Department of Psychology, University of Wisconsin, Madison

Lauren B. Alloy, Ph.D. Department of Psychology, Temple University, Philadelphia, Pennsylvania

Jessica S. Brown, M.S. Department of Psychology, Florida State University, Tallahassee

Joanne Davila, Ph.D. Department of Psychology, State University of New York at Stony Brook

Ian H. Gotlib, Ph.D. Department of Psychology, Stanford University, Stanford, California

Constance Hammen, Ph.D. Department of Psychology, University of California, Los Angeles

Steven D. Hollon, Ph.D. Department of Psychology, Vanderbilt University, Nashville, Tennessee

Sheri L. Johnson, Ph.D. Department of Psychology, University of Miami, Coral Gables, Florida

Thomas E. Joiner, Ph.D. Department of Psychology, Florida State University, Tallahassee

Daniel N. Klein, Ph.D. Department of Psychology, State University of New York at Stony Brook

Janet Kistner, Ph.D. Department of Psychology, Florida State University, Tallahassee

Peter M. Lewinsohn, Ph.D. Oregon Research Institute, Eugene

Björn Meyer, Ph.D. Clinical and Health Psychology Research Centre, University of Roehampton, London, United Kingdom

Paul Rohde, Ph.D. Oregon Research Institute, Eugene

William P. Sacco, Ph.D. Department of Psychology, University of South Florida, Tampa

John R. Seeley, Ph.D. Oregon Research Institute, Eugene

Sara J. Steinberg, M.A. Department of Psychology, State University of New York at Stony Brook

Christine A. Vaughan, M.A. Department of Psychology, University of South Florida, Tampa

Ray W. Winters, Ph.D. Department of Psychology, University of Miami, Coral Gables, Florida

Preface

At a time when depression research was dominated by strictly behavioral and cognitive approaches, an interpersonal approach to depression emerged as an alternative. This was a milestone in psychological depression research, in that it opened up new vistas for understanding depression in real context and is the antecedent of current efforts to integrate intrapsychic and interpersonal views of depression. The goal of this volume is to concretize and celebrate this milestone development and to foster its sequelae, by bringing together the primary figures from interpersonal, cognitive, and behavioral viewpoints for a state-of-the-art treatment of the psychology of depression.

There is a healthy tension in the field of psychological depression research among these various perspectives. The true integration of interpersonal, social psychological, and cognitive-behavioral approaches is the most important theoretical issue in the field of the psychology of depression, and yet we feel it has not been well addressed in any forum. This book was written to provide cutting-edge research and theoretical perspectives on this issue, and therefore is an essential resource for current researchers. However, this book is also appropriate for clinicians, because it has direct clinical relevance. It is our hope that this book will be read by researchers and practitioners in a variety of fields, such as psychology, psychiatry, and sociology. Our goal is both to inform and enhance treatment as well as to stimulate future, more integrative research into the nature of depression.

In true integrative fashion, this book does not limit itself to the nature of depression in adulthood—research on potential causes and predictors of depression in childhood, adolescence, young adulthood, and beyond is additionally addressed. Also included is a review of current treatments for depression. A model of bipolar disorder is presented that explains the development of both depressed and manic phases. There is research that focuses more on women, as well as research that focuses on both genders.

OVERVIEW OF THE BOOK

The first chapter, by Kistner, addresses actual peer acceptance and perceived peer acceptance in children as they relate to depression. This chapter extends interpersonal and cognitive approaches to children, and insofar as it emphasizes both actual and perceived interpersonal acceptance, is a promising approach for theoretical integration. This is a relatively new area of research, and this chapter both provides a valuable review of the state of this literature and illuminates where more research is needed. Additionally, by understanding the risk factors discussed in the chapter, clinicians may be better able to identify and address depression in children.

The second chapter, by Davila and Steinberg, focuses on a specific type of interpersonal dysfunction in depressed adolescents: romantic dysfunction. Because adolescence is a time when romantic relationships first develop and set the stage for adult relationships, the interference of depression on this important developmental process is an area of concern. Furthermore, this line of research has been woefully neglected to date.

The third chapter, by Lewinsohn, Rohde, Seeley, Klein, and Gotlib, reviews the Oregon Adolescent Depression Project, which has followed approximately 1,500 people for 10 years, starting when participants were 14 to 18 years old. Participants were regularly assessed on a range of diagnostic, psychological, social, demographic, and other indexes. This chapter examines the relation between an episode of major depression in adolescence and the development of later episodes of psychopathology, and on what interpersonal and psychological variables predict good and poor psychosocial outcome among people with a history of adolescent depression. Given the high recurrence rates of depression, these findings are useful not only in predicting recurrence, but also for developing treatments that may lower risk of recurrence.

The fourth chapter, by Hammen, focuses on the effect of depression on personal relationships among women. This chapter reviews new data from a 5-year longitudinal study of risk for depression among young women in the transition from high school to young adulthood. Given that the average age of onset of depression is the early to mid-20s, research on depression risk in this age group is of the utmost importance. A model of risk for depression is postulated in this chapter that includes not only interpersonal processes, but also cognitive and social processes.

In the fifth chapter, Abramson and Alloy review the cognitive vulnerability to depression hypothesis and discuss new research that tests it. This review focuses on the recent large-scale Temple–Wisconsin Cognitive Vulnerability to Depression Project, which has produced compelling support for the cognitive view of depression. New directions are discussed, including the possible developmental origins of negative cognitive style.

The sixth chapter, by Sacco and Vaughan, presents a social-cognitive model of interpersonal processes in depression. The model proposes that adverse interpersonal outcomes in the lives of depressed persons are primarily influenced by two sources: socially unskilled behavior on the part of depressed people, and the negative mental construction in the minds of others who interact with depressed people. This model thus spans interpersonal, social-cognitive, and behavioral viewpoints, and represents a possible direction for true theoretical integration.

The seventh chapter, by Hollon, reviews the use of cognitive therapy as a treatment for depression. It describes a series of studies that have tested the notion that cognitive therapy works to reduce existing distress via the disconfirmation of negative expectations (a proximal mediator) while also working to prevent symptom return and the onset of future episodes via the amelioration of the propensity to generate negative self-referential causal attributions for negative life events. The studies involve both acute treatment trials with depressed clinical populations and pure prevention studies with nonclinical populations at elevated risk.

Finally, the last chapter, by Johnson, Winters, and Meyer, looks at life stress and the social environment, particularly as they relate to bipolar disorder. Research on these areas is presented as it relates to both episodes of depression and episodes of mania. This work is an example of a new direction in mood disorders research—namely, the extension of interpersonal and cognitive approaches from depression to bipolar disorder.

CONCLUDING REMARKS

We hope that by providing reviews of new theoretical models of the development and maintenance of depression, further research on this important subject will be stimulated. We also hope that trainees and practitioners find that these reviews shed light on the treatments for this disorder. Depression is a complex disorder that cannot fully be understood by examining it from only one angle. True integrative models of depression are our only hope for a complete understanding of this disorder.

Chapter 1

Children's Peer Acceptance, Perceived Acceptance, and Risk for Depression

Janet Kistner
Florida State University

Understanding the etiology of depression is one of the most important goals of depression researchers. Ingram (2001) went so far as to assert that "the future of depression research is back," a reference to the importance of investigating characteristics and experiences of childhood as possible causes and contributors to the later development of depression. Prospective longitudinal studies that assess hypothesized childhood precursors of depression are critical for answering some of the most pressing questions about the origins of depression. In the late 1990s and into the 2000s, the number of such studies increased dramatically. Most of these studies focused on contributions of family factors to the origins of depression (cf., Goodman & Gotlib, 1999). This is an important area of study, but relationships outside the family—particularly children's relationships with peers—also contribute to children's risk for later psychopathology (Parker & Asher, 1987). This chapter focuses on children's peer acceptance and risk for depression.

A few caveats are in order before proceeding to review research on peer acceptance and depression. First, there is strong consensus that there are multiple causes of depression; low peer acceptance is but one of many possible contributors to the development of depression. Second, the impact of low social acceptance is not specific to depression; low peer acceptance is associated with a wide range of negative outcomes. Nonetheless, studies of prospective associations between peer acceptance in childhood and risk for depression are informative, because of the central role accorded to social acceptance by leading psychosocial theories of depression (e.g., Cole, 1990; Coyne, 1976; Lewinsohn, 1974). Also, the link between children's perceptions of their acceptance and later depression are pertinent to cognitive theories of depression (e.g., Beck, 1967).

This chapter reviews associations among peer acceptance, perceived acceptance, and depressive symptoms in the period of middle childhood. This is an important age group to target for research on these associations, for several reasons. First, there is growing evidence of increased prevalence of depression in adolescence as well as a decrease in the age of first onset of depression (Lewinsohn, Hops, Roberts, Seeley, & Andrews, 1993; Verhulst, Van Der Ende, Ferdinand, & Kasius, 1997). These statistics underscore the need to identify preadolescents who are at risk for depression, and to increase our understanding of the factors that contribute to the development of depression. Second, establishing positive peer relationships is a developmentally appropriate and important task in middle childhood, and thus is an area of competence that is likely to affect children's risk for depression. Third, by middle childhood, children's perceptions of their social acceptance are fairly well established and can be reliably and validly measured. Prior to age 8, children's self-perceptions tend to be glowingly positive and unrealistic (Harter, 1998). As children's cognitive abilities develop and they begin to rely on social comparisons to evaluate themselves, self-enhancing biases give way to more realistic self-perceptions. Still, there are individual differences in perceptual discrepancies in middle childhood, just as there are at older ages; the implications of discrepant perceptions are important for understanding the developmental origins of depression.

The emphasis in this chapter is on prospective longitudinal studies that test hypotheses about causal associations among children's perceived and actual peer acceptance and risk for depression. For the most part, these studies investigate associations between children's peer acceptance and depressive symptoms rather than clinically diagnosed cases of depression. Although there are differing points of view about generalizing results from research on depressive symptoms in a typical population to clinically diagnosed depression (Benazon & Coyne, 1999; Joiner, Metalsky, Katz, & Beach, 1999a), identifying childhood predictors of increases in depressive symptoms is important for understanding the origins of depression. Three questions pertaining to causal associations among children's peer relationships and risk for depression are addressed in this chapter: Is low peer acceptance a cause or consequence of depression? What role do children's perceptions of peer acceptance play in risk for depression? Are negatively biased perceptions of peer acceptance a cause or consequence of children's depression? Before reviewing the research that bears on these questions, a brief description of the most commonly used measures of peer acceptance is presented.

MEASURES OF CHILDREN'S PEER RELATIONSHIPS

Obtaining reliable and valid measures of how well people are liked by persons with whom they have regular contact is a challenge for researchers, particularly when the focus of research is adults' social acceptance. It is impractical (and probably objectionable to research participants) to gather information about acceptance from coworkers, friends, and acquaintances. This is likely the reason that researchers have relied on self-report measures of acceptance or laboratory measures of social interactions. Self-report measures are problematic because they fail to distinguish between cognitive distortions and veridical appraisals of acceptance, and the validity of observers' ratings of brief social interactions with unfamiliar persons in laboratory settings has been challenged (Ackerman & DeRubeis, 1991). Some researchers have responded to these criticisms by gathering information about acceptance from familiar others, such as spouses, college roommates, or close friends, and much has been learned from these studies (e.g., Hammen et al., 1995; Hokanson, Rubert, Welker, Hollander, & Hedeen, 1989). Still, these ratings are typically based on a single informant who is in a unique relationship with the target individual, so the degree to which findings based on these measures generalize to relationships with others is open to question.

One advantage that child researchers have over those that conduct research with adults is the availability of reliable and valid measures of children's social acceptance by familiar peers (Kupersmidt & Dodge, 2004). Ratings or nominations of acceptance are obtained from peers (typically classmates) or adult informants who are very knowledgeable about children's acceptance by peers (e.g., parents, teachers). For the rating scale measures, children indicate how much they like to play or spend time with individual peers; comparable measures assess parents' and teachers' perceptions of children's peer acceptance. Nomination measures ask children to identify peers they like most (LM) and those they like least (LL). Nominations may be used as separate indexes of children's social status among peers or combined to form a single measure of peer acceptance by subtracting standardized LL from LM nominations (often referred to as *social preference scores*). In addition, classifications based on sociometric nominations have been developed to distinguish between "rejected" children (those who receive high numbers of LL nominations and few or no LM nominations) and "neglected" children (those who receive very few or no nominations of either type). For the purposes of this chapter, *peer acceptance* refers to individual differences in children's social acceptance by peers. When distinctions among measures are important for interpreting results across studies reviewed in this chapter, they are noted.

LOW PEER ACCEPTANCE: CAUSE, CONSEQUENCE, OR CORRELATE OF DEPRESSION

There is no question that low peer acceptance is associated with depression, both elevated depressive symptoms and clinically diagnosed depression (for review, see Segrin, 2000). What is not clear is whether this association is a causal one and, if causally linked, what is the direction of the causal flow: Does low acceptance lead to depression, or does depression lead to low acceptance?

In Lewinsohn's behavioral theory of depression (1974), social skills deficits are viewed as causal antecedents to depression (i.e., persons with social skills deficits are likely to be avoided by others, leading to low rates of social reinforcement, which in turn cause depression). Similarly, Cole (1990, 1991) posited that low social acceptance and other competence deficits causally contribute to depression in childhood. Social acceptance is also central in Coyne's interactional model of depression (Coyne, 1976). This model argues that interpersonal behaviors of distressed and mildly depressed persons lead to social avoidance and rejection by others. These negative social consequences, in turn, exacerbate depressive symptoms, leading to more severe and chronic depression. Later revisions of Lewinsohn's behavioral theory of depression also highlight an emphasis on the negative impact of depression on social acceptance (Lewinsohn, Hoberman, Teri, & Hautzinger, 1985). Depressive episodes were hypothesized to leave residual "scars" in the form of disrupted social relationships (Rohde, Lewinsohn, & Seeley, 1990; Zeiss & Lewinsohn, 1988).

Children's perceptions of their peer acceptance are also important for understanding the origins of depression. In Cole's model of depression in childhood, low peer acceptance, as well as competence deficits in other domains, increases risk for depression through its impact on children's self-perceptions. This model posits that negative feedback experienced by children with competence deficits inhibits the emergence and differentiation of positive self-perceptions, and this then predisposes children to become depressed. Self-perceptions also play a central role in cognitive theories of depression (e.g., Beck, 1967), although these theories focus on distorted rather than accurate self-perceptions. Prospective studies of associations among children's peer acceptance, perceptions of their acceptance, and risk for depression provide ideal opportunities to test hypotheses about whether perceived and/or actual problems of social acceptance are causal antecedents, consequences, or merely correlates of depression.

In a review of research investigating associations between social acceptance and depression, Segrin (2000) concluded that there was little empirical support for causal links. A majority of the longitudinal studies that had been conducted at the time of Segrin's review failed to support the hypothesis that problematic social interactions predicted changes in depression among adults. Nor was there much support for the hypothesis that depression leads to impaired social acceptance. Based on results of a couple of longitudinal studies of children that were described in that review, Segrin speculated that causal associations between social acceptance and depression might be stronger in childhood. A number of prospective longitudinal studies investigating associations among children's peer acceptance and depression have been published since Segrin's review. Results of these studies are reviewed next.

Depression as a Cause of Children's Low Peer Acceptance

Depressed children tend to elicit negative responses from peers, even when their social contact is limited to brief interactions with unfamiliar peers (e.g., Baker, Milich, & Manolis, 1996; Connolly, Geller, Marton, & Kutcher, 1992; Rudolph, Hammen, & Burge, 1994). For example, Baker et al. (1996) found that girls who were randomly paired to interact with a dysphoric peer were rated as being less happy and less positive toward their partners than were girls who interacted with nondysphoric peers. These findings are consistent with results of prior research and provide support for the hypothesis that social interactions with depressed children have a negative impact on peers. The concurrent, correlational nature of these studies, however, does not allow one to draw conclusions about a causal link.

Only two prospective studies examined the contribution of depression to later acceptance by familiar peers, controlling for initial acceptance. Cole, Martin, Powers, and Truglio (1996) examined changes in depressive symptoms across a school year for children in Grades 3 and 6. Depressive symptoms at Time 1 did not predict peer acceptance at Time 2, after controlling for peer acceptance at Time 1. Similar results were reported by Nolan, Flynn, and Garber (2003) for a sample of young adolescents (Grades 6–8). Depressive symptoms, assessed via self- and parent reports, did not predict changes in peer rejection over a 3-year interval.

To date, little attention has been given to possible moderators of associations between depression and peer acceptance. Little and Garber (1995) found that predictive associations between depressive symptoms and peer acceptance among fifth and sixth graders were moderated by the level of stress that the children were experiencing. Decrements in children's peer acceptance were found for children with elevated depressive symptoms at Time 1, but only those who reported few or no stressors. Among children who were experiencing high levels of stress at the start of the study, depression was unrelated to changes in acceptance. This moderating effect of stress on the link between depression and acceptance is consistent with results of an experimental study by Peterson, Mullins, and Ridley-Johnson (1985). Peterson et al. (1985) presented children with videotapes of confederates portraying either a depressed or nondepressed child who was experiencing few or many stressful life events. The children were then asked to rate how much they would like to interact with each confederate. The depressed confederate was more rejected than was the nondepressed confederate, but only in the low-stress condition. The depressed confederate who was depicted as experiencing major stressful events was as accepted as the nondepressed confederate and was significantly more accepted than the depressed confederate in the low-stress condition. These findings suggest that children may have greater tolerance for depressed behaviors of peers if they are experiencing stressful life events.

In addition to greater tolerance of peers, Little and Garber (1995) speculated that the moderating effect of stress on the link between depression and changes in peer acceptance in naturalistic settings may be influenced by other factors. Depressive symptoms may be more transient among children who are experiencing stressful life events (i.e., depressive symptoms and associated behaviors that were likely to elicit negative reactions from peers may quickly diminish when stressful events dissipate), whereas depressive symptoms may be more chronic among depressed children who report few stressors and thus have a more negative impact on children's relationships with peers. Alternatively, the expression of depression and/or behavioral correlates of depression may differ between low- and high-stress groups in ways that affect peer reactions. For example, depressed children with low stress may exhibit more irritability, whereas depressed children experiencing high stress may exhibit more sadness. Behaviors associated with sadness are likely to evoke less negative reactions from peers than are behaviors associated with irritability. Unfortunately, little is known about the mechanisms by which depression may negatively affect children's acceptance or the mechanisms that may account for moderating effects of stress on the association between depression and acceptance.

Low Peer Acceptance as a Cause of Depression

Relative to the number of studies that investigated the contribution of depression to children's peer acceptance, much more research has investigated the contribution of low peer acceptance to children's risk for depression. The disproportionate attention to the latter causal path reflects the strong influence of the developmental psychopathology model. Identification of risk factors for later psychopathology, a major goal of this model, has resulted in a substantial body of research examining negative outcomes associated with low peer acceptance in childhood. Results of longitudinal studies in which predictive associations between peer acceptance and depression were examined generally support the hypothesis that low-accepted children are at greater risk for depression (Boivin, Hymel, & Bukowski, 1995; Coie, Lochman, Terry, & Hyman, 1992; Coie, Terry, Lenox, Lochman, & Hyman, 1995; Cole et al., 1996; DeRosier, Kupersmidt, & Patterson, 1994; Kupersmidt & Patterson, 1991; Lochman & Wayland, 1994; Morison & Masten, 1991; Panak & Garber, 1992), although a few studies did not (Hoza, Molina, Bukowski, & Sippola, 1995; Hymel, Rubin, Rowden, & LeMare, 1990; Kistner, Balthazor, Risi, & Burton, 1999; Ollendick, Weist, Borden, & Green, 1992). However, few of these longitudinal studies controlled for initial depression.

Of the five prospective studies that controlled for initial depression, three discerned significant predictive links (Boivin et al., 1995; Cole et al., 1996; Kistner, David, Repper, & Joiner, in press), whereas two did not (Kistner et al., 1999; Panak & Garber, 1992). Boivin et al. (1995) found that low peer acceptance predicted modest but significant changes in depression over a 2-year interval for children ages 9 to 12. Similarly, Kistner et al., (in press) discovered that peer acceptance predicted changes in depressive symptoms over a 6-month interval for children in Grades 3 to 5, although the magnitude of this predictive link was small ($pr = .08, p < .05$). Cole et al. (1996) found that peer acceptance predicted changes in depressive symptoms for sixth graders but not third graders. The two studies that failed to find a significant association between peer acceptance and changes in depressive symptoms had smaller samples than did those that reported significant associations, suggesting that the null findings may be due to insufficient power to detect a small effect size.

Baron and Kenney (1986) suggested that when associations among variables are small and inconsistent across studies, this may reflect unassessed moderating variables. Results of the study conducted by Cole and his colleagues (Cole et al., 1996) offer some support for a moderating effect of developmental level. Peer acceptance predicted changes in depressive symptoms over a 6-month interval for sixth graders but not for third graders. Another possible moderator of the association between peer acceptance and depression is the stability of low peer acceptance. Assessment of peer acceptance at a single point in time, which is typical of most of the research reviewed, does not take into account the stability of low acceptance. Boivin et al. (1995) found a more robust association with depression when change in peer acceptance between Time 1 and Time 2, rather than level of acceptance at Time 1, was the predictor variable. Consistent with these results, Panak and Garber (1992) noted that change in peer acceptance, but not initial peer acceptance, predicted changes in depression for their sample. One interpretation of these results is that children with low acceptance at two points in time, as well as those whose acceptance is in decline, are at greater risk for depression than are children with milder and more transient social difficulties.

One potential moderator that may also function as a mediator of the link between low acceptance and depression is children's self-perceptions of acceptance. In Cole's competence-based model of depression, internalization of negative feedback is what increases risk for depression. Internalization of negative feedback may be affected by developmental level as well as the stability of peer relationship problems. Older children and children with chronic social difficulties are likely to have a longer and more consistent history of negative feedback about their acceptance and thus are more likely to internalize negative external appraisals than are younger children and those with more mild and transient problems in getting along with peers. The role of perceived acceptance in understanding the developmental origins of depression is considered next.

CHILDREN'S PERCEPTIONS OF THEIR PEER ACCEPTANCE AND RISK FOR DEPRESSION

Rudolph and Clark (2001) noted a paradox between interpersonal and cognitive theories of depression regarding accuracy of self-perceptions and implications for depression. Interpersonal theories assume at least some awareness of interpersonal problems among depressed persons (i.e., presumably attempts to seek reassurance from others is stimulated by perceptions of depressed persons that others are withdrawing from them). Cole's competency-based model focuses on increased risk of depression of children who internalize negative peer feedback (i.e., accurately perceive that they have competence deficits); however, children may not accurately perceive their acceptance. If low-accepted children have positively biased perceptions of their acceptance, their risk of depression should be lower than that of low-accepted children who are aware of how peers feel about them. Cognitive theories of depression emphasize the role of negatively distorted perceptions in developing and/or maintaining depression (e.g., Beck, 1967). Children with negatively biased self-perceptions are expected to be at increased risk for depression. In the next two sections of this chapter, research on the role of self-perceptions on risk for depression is reviewed. Studies that examined predictive associations between children's perceived acceptance and depression are described first, followed by a review of studies that assessed accuracy of children's perceived acceptance and the implications of accuracy for predicting depressive symptoms.

Negative Perceptions of Peer Acceptance: Cause or Consequence of Depression?

According to Cole's (1990) competency-based model of depression, children with competence deficits (including low peer acceptance) are expected to receive negative feedback from others. Repeated exposure to negative feedback in one or more domains of importance to children is purported to inhibit the emergence and differentiation of positive self-schemas and increase children's risk for depression. Thus, children's perceptions of their peer relations are proximal causes of depression, and their self-perceptions of competence mediate the link between competence deficits and risk for depression.

Longitudinal studies offer support for predictive associations between perceived acceptance and depressive symptoms over 1-month (Wierzbicki & McCabe, 1988), 2-year (McGrath & Repetti, 2002; Panak & Garber, 1992), and 7-year intervals (Kistner et al., 1999), after controlling for initial depression. Studies conducted by Cole and his colleagues that examined children's perceptions of competence across multiple domains, one of which was peer acceptance, offered additional support for the hypothesis that negative perceptions of peer acceptance causally contribute to increased depressive symptoms (Cole, Jacquez, & Maschman, 2001; Cole, Martin, & Powers, 1997; Tram & Cole, 2000). One of these studies also demonstrated that children's self-perceptions mediated associations between actual competence deficits and changes in depression (Cole et al., 1997).

Three studies tested the reverse hypothesis—that depression contributes to changes in children's perceived peer acceptance (Cole et al., 1996; Kistner, David, et al., 2005; McGrath & Repetti, 2002); a convergent pattern of results across studies support this hypothesis. McGrath and Repetti (2002) found that depression predicted changes in children's perceptions of peer acceptance across 1- and 2-year intervals for their sample of fourth graders. Similarly, Kistner et al. (in press) noted that for children in Grades 3 through 5, depressive symptoms at Time 1 predicted perceived peer acceptance at Time 2, controlling for initial perceptions of acceptance. Cole et al. (1996) partially replicated these results; depressive symptoms predicted decrements in self-perceptions of third graders but not sixth graders. The investigators speculated that as children's perceptions of acceptance become more stable, the influence of depression on self-perceptions decreases, thus accounting for the findings that depression predicted changes in perceptions of third graders but not sixth graders. Additional research on moderating effects of developmental level on associations between self-perceptions and depression is needed, with an effort focused on discovering the mechanisms that may account for it.

In summary, there is some support for reciprocal effects: Negative perceptions of acceptance predicted increases in depression, and depression predicted decrements in children's perceptions of their peer acceptance. What cannot be discerned from these studies is whether the negative self-perceptions associated with depression reflect veridical appraisals of children's social standing among peers or negatively biased self-perceptions. To draw conclusions about the role that biased or distorted self-perceptions play in the origins of depression requires that children's self-perceptions be compared to some criterion in order to assess discrepancies. The next section reviews studies that assessed links between discrepant self-perceptions and children's risk for depression.

Negatively Biased Self-Perceptions and Children's Risk for Depression

Much of the research on discrepant self-perceptions and depression has focused on children's academic competence or task performance rather than social acceptance. This is understandable, because criterion measures against which to compare self-perceptions are more readily available in nonsocial domains. Due to the dearth of studies that focus specifically on discrepant social self-perceptions and depression, this review includes the findings of research on associations between depression and negatively biased perceptions in multiple domains.

Evidence for concurrent associations between children's depressive symptoms and negatively biased self-perceptions is drawn from three types of studies. Comparisons of children grouped according to high and low depressive symptoms have revealed more negative self-perceptions in depressed groups, despite equivalent academic and laboratory task performance (e.g., Asarnow, Carlson, & Guthrie, 1987; Kendall, Stark, & Adam, 1990; Meyer, Dyck, & Petrinack, 1989) and teacher-rated social acceptance (Rudolph & Clark, 2001). Studies of children with comparable competence and congruent versus negatively biased perceptions have reported more depression among children with negatively biased perceptions (Miserandino, 1996; Phillips, 1984). Finally, correlations between discrepant self-perceptions and depressive symptoms have offered additional support for the hypothesis that negatively biased perceptions are associated with elevated depressive symptoms (Cole, Martin, Peeke, Seroczynski, & Fier, 1999; Cole, Martin, Peeke, Seroczynski, & Hoffman, 1998), although one study failed to support this hypothesis (Proffitt & Weisz, 1992).

Taken together, there is consistent evidence of concurrent associations between negatively biased perceptions and depression. These findings have often been interpreted as evidence of a cognitive vulnerability to depression (i.e., negatively biased perceptions lead to depression), but one could just as plausibly interpret concurrent correlations as support for the hypothesis that depression leads to the development of negatively biased perceptions. Lewinsohn and his colleagues (Rohde et al., 1990; Zeiss & Lewinsohn, 1988) hypothesized that depression may leave residual negative effects on functioning, or "scars." Depression has been shown to affect memory and lead to negative cognitive errors in adults (e.g., Segal, 1988) and children (e.g., Whitman & Leitenberg, 1990). These cognitive disturbances may impair children's abilities to form accurate/unbiased views about their social standing among peers. Longitudinal studies are important for assessing causal links and determining the direction of influence between biased perceptions and depression.

Six longitudinal studies (Brendgen, Vitaro, Turgeon, Poulin, & Wanner, 2004; Cole et al., 1998, 1999; Hoffman, Cole, Martin, Tram, & Seroczynski, 2000; Kistner et al., 2005a; McGrath & Repetti, 2002) examined the contribution of negatively biased perceptions of acceptance to changes in children's depressive symptoms. In three of these six studies, negatively biased perceptions did not significantly predict changes in depression (Cole et al., 1998; Kistner et al., in press; McGrath & Repetti, 2002). Brendgen et al. (2004) found that underestimation was predictive of increased depression for a large sample of children in Grades 4 through 6. Cole et al. (1999) discerned limited support for a predictive link between underestimation of academic competence and depressive symptoms, with less robust findings for children (Grades 3–6) relative to young adolescents (Grades 6–8). Finally, Hoffman et al. noted that negatively biased perceptions predicted changes in depressive symptoms in a sample of children and adolescents. This study differed from the other studies in how depression was measured; a composite measure of depression based on maternal ratings and self-report was used instead of relying solely on self-report. Given the low agreement between maternal and child reports of depressive symptoms (for review, see Kazdin, 1994), the validity of this composite measure is questionable. It seems likely that this measurement difference accounts for the different pattern of results obtained in this study relative to others.

In contrast to weak and inconsistent support for the hypothesis that discrepant self-perceptions causally contribute to depression, all five of the longitudinal studies that examined the impact of depressive symptoms on negatively biased perceptions of acceptance supported the reverse hypothesis (Cole et al., 1998, 1999; Hoffman et al., 2000; Kistner et al., in press; McGrath & Repetti, 2002): Higher levels of depressive symptoms predicted underestimation of competence at Time 2, controlling for initial tendencies to underestimate competence.

In summary, there is some support for bidirectional influences of negatively biased perceptions and depression, with stronger support for the hypothesis that depressive symptoms lead to negatively biased perceptions than for the reverse. Thus, contrary to what cognitive theories of depression predict, negatively biased self-perceptions appear to be a product of depressive symptoms rather than a cause of them. Future research should focus on the mechanisms by which depression influences children's self-perceptions of acceptance.

DIRECTIONS FOR FUTURE RESEARCH

In his review of the adult literature, Segrin (2000) concluded that there was little evidence of causal associations between low social acceptance and depression. Longitudinal studies resulted in many null findings when testing the hypothesis that low social acceptance causally contributes to depression. Similarly, little support was found for the hypothesis that depression causally contributes to decreases in social acceptance. Based on just a couple of studies conducted with children that were included in his review, Segrin speculated that stronger support for one or both of these hypotheses might be found in childhood.

A review of the child literature does yield more support for hypothesized causal associations between low acceptance and depression in children than was found in the adult literature, but this evidence is neither robust nor clear-cut. Much remains to be learned about what leads some low-accepted children to become depressed whereas others do not. Also, depression may result in impaired social relationships, but not for all children. What variables moderate prospective links between peer acceptance and depression? Answers to these questions have both theoretical and clinical implications.

When Is Depression Likely to Negatively Impact Children's Peer Acceptance?

Depressed children, on average, elicit more negative reactions from peers than do nondepressed children, but little is known about the specific behaviors that account for negative peer reactions. Also, some depressed children are well liked by peers; how do these children differ from those with low acceptance? Perhaps only when depression reaches a certain threshold of severity does it negatively affect children's peer acceptance. Alternatively, specific behaviors that characterize some but not all depressed children may result in impaired social relationships. One behavior that has gained attention in studies of adult depression is excessive reassurance seeking (Coyne, 1976; Joiner, Metalsky, Katz, & Beach, 1999b). A study by Abela et al. (2005) extended this line of research to adolescents. Reassurance seeking, in combination with insecure attachment, was associated with increased risk of depression among adolescents of depressed mothers. Assessment of reassurance-seeking behaviors among depressed children with and without peer relationship problems is a promising direction for future research.

Investigating the mechanisms that account for the moderating effect of stress on the association between depression and children's peer acceptance reported by Little and Garber (1995) is also a promising direction for future research. Stress is often found to moderate associations among risk and outcome variables, but what makes this particular finding so intriguing is that it was the combination of *low* stress and elevated depressive symptoms that predicted negative consequences for children's acceptance by peers. Were it not for the fact that a similar finding was obtained in a prior study using an experimental design (Peterson et al., 1985), this finding might be dismissed as spurious. With two studies using very different methods producing the same results, further examination of a moderating effect of stress on the depression–peer acceptance association is warranted. Is this effect accounted for by increased tolerance of peers due to the difficult circumstances experienced by some children, or are there behavioral differences between depressed children with high versus low stress that contribute to differences in acceptance?

Children's Self-Perceptions and Risk for Depression: Is Ignorance Bliss?

As Parker and Asher (1987) noted in their review of outcomes associated with low peer acceptance, "[I]ntuitively, we might expect children who are cognizant of their negative peer adjustment to show a pattern of adjustment different from that of children who are equally unpopular but unaware of it" (p. 383). Perceptions of peer acceptance seem particularly relevant to low-accepted children's risk for depression. Perceived competence is a more robust predictor of depression than are external appraisals of competence, and it mediates the association between competence deficits and depression. These findings are consistent with Cole's model of depression; it is the internalization of negative feedback (i.e., the resulting self-perceptions of acceptance) that is the proximal cause of depression. This leads to the following questions: Is ignorance bliss? Do positively biased perceptions protect low-accepted children from depression? Why are some children aware of negative external appraisals and others are not?

Overly positive and unrealistic self-perceptions are common among young children; just about all preschoolers think of themselves as very smart and popular. Sometime in the early grade school years, children become increasingly accurate about their competence. These developmental changes in accuracy of children's perceptions are attributed to changes in cognitive abilities (e.g., development of social comparison processes; increased understanding of inverse relations between effort and ability) as well as changes in their experiences (e.g., increases in negative feedback; grading practices that emphasize comparisons to others). These age-related cognitive and experiential changes account for why younger children, on average, are more likely to have overly positive self-perceptions, but they do not inform us about individual differences among children of the same ages. Attempts to understand why some low-accepted children internalize negative feedback (i.e., have negative, albeit accurate, perceptions of their peer acceptance) and others do not may shed some light on developmental precursors of depression.

Findings of several studies suggest that overly positive perceptions of peer acceptance do provide some "protection" from negative self-views and depressive symptoms. Brendgen et al. (2004) discerned that overly positive perceptions of acceptance predicted decrements in depressive symptoms and gains in peer acceptance across a school year. Similarly, Kistner, Stone, Ferdon, and Repper (2005) noted that overestimation of peer acceptance was associated with gains in feelings of self-worth and peer acceptance over a 6-month interval. In the latter study, two types of inflated perceptions of acceptance were assessed: A general measure asked children to rate their peer acceptance without specifying a peer referent group, and a more specific measure asked children to predict the acceptance ratings they would receive from specific peers. The benefits of overly positive perceptions (i.e., gains in self-worth and peer acceptance) were associated with general but not specific perceptions of peer acceptance. These results are consistent with an explanation generated by Taylor, Lerner, Sherman, Sage, and McDowell (2003) to reconcile discrepant results in the adult literature pertaining to whether inflated self-perceptions are adaptive or maladaptive. Taylor et al. (2003) proposed that self-enhancing perceptions that are more abstract in nature and not easily confirmed or disconfirmed are likely to be adaptive, whereas self-enhancement of more specific, verifiable perceptions are likely to be maladaptive.

Although ignorance may bliss for children with inflated self-perceptions, it may not be bliss for those who must interact with these children. Children with overly positive perceptions of their peer acceptance are more likely to exhibit aggression than are children with more realistic self-perceptions (e.g., David & Kistner, 2000; Hymel, Bowker, & Woody, 1993; Patterson, Kupersmidt, & Griesler, 1990; Zakriski & Coie, 1996). Several explanations have been generated for this association between aggression and positively biased perceptions of acceptance. Peers may be reluctant to give negative feedback to aggressive children, so the children's distorted perceptions may simply reflect lack of feedback rather than cognitive distortions. Alternatively, aggression may be a consequence of positively biased perceptions; to maintain positive self-perceptions, children may reject negative feedback, sometimes resulting in aggression toward peers (Baumeister & Boden, 1998; Baumeister, Smart, & Boden, 1996). Longitudinal studies are needed to address questions about the temporal order of influence of associations among aggression, depression, and discrepant self-perceptions.

Beyond Bias: Perceptual "Accuracy" and Children's Risk for Depression

For the most part, the only types of discrepant self-perceptions that have been studied in relation to depression are those that systematically overestimate (positive bias) or underestimate (negative bias) one's acceptance. What about children whose perceptions are discrepant in unsystematic ways, children who seem to lack awareness of who likes them more and who likes them less? Are depressed children less accurate in perceiving their social status among peers?

Assessing accuracy of self-perceptions requires comparison to a valid, objective criterion, a requirement that is difficult to meet when one is studying social self-perceptions. Kistner et al. (in press) developed a measure of perceptual accuracy by comparing acceptance ratings that children expected to receive from classmates to the ratings they actually received. To tease apart associations of bias and accuracy, Kistner et al. measured children's expected and received peer acceptance ratings along with CDI scores for a sample of third through fifth graders at the start and end of the school year. Multiple regression analyses were used to test for contributions of inaccurate and biased perceptions and depressive symptoms. Inaccurate but not biased perceptions predicted changes in depressive symptoms.

The mechanism by which inaccurate perceptions contribute to increased risk for depression merits further study. Self-verification theory posits that congruence of self-perceptions with external appraisals is important for developing a sense of certainty and predictability (Swann, Stein-Seroussi, & Giesler, 1992). The logical extension of this theory is that self-perceptions that are discrepant from the feedback, regardless of whether the discrepancies are positive or negative, are likely to lead to distress and possibly depression (Giesler, Josephs, & Swann, 1996).

Integrative Cognitive-Interpersonal Approaches

There is strong consensus that depression has multiple etiologies, yet studies are typically designed to pit one hypothesized cause against another. There are some exceptions to this general observation that may serve as examples for future investigations. For example, Rudolph and Clark (2001) tested skill-deficit and cognitive-distortion models of depression in children. As predicted by a skill-deficit model, depressed children were aware of their social standing among peers. In keeping with the cognitive-distortion model, depressed children were also more likely than were nondepressed children to have negatively biased self-perceptions of acceptance. Thus, both models of depression were supported by the results of this study.

Another example of testing for multiple contributors to depression comes from a study by Cole and his colleagues (Hoffman et al., 2000). Perceived competence was regressed onto externals appraisals of competence to form a measure of reflected appraisals (i.e., predictor scores) and discrepant perceptions (residual scores). Both reflected appraisals and discrepant perceptions made unique contributions to the prediction of changes in depressive symptoms. Interestingly, looking at the reverse hypothesis, the impact of depression was significant only for the measure of discrepant perceptions; elevated depression predicted perceptions that became more negatively biased over time. Unfortunately, as previously discussed, this study used maternal and self-ratings of depression to form a composite measure, so comparison of the results of this study to other studies may not be appropriate.

Finally, attention to the presence of subgroups within samples is important for advancing our understanding of multiple paths to depression. Some children may have a cognitive vulnerability to depression, whereas for others increased risk for depression stems from (accurate) internalization of negative feedback from others. Failure to consider these different subgroups is likely to lead to misleading results. For example, Kistner et al. (1999) analyzed the data for their full sample and found little to no support for either a skill-deficit or cognitive-distortion hypothesis. Further examination of the data revealed two subgroups of depressed children: those who were disliked by peers and were aware of their negative social status, and those who perceived themselves to be disliked by peers when, in fact, they were well accepted.

One of the unnecessary limitations of research investigating associations between social acceptance and depression is approaching studies with "either/or" questions such as "Is low acceptance a cause or consequence of depression?" and "Do negative perceptions of depressed children reflect negatively biased cognitions or veridical appraisals of competence deficits?" Future research should utilize research designs that are more consistent with the view that depression has multiple etiologies. For some children, a combination of skill deficits and biased perceptions may best account for depression. Alternatively, multiple paths to the depressive outcomes are likely, and this behooves researchers to test for subgroups within samples.

CONCLUSION

Research on reciprocal relations among children's peer acceptance, perceived peer acceptance, and risk for depression has the potential to advance our understanding of the developmental origins of depression. This area of research provides unique opportunities to refine our theories of depression by testing hypotheses about causal direction of influence, moderating variables, and likely underlying mechanisms. Furthermore, this research has implications for identifying those children at greatest risk for depression and for developing preventive interventions.

REFERENCES

Abela, J. R., Hankin, B. L., Haigh, E. A., Adams, P., Vinokuroff, T., & Trayhern, L. (2005). Interpersonal vulnerability to depression in high-risk children: The role of insecure attachment and reassurance seeking. *Journal of Clinical Child and Adolescent Psychology, 34,* 182–192.

Ackerman, R., & DeRubeis, R. J. (1991). Is depressive realism real? *Clinical Psychology Review, 11,* 565–584.

Asarnow, J. R., Carlson, G. A., & Guthrie, D. (1987). Coping strategies, self-perceptions, hopelessness, and perceived family environments in depressed and suicidal children. *Journal of Consulting and Clinical Psychology, 55,* 361–366.

Baker, M., Milich, R., & Manolis, M. B. (1996). Peer interactions of dysphoric adolescents. *Journal of Abnormal Child Psychology, 24,* 241–255.

Baron, R. M., & Kenny, D. A. (1986). The moderator–mediator variable distinction in social psychological research: Conceptual, strategic, and statistical considerations. *Journal of Personality and Social Psychology, 51,* 1173–1182.

Baumeister, R. F., & Boden, J. M. (1998). Aggression and the self: High self-esteem, low self-control, and ego threat. In R. G. Geen & E. Donnerstein (Eds.), *Human aggression: Theories, research, and implications for social policy* (pp. 111–137). San Diego: Academic Press.

Baumeister, R. F., Smart, L., & Boden, J. M. (1996). Relation of threatened egotism to violence and aggression: The dark side of high self-esteem. *Psychological Review, 103,* 5–33.

Beck, A. T. (1967). *Depression: Clinical, experimental, and theoretical aspects.* New York: Harper & Row.

Benazon, N. R., & Coyne, J. C. (1999). The next step in developing an interactional description of depression? *Psychological Inquiry, 10,* 279–304.

Boivin, M., Hymel, S., & Bukowski, W. M. (1995). The roles of social withdrawal, peer rejection, and victimization by peers in predicting loneliness and depressed mood in childhood. *Development and Psychopathology, 7,* 765–786.

Brendgen, M., Vitaro, F., Turgeon, L., Poulin, F., & Wanner, B. (2004). Is there a dark side of positive illusions? Overestimation of social competence and subsequent adjustment in aggressive and nonaggressive children. *Journal of Abnormal Child Psychology, 32,* 305–320.

Coie, J. D., Lochman, J. E., Terry, R., & Hyman, C. (1992). Predicting early adolescent disorder from childhood aggression and peer rejection. *Journal of Consulting and Clinical Psychology, 60,* 783–792.

Coie, J. D., Terry, R., Lenox, K., Lochman, J., & Hyman, C. (1995). Childhood peer rejection and aggression as predictors of stable patterns of adolescent disorder. *Development and Psychopathology, 7,* 697–714.

Cole, D. A. (1990). Relation of social and academic competence to depressive symptoms in childhood. *Journal of Abnormal Psychology, 99,* 429.

Cole, D. A. (1991). Preliminary support for a competency-based model of depression in children. *Journal of Abnormal Psychology, 100,* 181–190.

Cole, D. A., Jacquez, F. M., & Maschman, T. L. (2001). Social origins of depressive cognitions: A longitudinal study of self-perceived competence in children. *Cognitive Therapy and Research, 25,* 377–395.

Cole, D. A., Martin, J. M., Peeke, L. G., Seroczynski, A. D., & Fier, J. (1999). Children's over- and underestimation of academic competence: A longitudinal study of gender differences, depression, and anxiety. *Child Development, 70*, 459–473.

Cole, D. A., Martin, J. M., Peeke, L. G., Seroczynski, A. D., & Hoffman, K. (1998). Are cognitive errors of underestimation predictive or reflective of depressive symptoms in children: A longitudinal study. *Journal of Abnormal Psychology, 107*, 481–496.

Cole, D. A., Martin, J. M., & Powers, B. (1997). A competency-based model of child depression: A longitudinal study of peer, parent, teacher, and self-evaluations. *Journal of Child Psychology and Psychiatry, 38*, 505–514.

Cole, D. A., Martin, J. M., Powers, B., & Truglio, R. (1996). Modeling causal relations between academic and social competence and depression: A multitrait-multimethod longitudinal study of children. *Journal of Abnormal Psychology, 105*, 258–270.

Connolly, J., Geller, S., Marton, P., & Kutcher, S. (1992). Peer responses to social interaction with depressed adolescents. *Journal of Clinical Child Psychology, 21*, 365–370.

Coyne, J. C. (1976). Toward an interactional description of depression. *Psychiatry, 39*, 28–40.

David, C., & Kistner, J. (2000). Do positive self-perceptions have a "dark side"? Examination of the link between perceptual bias and aggression. *Journal of Abnormal Child Psychology, 28*, 327–337.

DeRosier, M. E., Kupersmidt, J. B., & Patterson, C. J. (1994). Children's academic and behavioral adjustment as a function of the chronicity and proximity of peer rejection. *Child Development, 65*, 1799–1813.

Giesler, R. B., Josephs, R. A., & Swann, W. B. (1996). Self-verification in clinical depression: The desire for negative evaluation. *Journal of Abnormal Psychology, 105*, 358–368.

Goodman, S. H., & Gotlib, I. H. (1999). Risk for psychopathology in the children of depressed mothers: A developmental model for understanding mechanisms of transmission. *Psychological Review, 106*, 458–490.

Hammen, C., Burge, D., Daley, S., Davila, J., Paley, B., & Rudolph, K. (1995). Interpersonal attachment cognitions and prediction of symptomatic responses to interpersonal stress. *Journal of Abnormal Psychology, 104*, 436–443.

Harter, S. (1998). The development of self-representations. In W. Damon (Series Ed.) & N. Eisenberg (Vol. Ed.), *Handbook of child psychology: Vol. 3. Social, emotional, and personality development* (pp. 103–196). New York: Guilford.

Hoffman, K. B., Cole, D. A., Martin, J. M., Tram, J., & Seroczynski, A. D. (2000). Are the discrepancies between self- and others' appraisals of competence predictive or reflective of depressive symptoms in children and adolescents: A longitudinal study, Part II. *Journal of Abnormal Psychology, 109*, 651–662.

Hokanson, J. E., Rubert, M. P., Welker, R. A., Hollander, G. R., & Hedeen, C. (1989). Interpersonal concomitants and antecedents of depression among college students. *Journal of Abnormal Psychology, 98*, 209–217.

Hoza, B., Molina, B., Bukowski, W., & Sippola, L. (1995). Peer variables as predictors of later childhood adjustment. *Development and Psychopathology, 7*, 787–802.

Hymel, S., Bowker, A., & Woody, E. (1993). Aggressive versus withdrawn unpopular children: Variations in peer and self-perceptions in multiple domains. *Child Development, 64*, 879–896.

Hymel, S., Rubin, K., Rowden, L., & LeMare, L. (1990). Children's peer relationships: Longitudinal prediction of internalizing and externalizing problems from middle to late childhood. *Child Development, 61*, 2004–2021.

Ingram, R. E. (2001). Developing perspectives on the cognitive-developmental origins of depression: Back is the future. *Cognitive Therapy and Research, 25*, 497–504.

Joiner, T. E., Metalsky, G. I., Katz, J., & Beach, S. R. H. (1999a). Be (re)assured: Excessive reassurance-seeking has (at least) some explanatory power regarding depression. *Psychological Inquiry, 10*, 305–308.

Joiner, T. E., Metalsky, G. I., Katz, J., & Beach, S. R. H. (1999b). Depression and excessive reassurance-seeking. *Psychological Inquiry, 10*, 269–278.

Kazdin, A. E. (1994). Informant variability in the assessment of childhood depression. In W. Reynolds & H. Johnston (Eds.), *Handbook of depression in children and adolescents* (pp. 249–271). New York: Plenum.

Kendall, P. C., Stark, K. D., & Adam, T. (1990). Cognitive deficit or cognitive distortion in childhood depression. *Journal of Abnormal Child Psychology, 18*, 255–270.

Kistner, J. A., Balthazor, M., Risi, S., & Burton, C. (1999). Predicting dysphoria in adolescence from actual and perceived peer acceptance in childhood. *Journal of Clinical Child Psychology, 28*, 94–104.

Kistner, J. A., Balthazor, M., Risi, S., & David, C. (2001). Adolescents' perceptions of peer acceptance: Is dysphoria associated with greater realism? *Journal of Social and Clinical Psychology, 20*, 69–84.

Kistner, J. A., David-Ferdon, C. F., Repper, K., & Joiner, T. E. (in press). Bias and accuracy of children's perceptions of peer acceptance: Prospect associations with depressive symptoms. *Journal of Abnormal Child Psychology.*

Kistner, J. A., Stone, H., Ferdon, C. F., & Repper, K. (2005, April). *Are positive illusions adaptive or maladaptive? Implications for children's self-worth and peer relationships.* Poster presented at the biennial meeting of the Society for Research in Child Development, Atlanta.

Kupersmidt, J. B., & Dodge, K. A. (2004). *Children's peer relations: From development to intervention.* Washington, DC: American Psychological Association.

Kupersmidt, J. B., & Patterson, C. J. (1991). Childhood peer rejection, aggression, withdrawal, and perceived competence as predictors of behavior problems in preadolescence. *Journal of Abnormal Child Psychology, 19*, 427–449.

Lewinsohn, P. M. (1974). A behavioral approach to depression. In R. J. Friedman & M. M. Katz (Eds.), *The psychology of depression: Contemporary theory and research* (pp. 157–185). Washington, DC: Winston-Wiley.

Lewinsohn, P. M., Hoberman, H., Teri, L., & Hautzinger, M. (1985). An integrative theory of depression. In S. Reiss & R. Bootzin, (Eds.), *Theoretical issues in behavior therapy* (pp. 334–361). New York: Academic Press.

Lewinsohn, P. M., Hops, H., Roberts, R. E., Seeley, J. R., & Andrews, J. A. (1993). Adolescent psychopathology: I. Prevalence and incidence of depression and other DSM-III-R disorders in high school students. *Journal of Abnormal Psychology, 102*, 133–144.

Little, S. A., & Garber, J. (1995). Aggression, depression, and stressful life events predicting peer rejection in children. *Development and Psychopathology, 7*, 845–856.

Lochman, J. E., & Wayland, K. K. (1994). Aggression, social acceptance, and race as predictors of negative adolescent outcomes. *Journal of the American Academy of Child and Adolescent Psychiatry, 33*, 1026–1035.

McGrath, E. P., & Repetti, R. L. (2002). A longitudinal study of children's depressive symptoms, self-perceptions, and cognitive distortions about the self. *Journal of Abnormal Psychology, 111*, 77–87.

Meyer, N. E., Dyck, D. G., & Petrinack, R. J. (1989). Cognitive appraisal and attributional correlates of depressive symptoms in children. *Journal of Abnormal Child Psychology, 17*, 325–336.

Miserandino, M. (1996). Children who do well in school: Individual differences in perceived competence and autonomy in above-average children. *Journal of Educational Psychology, 88*, 203–214.

Morison, P., & Masten, A. S. (1991). Peer reputation in middle childhood as a predictor of adaptation in adolescence: A seven-year follow-up. *Child Development, 62*, 991–1007.

Nolan, S. A., Flynn, C., & Garber, J. (2003). Prospective relations between peer rejection and depression in young adolescents. *Journal of Personality and Social Psychology, 85*, 745–755.

Ollendick, T. H., Weist, M. D., Borden, M. C., & Green, R. W. (1992). Sociometric status and academic, behavioral, and psychological adjustment: A five-year longitudinal study. *Journal of Consulting and Clinical Psychology, 60*, 80–87.

Panak, W., & Garber, J. (1992). Role of aggression, rejection, and attributions in the prediction of depression in children. *Development and Psychopathology, 4*, 145–165.

Parker, J. G., & Asher, S. R. (1987). Peer relations and later personal adjustment: Are low accepted children at risk? *Psychological Bulletin, 102*, 357–389.

Patterson, C. J., Kupersmidt, J. B., & Griesler, P. C. (1990). Children's perceptions of self and of relationships with others as a function of sociometric status. *Child Development, 61*, 1335–1349.

Peterson, L., Mullins, L. L., & Ridley-Johnson, R. (1985). Childhood depression: Peer reactions to depression and life stress. *Journal of Abnormal Child Psychology, 13*, 597–609.

Phillips, D. A. (1984). The illusion of incompetence among academically competent children. *Child Development, 55*, 2000–2016.

Proffitt, V. D., & Weisz, J. R. (1992). *Perceived incompetence and depression in childhood: Cognitive distortion or accurate appraisal.* Unpublished manuscript.

Rohde, P., Lewinsohn, P. M., & Seeley, J. R. (1990). Are people changed by the experience of having a depressive episode? A further test of the scar hypothesis. *Journal of Abnormal Psychology, 99*, 264–271.

Rudolph, K. D., & Clark, A. G. (2001). Conceptions of relationships in children with depressive and aggressive symptoms: Social-cognitive distortion or reality? *Journal of Abnormal Child Psychology, 29*, 41–56.

Rudolph, K. D., Hammen, C., & Burge, D. (1994). Interpersonal functioning and depressive symptoms in childhood: Addressing the issues of specificity and comorbidity. *Journal of Abnormal Child Psychology, 22*, 355–371.

Segal, Z. V. (1988). Appraisal of the self-schema construct in cognitive models of depression. *Psychological Bulletin, 103*, 147–162.

Segrin, C. (2000). Social skills deficits associated with depression. *Clinical Psychology Review, 20*, 379–403.

Swann, W. B., Stein-Seroussi, A., & Giesler, B. (1992). Why people self-verify. *Journal of Personality and Social Psychology, 62*, 392–401.

Taylor, S. E., Lerner, J. S., Sherman, D. K., Sage, R. M., & McDowell, N. K. (2003). Portrait of the self-enhancer: Well adjusted and well liked or maladjusted and friendless? *Journal of Personality and Social Psychology, 84*, 165–176.

Tram, J. M., & Cole, D. A. (2000). Self-perceived competence and the relation between life events and depressive symptoms in adolescence: Mediator or moderator? *Journal of Abnormal Psychology, 109*, 753–760.

Verhulst, F. C., Van Der Ende, J., Ferdinand, R. F., & Kasius, M. C. (1997). The prevalence of DSM-III-R diagnoses in a national sample of Dutch adolescents. *Archives of General Psychiatry, 54*, 329–336.

Whitman, P. B., & Leitenberg, H. (1990). Negatively biased recall in children with self-reported symptoms of depression. *Journal of Abnormal Child Psychology, 18,* 15–27.

Wierzbicki, M., & McCabe, M. (1988). Social skills and subsequent depressive symptomatology in children. *Journal of Clinical Child Psychology, 17,* 203–208.

Zakriski, A., & Coie, J. D. (1996). A comparison of aggressive-rejected and nonaggressive-rejected children's interpretations of self-directed and other-directed rejection. *Child Development, 7,* 1048–1070.

Zeiss, A. M., & Lewinsohn, P. M. (1988). Enduring deficits after remissions of depression: A test of the scar hypothesis. *Behavior Research and Therapy, 26,* 151–158.

Chapter 2

Depression and Romantic Dysfunction During Adolescence

Joanne Davila
Sara J. Steinberg
State University of New York at Stony Brook

Although many aspects of the association between depression and poor interpersonal functioning in adolescence are well documented, examination of one aspect—the association between depression and romantic dysfunction—is noticeably lacking. The goals of this chapter are to describe why adolescent depression and romantic dysfunction are likely to be associated, identify factors that might explain their association, and discuss how their association might set the stage for continued depression and romantic dysfunction in adulthood.

Adolescent depression, sadly, is a relatively common occurrence. As revealed in several studies, lifetime prevalence rates of major depressive disorder typically range from 15% to 20% (e.g., Essau, Conradt, & Petermann, 2000; Lewinsohn, Rohde, Seeley, Klein, & Gotlib, 2000). Incidence rates of first onsets in a 1-year period are 7.1% for girls and 4.4% for boys, and incidence rates of recurrences in a 1-year period are 21.1% for girls and 9.1% for boys (see Lewinsohn & Essau, 2002). Rates of depression in adulthood are similar. Lifetime prevalence rates for a major depressive episode are approximately 16% (Kessler et al., 1994). The fact that prior episodes, or even prior subclinical symptoms, in adolescence (e.g., Pine, Cohen, Cohen, & Brook, 1999) predict future episodes in adulthood testifies to the recurrent nature of the disorder and the risks associated with adolescent depression.

Romantic dysfunction, unfortunately, is also a common occurrence. Although there is little research on romantic difficulties in adolescence, what does exist suggests that the romantic aspect of adolescents' lives is prominent, affects how adolescents view the self, and is marked by intense emotional ups and downs (e.g., Connolly & Konarski, 1994; Larson, Clore, & Wood, 1999). The high rates of adolescent dating aggression also attest to the serious dysfunction that can occur in the romantic lives of adolescents (see Lewis & Fremouw, 2001). The data on adult romantic dysfunction is abundant and clearly indicates that many individuals and couples face significant stress in their romantic lives and have difficulty adaptively managing their relationships. Relationship problems are one of the primary reasons that adults seek therapy, and the divorce rate suggests that nearly half of all people who marry experience problems that are significant enough to lead to dissolution of the relationship (U.S. Census Bureau, 2002).

Hence, on their own, depression and romantic dysfunction are serious mental and public health problems. We know that depression and romantic dysfunction are related in adulthood, thereby increasing the risk for both (Davila, Karney, Hall, & Bradbury, 2003; Whisman, 2001). We believe that this association may begin earlier, in adolescence, and we hope to identify the nature of this association and how it may set the stage for continued risk for both depression and romantic problems into adulthood. We start our analysis of this issue by briefly reviewing bodies of literature addressing three issues: the association between depression and romantic dysfunction in adulthood, the association between depression and other types of interpersonal dysfunction in adolescence, and adolescent romantic dysfunction. We then discuss how depression may relate to romantic dysfunction in adolescence, with a focus on potential mediators and moderators of their association. We finish with a discussion of how adolescent experiences may relate to adult experiences.

DEPRESSION AND ROMANTIC DYSFUNCTION IN ADULTHOOD

As noted earlier, the association between depression and romantic dysfunction in adulthood is clearly documented. There is evidence that greater depressive symptoms are associated with greater relationship dysfunction across different samples (individuals, newlyweds, established marriages), different levels of symptoms (e.g., subclinical, diagnosable), and different types of romantic dysfunction (e.g., self-reported dissatisfaction, observable maladaptive behavior). This is true cross-sectionally. It is also true with symptoms predicting certain types of dysfunction, and with certain types of dysfunction predicting symptoms (e.g., Beach, Sandeen, & O'Leary, 1990; Burns, Sayers, & Moras, 1994; Davila et al., 2003; Davila,

Bradbury, Cohan, & Tochluk, 1997; Fincham, Beach, Harold, & Osborne, 1997; Karney, 2001; Kurdek, 1998; for reviews, see Gotlib & Beach, 1995; Whisman, 2001).

One of the most commonly studied romantic correlates of depression is relationship distress or lack of satisfaction. They are reliably associated concurrently (e.g., Whisman, 2001), they seem to affect one another reciprocally or bidirectionally (e.g., Beach & O'Leary, 1993a, 1993b; Fincham et al., 1997), and the associations exist longitudinally, even at the within-subject level (e.g., Davila et al., 2003; Karney, 2001; Kurdek, 1998). Research has begun to identify moderators of their association in an attempt to identify whether some individuals are more prone than others to feeling depressed in response to marital distress, or vice versa (e.g., Whisman, 2001; Whisman & Bruce, 1999). Only a few variables have been studied to date; they include gender and neuroticism. Results for gender have been equivocal, and gender differences may be weak at best when basic associations between depression and relationship distress are examined (Davila et al., 2003; Fincham et al., 1997; Kurdek, 1998, 1999; Whisman & Bruce, 1999). However, two studies have shown that gender interacts with the effects of neuroticism on the association between depression and relationship distress. Specifically, for women, neuroticism is associated with stronger associations between depression and relationship distress, whereas for men, neuroticism is associated with weaker associations (Davila et al., 2003; Karney, 2001). Although a more in-depth discussion of these issues is precluded due to space limitations, these findings highlight the fact that it is likely to be useful to not only document basic associations between depression and romantic distress (or dysfunction more broadly), but also to identify for whom these associations are most strong.

Another set of commonly studied correlates of depression is relationship stressors and romantic events. For example, relationship breakups, conflicts, and divorce have been shown to lead not only to depressive symptoms, but also to onsets of clinically significant depression (e.g., Kendler et al., 1995; Monroe, Rohde, Seeley, & Lewinsohn, 1999). Similarly, ongoing relationship stress predicts increases in depressive symptoms among newly married couples, and depressive symptoms also predict increases in stress, again supporting a bidirectional association between these variables (Davila et al., 1997).

Depression is also associated with how people behave in relationships. Davila et al. (1997) observed newlywed spouses interacting with one another while one partner talked about a nonmarital problem with which he or she was struggling. Depressive symptoms were associated with less adaptive seeking and provision of support. A number of studies have observed couples with a depressed spouse (typically the wife) as they try to solve a marital problem. This research indicates that depressed spouses tend to exhibit high levels of conflict, tension, negativity, ambivalence, hostility, and criticism (e.g., Gotlib & Whiffen, 1989; for a review, see Gotlib & Beach, 1995). In addition, depressed spouses may exhibit "depressive be-haviors," such as depressed affect, self-degradation, and physical and psy-chological complaints during interaction (e.g., Biglan et al., 1985). Partners of depressed spouses also behave in a negative fashion during in-teraction, and they disagree with and evaluate their spouses negatively (e.g., Hautzinger, Linden, & Hoffman, 1982).

There is also a growing literature indicating that depression is associ-ated with feelings of insecurity in romantic relationships. For example, Carnelly, Pietromonaco, and Jaffe (1994) found that dysphoric college-age women and recovering depressed married women reported higher levels of fearful avoidance in romantic relationships. The dysphoric college-age women also reported higher levels of preoccupation. Whiffen, Kallos-Lilly, and MacDonald (2001) also noted that depressed wives were more inse-cure than were their nondepressed counterparts. Moreover, the husbands of chronically depressed wives were particularly insecure, and their insecu-rity predicted the maintenance of their wives' depressive symptoms.

In summary, this brief review clearly indicates that, in adulthood, de-pression is associated with various types of romantic dysfunction, including relationship distress, relationship stressors, maladaptive relationship be-havior, and relationship insecurity. As shown in the next section, the same is true for the association between adolescent depression and more general interpersonal dysfunction.

DEPRESSION AND INTERPERSONAL FUNCTIONING IN ADOLESCENTS

There is growing evidence that depressed adolescents suffer from inter-personal impairment in their family and peer relations. One domain in which this is true regards support, conflict, and cohesiveness in adoles-cents' family environments. For example, less supportive and more con-flictual family environments (as reported by adolescents and mothers) relate to adolescent depressive symptoms concurrently, and also predict adolescent depressive symptoms 1 year later (Sheeber, Hops, Albert, Da-vis, & Andrews, 1997). Adolescent depressive symptoms have been linked with adolescents' perceptions of lower levels of family cohesiveness among nonclinical (McKeown et al., 1997) and clinical samples (Cumsille & Ep-stein, 1994). Preadolescents who thought of and attempted suicide tended to perceive their family environments as unsupportive and stressful, with poor control, high conflict, and a lack of cohesiveness (Asarnow, Carlson, & Guthrie, 1987). Preadolescent children who were depressed considered their families to be less supportive, less involved in recreational/social ac-tivities, and more enmeshed. These children also felt that they had less in-volvement in decision making (Stark, Humphrey, Crook, & Lewis, 1990).

Although not longitudinal studies, these preadolescent studies are important because they suggest that certain family environment factors might be in place even before adolescence.

Parenting styles and behaviors have also been linked to adolescent depression. For example, depressed youth tend to have parents who are controlling, autocratic, and likely to use coercive behavior (Amanat & Butler, 1984; Dadds, Sanders, Morrison, & Rebgetz, 1992; Friedrich, Reams, & Jacobs, 1988; Stark et al., 1990). Parents may also reinforce adolescent depression through their behavior. For instance, mothers of depressed adolescents were more likely than were mothers of nondepressed adolescents to increase facilitative behavior in response to adolescent depressive behavior, and fathers of depressed adolescents were more likely to decrease aggressive behavior subsequent to adolescent depressive behavior (Sheeber, Hops, Andrews, Alpert, & Davis, 1998). Interactions between depressed adolescents and their parents are also typified by low levels of friendliness and involvement (Lasko et al., 1997).

Adolescents' security with their parents and their ability to successfully develop autonomy from their parents are another set of important factors in adolescent depression. For example, adolescents with depressed affect have difficulty establishing autonomy (Allen, Hauser, Eickholt, Bell, & O'Connor, 1994). Specifically, adolescents who report being either alienated or highly dependent on their parents report more symptoms of depression than do adolescents without these difficulties (Frank, Poorman, Van Egeren, & Field, 1997). Depressed adolescents also tend to have less secure attachment relationships with their parents (Armsden, McCauley, Greenberg, Burke, & Mitchell, 1990; Essau, 2004; Laible, Carlo, & Raffaelli, 2000) and particularly demonstrate hyperactivating and preoccupied patterns of attachment (Cole-Detke & Kobak, 1996).

The peer relations of depressed youth also tend to be impaired. One important indicator of this is that depressed youth are regarded as less likeable than are others (Peterson, Mullins, & Ridley-Johnson, 1985). Furthermore, adolescents who are depressed report having less emotional support from friends (Lewinsohn et al., 1994), less perceived warmth from peers (Greenberger, Chen, Tally, & Dong, 2000), less reciprocal friendship relations, and higher levels of hostility with close friends (Windle, 1994). Depressed youth tend to feel insecure in their relationships with their peers (Armsden et al., 1990; Formoso, Gonzales & Aiken, 2000) and demonstrate poor social problem-solving skills (Rudolph, Hammen, & Burge, 1994). Depressed children often spend more time alone, have interactions with peers that are more negative and more aggressive, and perceive themselves as being less socially competent (Altmann & Gotlib, 1988).

As these findings indicate, the peer relations of depressed adolescents are impaired in a variety of ways. It is also the case that problems in peer functioning may lead to depression. For example, girls who are rejected by their peers and feel withdrawn tend to show higher levels of depressive symptoms (Bell-Dolan, Foster, & Christopher, 1995). In addition, children who perceive themselves as being unpopular at age nine have an increased risk for developing depressive symptoms in adolescence (Reinherz et al., 1993). Although some of this research is longitudinal (e.g., Reinherz et al., 1993), most is cross-sectional, making it difficult to forge statements about temporal associations. However, it is likely that there is a reciprocal process in which depressed adolescents may have difficulty forming or maintaining close friendships because of their interpersonal deficits, and also become more depressed in response to social isolation.

It is evident from this brief review that depressed adolescents have impaired peer and family relationships, and that similar aspects of functioning are impaired across these relationships. For example, depressed adolescents tend to feel insecure in their relationships with parents and peers (e.g., Armsden et al., 1990), and they often hold more negative perceptions of their family environments (see Sheeber, Hops, & Davis, 2001 for a review) and peer relations (e.g., Altman & Gotlib, 1987). As is evident in the rest of this chapter, many of the interpersonal styles, characteristics, or difficulties experienced by depressed adolescents in parent and peer relationships are relevant for romantic functioning in adolescence. The next section reviews important aspects of romantic functioning in adolescence.

ROMANTIC FUNCTIONING IN ADOLESCENCE

In order to understand why an association may exist between adolescent romantic functioning and depression, it is necessary to be aware of current models of romantic functioning in adolescence. In this section we briefly describe a model of the developmental stages of romantic functioning in adolescence, followed by a number of peer, family, and individual factors that are linked to adolescent romantic functioning and that ultimately may have implications for the association between romantic functioning and depression.

Many researchers have identified stages of romantic relationships in adolescence (e.g., Brown, 1999; Connolly & Goldberg, 1999; Furman & Wehner, 1994), and although differences exist between these models, there are notable similarities. Specifically, romantic relationships in early adolescence are typically marked by affiliation and companionship, rather than intimacy, and romantic interactions typically occur in mixed-gender group interactions (Shulman & Scharf, 2000). Adolescents in the early stages of romantic development are beginning to explore their sexual feelings, and romantic partners typically serve as companions or friends by providing experiences of cooperation and reciprocity (Furman & Wehner,

1994). During late adolescence, intimate and committed relationships are often formed as group dating emerges into couple dating. It is in late adolescence that caretaking, greater levels of intimacy and closeness, deeper mutual feelings, and often more extensive sexual activity occurs (Connolly & Goldberg, 1999; Shulman & Scharf, 2000). During the later stages when a partner is more expected to provide support, comfort, and caregiving, the aspects of companionship and friendship in the romantic relationship are less prominent (Furman & Wehner, 1994).

The stages of romantic development just described indicate that peers may play a prominent role in adolescent romantic functioning, and particularly in the development of interpersonal skills. Romantic partners are often met through the peer group (Brown, 1999), and the interpersonal skills necessary to have a successful relationship are often the same as those underlying successful friendships. For example, in one study, same-gender cliques in Grade 9 fostered the emergence of mixed-gender peer groups in Grade 10, which in turn increased the likelihood of having romantic relationships in Grade 11 (Connolly, Furman, & Konarski, 1995). The affiliative features of adolescent romantic relationships suggest that competencies underlying reciprocity, validation of worth, and intimacy are likely to be important in the development of both friendships and romantic relationships (Furman, 1999). Therefore, experiences in peer relationships may serve as one of the primary foundations for the development of affiliative competencies that are fundamental in romantic relationships (Furman, 1999).

The absence of a peer group can also affect the romantic lives of adolescents. Adolescents with more opposite-gender friends and larger peer groups are more likely to report being in a romantic relationship (Connolly & Johnson, 1996), whereas adolescents who are rejected and neglected by their peers date less frequently than do others (Franzoi, Davis, & Vasquez-Suson, 1994). In addition, perceptions of social support and negative interactions in adolescent close friendships predicted similar qualities in adolescent romantic relationships 1 year later (Connolly, Furman, & Konarski, 2000). It is also possible that certain peer groups can have a negative impact on adolescent romantic functioning if they are maladaptive for the adolescent. For example, males who are involved in a deviant peer group during adolescence (i.e., who have a peer group that is involved in antisocial behavior and engages in hostile talk about women) are more likely to act aggressively toward their romantic partners as adults (Capaldi, Dishion, Stoolmiller, & Yoerger, 2001).

The peer group clearly plays a major role in the development of adolescent romantic experience and functioning. In fact, there is some evidence that aspects of peer relationships are more important than the parent–adolescent relationship for certain types of romantic functioning. For example, affective intensity, or level of closeness, with a romantic partner has been shown to relate to the quality of relationship with a same-gender close friend, but not to the quality of the parent–child relationship (Shulman & Scharf, 2000). In addition, romantic relational styles of high school girls are related to those with friends but not with parents (Furman & Wehner, 1993).

Despite these findings, the family environment may be important for various aspects of adolescent romantic development. For example, nurturant, involved parenting in early adolescence predicted romantic behaviors in late adolescence that were warm, supportive, and low in hostility (Conger, Cui, Bryant, & Elder, 2000). In line with this, it has been proposed that a secure attachment with one's parents provides the foundation to develop a secure attachment to a romantic partner, which would facilitate a successful relationship (Gray & Steinberg, 1999). Attachment theory suggests that past relationship experiences influence internal representations of relationships and the nature and course of relationships throughout the life span (Bowlby, 1969). Hence, adolescents who were securely attached to their parents should be more likely to develop a capacity for intimacy with their peers and romantic partners. In fact, the quality of infant–parent attachment is associated with the quality of children's social interactions with peers (for a review, see Elicker, Englund, & Sroufe, 1992). Furthermore, adolescents' representation of their attachment relationship with their parents is associated with the quality of their behaviors with romantic partners 8 years later (Roisman, Madsen, Hennighausen, Sroufe, & Collins, 2001).

One important aspect of adolescent romantic functioning that is influenced by the parent–adolescent relationship is conflict resolution. For example, late adolescents with more insecure attachment orientations have more difficulties managing conflict in their romantic relationships (Creasey & Hesson-McInnis, 2001; Creasey, Kershaw, & Boston, 1999; Levy & Davis, 1988). Furthermore, parent–adolescent conflict is associated with adolescents' romantic conflict resolution strategies (Reese-Weber & Bartle-Haring, 1998; Reese-Weber & Marchand, 2002). Adolescent relationships may also be shaped by the marital relationship of the parents. Boys who witnessed their parents engaging in more aggressive conflicts had an increased likelihood of acting aggressively toward their romantic partners. However, this effect did not hold for girls, because parental conflict was not associated with conflict in romantic relationships (Kinsfogel & Grych, 2004).

In addition to parent and peer influences on adolescent romantic functioning, individual differences may also play an important role. This may occur in a variety of ways. For example, characteristics of individuals typically determine their interpersonal desirability to others, suggesting that traits may influence partner selection. Personality traits are also likely to influence actual romantic functioning. For instance, late adolescents with personality pathology tend to demonstrate dysfunctional romantic relationships (Daley, Burge, & Hammen, 2000). In addition, important gender differences have been documented regarding differences in how boys and girls view romantic involvements. One study found that adolescent girls cited a higher level of affective intensity with their romantic partners than did boys (Shulman & Scharf, 2000). In addition, girls reported valuing attachment and care in their relationships more than boys did (Shulman & Scharf, 2000).

Individual differences in emotional experience can also affect romantic relationships in adolescence. Developing adolescents face numerous changes that can affect their experience of emotion, including puberty, cognitive development, and sociocultural experiences and changes. These emotions can have disruptive effects on adolescent romantic functioning (Larson et al., 1999). In addition, adolescents also experience a wide array of emotions as they develop romantic interests—emotions with which they may have difficulty coping. In fact, young adolescents who report experiencing passionate love also report higher levels of anxiety (Hatfield, Brinton, & Cornelius, 1989).

Individual differences in adolescent identity development, particularly with regard to separation and individuation from parents, may also be important for romantic functioning. It has been suggested that individuation from parents may influence the development of romantic interests (Buhrmester & Furman, 1987), and also that involvement in romantic relationships may influence separation from parents (Gray & Steinberg, 1999). Furthermore, as adolescents gain autonomy from parents and peers, experiences with intimacy and closeness with parents and peers may be influential in adolescents' perceptions about romantic relationships (Connolly & Goldberg, 1999).

In summary, there are a variety of peer, family, and individual factors that can affect the development and course of adolescent romantic functioning. The reader has likely noted that many of these factors have also been identified as playing a role in adolescent depression, as the review in our prior section suggested. Given that the same factors appear to be relevant to both romantic dysfunction and depression, it is likely that the two are associated. We discuss this possibility in greater detail in the following section.

ROMANTIC FUNCTIONING AND DEPRESSION IN ADOLESCENCE

The literature reviewed thus far indicates that depression in adolescence is associated with many aspects of interpersonal functioning with both parents and peers. In addition, depression among adults is associated with dissatisfaction, insecurity, poor support, and high conflict in romantic relationships. Given these associations, and the types of individual, family, and peer factors that are connected to romantic relating in adolescence, we would expect a link between depression and adolescent romantic functioning. A number of studies are beginning to support this notion. For example, having a romantic partner is related to poor emotional and behavioral adjustment for unpopular early adolescents (Brendgen, Vitaro, Doyle, Markiewicz, & Bukowski, 2002). Having a romantic partner in adolescence also appears to be associated with dysphoria (Gotlib, Lewinsohn, & Seeley, 1998; Joyner & Udry, 2000), especially for adolescents who display a preoccupied interpersonal style (Davila, Steinberg, Kachadourian, Cobb, & Fincham, 2004). Furthermore, a romantic breakup during adolescence increases the chances of experiencing a first major depressive episode in adolescence (Monroe, Rohde, & Seeley, 1999). Hence, evidence for the association between depression and romantic dysfunction in adolescence is beginning to emerge. However, there are numerous issues that remain to be addressed.

For example, research needs to identify specific aspects of romantic functioning that may be impaired when depressive symptoms are present. The most common association in the literature, as indicated earlier, is the one between depressive symptoms and romantic involvement. Very little is known about why this association exists, or about the qualities of romantic thoughts, feelings, behaviors, and experiences that are related to depression. Based on the findings linking adolescent depression to interpersonal impairment in peer and family relations, and linking adult depression to romantic impairments, we would expect similar aspects of adolescent romantic relationships to be impaired. For example, just as depressed adolescents have insecure relationships with their peers and their parents, and depressed adults have insecure relationships with their romantic partners, depressed adolescents may have insecure relationships with their romantic partners. In addition, depressed adolescents demonstrate higher levels of conflict with their parents and their peers, as do depressed adults with their romantic partners. Consequently, we might expect depressed adolescents to have higher levels of conflict, or poor conflict resolution strategies, with their romantic partners. Because depressed adolescents often feel isolated and rejected by their peers, and adolescents tend to meet romantic partners through their peer groups, depressed adolescents may have difficulty finding romantic partners and consequently progress differently through the romantic stages of adolescence.

In addition to identifying basic associations, research will also need to investigate factors that can help explain the context in which adolescent depression and romantic dysfunction develop, as well as mechanisms of their association. For example, it has been theorized that adolescents who diverge from the normative trajectory of romantic functioning, as described earlier, may be at an increased risk for depression (Welsh, Grello, & Harper, 2003). There are also several types of family factors that may be relevant in this endeavor. For example, one way that adolescents learn about interpersonal functioning is from observing their parents' relationship. Adolescents in families in which a parent is depressed and/or experiencing marital distress may be less likely than other adolescents to learn relationship skills that could lead to romantic competence. They would also be at greater risk for depression. This is consistent with research showing that mothers' marital satisfaction predicts emotional adaptation of adolescents when assessed 6 years later (Feldman, Fisher, & Seitel, 1997).

The adolescent–parent relationship may also be relevant to understanding the association between adolescent depression and romantic functioning. Failure to develop a sense of autonomy and independence from parents is related to the development of depression and romantic dysfunction, and may thus help explain their association. Conflict and insecurity in parent–child relationships may also lead to depressive symptoms and romantic difficulties. For example, adolescents whose emotional needs are not being met by their parents may seek out romantic partners for maladaptive reasons, and they may subsequently develop interpersonal tendencies that make them vulnerable to both depression and romantic difficulties (i.e., dependent personality style, preoccupied attachment strategies). In fact, evidence suggests that family relationships, particularly adolescent–parent attachment security, moderates the association between adolescent romantic relationships and adjustment (Doyle, Brendgen, Markiewicz, & Kamkar, 2003).

There are also several types of individual difference variables that may help us understand the association between adolescent depression and romantic dysfunction. Interpersonal and/or personality styles may help explain who is most likely to show strong associations or why depressive symptoms might result in romantic problems (Davila et al., 1997, 2003). Our own data support this hypothesis. In attempting to explain why depressive symptoms are associated with being in a romantic relationship in adolescence, we have found that the strongest associations emerge for adolescents who exhibit a preoccupied relational style (Davila et al., 2004). This style is characterized by the use of proximity seeking as an emotion regulation style and a desire for intense involvement and intimacy, but also a tendency to worry that they will be rejected or abandoned by others (e.g., Collins & Read, 1990; Hazan & Shaver, 1987). Therefore, young preoccupied adolescents who are dysphoric might seek out relationships in order to feel better, or preoccupied young people in relationships might be more prone to feeling depressed than others, given that they are likely to feel that their needs are never getting fully met and that they are sure to be rejected.

There also are likely to be other individual difference factors that may help us better understand how adolescent depression and romantic dysfunction are linked. For example, building on cognitive and interpersonal models of depression (e.g., Abramson, Seligman, & Teasdale, 1978; Gotlib & Hammen, 1992; Hammen, 1991) and marriage (e.g., Bradbury & Fincham, 1990), the attributions that adolescents make about romantic circumstances might increase their risk for romantic problems and depression. In addition, other risky behavior (e.g., substance abuse, delinquency, sexual risk taking) that tends to be associated with both depression and romantic dysfunction might further our understanding of which adolescents will become depressed in response to romantic problems, or vice versa.

Finally, there may be social and environmental factors that can help explain associations between depression and romantic dysfunction in adolescence. As noted earlier, peers play a critical role in both adolescent romantic development and depression. The nature of the peer group or the quality of specific peer relationships may thus provide important contextual information regarding the association between romantic dysfunction and depression. In addition, recent research is beginning to focus on how neighborhood factors and social norms affect adolescent outcomes (see Leventhal & Brooks-Gunn, 2000). It is not hard to imagine that the neighborhood in which adolescents live could, for example, increase their risk for depression, increase their exposure to deviant peers, and limit partner selection opportunities.

Of course, the variables that we have described are just a sampling of possible factors that may help us understand the association between adolescent depression and romantic dysfunction. They are by no means an exhaustive list. The first step for researchers must be the identification of basic associations between depression and specific aspects of romantic dysfunction in adolescence. The exploration of factors that help explain their association should follow from theory-driven models of why depression and romantic dysfunction may be related. We hope our brief review can offer some beginning directions in this regard.

LINKING ADOLESCENT AND ADULT DEPRESSION AND ROMANTIC DYSFUNCTION

As we stated at the beginning of this chapter, we believe that by failing to focus on the association between romantic dysfunction and depression in adolescence, researchers have neglected a critical aspect of adolescent life, and a set of experiences that potentially have serious implications for adult life. Although adolescent experiences of romantic dysfunction and depression may not have negative consequences for subsequent functioning for everyone, it is likely to be that case that, for at least some people, depression and romantic dysfunction in adolescence set the stage for depression and romantic dysfunction throughout the life course. There are a number of reasons to believe this is true. For example, from a developmental psychopathology perspective, to the extent that people do not successfully master relational skills or negotiate important relational tasks early on, this will put them at risk for depression and further interpersonal dysfunction throughout their lives (e.g., Cicchetti, Rogosch, & Toth, 1994). Therefore, failure to do well in early relationships may be an ongoing risk factor into adulthood. This is consistent with a number of other theoretical positions (e.g., attachment theory, social learning theory) suggesting that information and skills learned in earlier relationships set the stage for experiences and behavior in later relationships. These models would also posit that typical emotional responses and emotion regulation strategies that occur in the context of relationships would also carry forward. This is consistent with the notion that depression is a recurrent disorder. As such, depression and romantic dysfunction, once linked, may remain so over time.

This link has implications for various literatures. It is important to the study and treatment of both adolescent and adult depression, because it identifies a potential target of intervention and adds to understanding of the interpersonal dysfunction associated with depression and its chronicity. The link is important to scholars who want to understand marriage, particularly the association between marriage and depression, because it draws attention to the individual vulnerabilities that people may bring to marriage and the developmental course of these problems. The link may also have broader public policy implications regarding the prevention of depression and interpersonal dysfunction. If there is a group of people for whom the association between depression and romantic dysfunction begins early, then early efforts designed at preventing depression and educating young people about relationship skills may reduce the risk for adult depression, poor relationship choices, and possibly even divorce and its associated negative consequences.

CONCLUSION

In summary, we have posited that depression and romantic dysfunction are associated in adolescence, and we have suggested a number of mechanisms that might help us better understand their association. We have also hypothesized that the association between depression and romantic dysfunction in adolescence sets the stage for their association over the course of the life span, at least for some people. We hope that this review highlights the importance of examining the association between depression and romantic dysfunction in adolescence and motivates researchers to do so.

REFERENCES

Abramson, L. Y., Seligman, M. E. P., & Teasdale, J. D. (1978). Learned helplessness in humans: Critique and reformulation. *Journal of Abnormal Psychology, 87*, 49–74.

Allen, J. P., Hauser, S. T., Eickholt, C., Bell, K. L., & O'Connor, T. G. (1994). Autonomy and relatedness in family interactions as predictors of expressions of negative adolescent affect. *Journal of Research on Adolescence, 4*, 535–552.

Altman, E. O., & Gotlib, I. H. (1988). The social behavior of depressed children: An observational study. *Journal of Abnormal Child Psychology, 16*, 29–44.

Amanat, E., & Butler, C. (1984). Oppressive behaviors in the families of depressed children. *Family Therapy, 11*, 65–77.

Armsden, G. C., McCauley, E., Greenberg, M. T., Burke, P. M., & Mitchell, J. R. (1990). Parent and peer attachment in early adolescent depression. *Journal of Abnormal Child Psychology, 18*, 683–697.

Arsarnow, J. R., Carlson, G. A., & Guthrie, D. (1987). Coping strategies, self-perceptions, hopelessness, and perceived family environments in depressed and suicidal children. *Journal of Consulting and Clinical Psychology, 55*, 361–366.

Beach, S. R. H., & O'Leary, K. D. (1993a). Dysphoria and marital discord: Are dysphoric individual at risk for marital maladjustment? *Journal of Marital and Family Therapy, 19*, 355–368.

Beach, S. R. H., & O'Leary, K. D. (1993b). Marital discord and dysphoria: For whom does the marital relationship predict depressive symptomatology? *Journal of Social and Personal Relationships, 10*, 405–420.

Beach, S. R. H., Sandeen, E. E., & O'Leary, K. D. (1990). *Depression in marriage: A model for etiology and treatment.* New York: Guilford.

Bell-Dolan, D. J., Foster, S. L., & Christopher, J. S. (1995). Girls' relations and internalizing problems: Are socially neglected, rejected, and withdrawn girls at risk? *Journal of Clinical Child Psychology, 4*, 463–473.

Biglan, A., Hops, H., Sherman, L., Friedman, L. S., Arthur, J., & Osteen, V. (1985). Problem solving interactions of depressed women and their spouses. *Behavior Therapy, 16*, 431–451.

Bowlby, J. (1969). *Attachment and loss: Volume 1. Attachment.* New York: Basic Books.

Bradbury, T. N., & Fincham, F. D. (1990). Attributions in marriage: Review and critique. *Psychological Bulletin, 107*, 3–33.

Brendgen, M., Vitaro, F., Doyle, A. B., Markiewicz, D., & Bukowski, W. M. (2002). Same-sex peer relations and romantic relationships during early adolescence: Interactive links to emotional, behavioral, and academic adjustment. *Merrill-Palmer Quarterly, 48*, 77–103.

Brown, B. B. (1999). "You're going out with who?": Peer group influences on adolescent romantic relationships. In W. Furman, B. B. Brown, & C. Feiring (Eds.), *The development of romantic relationships in adolescence* (pp. 291–329). New York: Cambridge University Press.

Burmehster, D., & Furman, W. (1987). The development of companionship and intimacy. *Child Development, 58*, 1101–1113.

Burns, D. D., Sayers, S. L., & Moras, K. (1994). Intimate relationships and depression: Is there a causal connection? *Journal of Consulting and Clinical Psychology, 62*, 1033–1043.

Capaldi, D., Dishion, T. J., Stoolmiller, M., & Yoerger, K. (2001). Aggression toward female partners by at-risk young men: The contribution of male adolescent friendships. *Developmental Psychology, 37*, 61–73.

Carnelly, K. B., Pietromonaco, P. R., & Jaffe, K. (1994). Depression, working models of others, and relationship functioning. *Journal of Personality and Social Psychology, 66*, 127–140.

Cicchetti, D., Rogosch, F. A., & Toth, S. L. (1994). A developmental psychopathology perspective on depression in children and adolescents. In W. M. Reynolds & H. F. Johnson (Eds.), *Handbook of depression in children and adolescents* (pp. 123–141). New York: Plenum.

Cole-Detke, H., & Kobak, R. (1996). Attachment processes in eating disorders and depression. *Journal of Consulting and Clinical Psychology, 64*, 282–290.

Collins, N. L., & Read, S. J. (1990). Adult attachment, working models, and relationship quality in dating couples. *Journal of Personality and Social Psychology, 58*, 644–663.

Conger, R. D., Cui, M., Bryant, C. M., & Elder, G. (2000). Competence in early adult romantic relationships: A developmental perspective on family influences. *Journal of Personality and Social Psychology, 79*, 224–237.

Connolly, J. A., Furman, W., & Konarski, R. (1995, March). *The role of social networks in the emergence of romantic relationships in adolescence.* Paper presented at the biennial meetings of the Society for Research on Adolescence, Boston.

Connolly, J. A., Furman, W., & Konarski, R. (2000). The role of peers in the emergence of heterosexual romantic relationships in adolescence. *Child Development, 71*, 1395–1408.

Connolly, J. A., & Goldberg, A. (1999). Romantic relationships in adolescence: The role of friends and peers in their emergence and development. In W. Furman, B. B. Brown, & C. Feiring (Eds.), *The development of romantic relationships in adolescence* (pp. 266–290). New York: Cambridge University Press.

Connolly, J., & Johnson, A. (1996). Adolescents' romantic relationships and the structure and quality of their close interpersonal ties. *Personal Relationships, 2*, 185–195.

Connolly, J. A., & Konarski, R. (1994). Peer self-concept in adolescence: Analysis of factor structure and of associations with peer experience. *Journal of Research on Adolescence, 4*, 385–403.

Creasey, G., & Hesson-McInnis, M. (2001). Affective responses, cognitive appraisals, and conflict tactics in late adolescent romantic relationships: Associations with attachment orientations. *Journal of Counseling Psychology, 48*, 85–96.

Creasey, G., Kershaw, K., & Boston, A. (1999). Conflict management with friends and romantic partners: The role of attachment and negative mood regulation expectancies. *Journal of Youth and Adolescence, 28*, 523–543.

Cumsille, P. E., & Epstein, N. (1994). Family cohesion, family adaptability, social support, and adolescent depressive symptoms in outpatient clinic families. *Journal of Family Psychology, 8*, 202–214.

Dadds, M. R., Sanders, M. R., Morrison, M., & Rebgetz, M. (1992). Childhood depression and conduct disorder: II. An analysis of family interaction patterns in the home. *Journal of Abnormal Psychology, 101*, 505–513.

Daley, S. E., Burge, D., & Hammen, C. (2000). Borderline personality disorder symptoms as predictors of 4-year romantic relationship dysfunction in young women: Addressing issues of specificity. *Journal of Abnormal Psychology, 109*, 451–460.

Davila, J., Bradbury, T. N., Cohan, C., & Tochluk, S. (1997). Marital functioning and depressive symptoms: Evidence for a stress generation model. *Journal of Personality and Social Psychology, 73*, 849–861.

Davila, J., Karney, B. R., Hall, T., & Bradbury, T. N. (2003). Depressive symptoms and marital satisfaction: Within-subject associations and the moderating effects of gender and neuroticism. *Journal of Family Psychology, 17*, 557–570.

Davila, J., Steinberg, S., Kachadourian, L., Cobb, R., & Fincham, F. (2004). Romantic involvement and depressive symptoms in early and late adolescence: The role of a preoccupied relational style. *Personal Relationships, 11*, 161–178.

Doyle, A. B., Brendgen, M., Markiewicz, D., & Kamkar, K. (2003). Family relationships as moderators of the association between romantic relationships and adjustment in early adolescence. *Journal of Early Adolescence, 23*, 316–340.

Elicker, J., Englund, M., & Sroufe, L. A. (1992). Predicting peer competence and peer relationships in childhood from early parent–child relationships. In R. D. Parke & G. W. Ladd (Eds.), *Family–peer relationships: Modes of linkage* (pp. 77–108). Hillsdale, NJ: Lawrence Erlbaum Associates.

Essau, C. A. (2004). The association of family factors and depressive disorders in adolescents. *Journal of Youth and Adolescence, 33*, 365–372.

Essau, C. A., Conradt, J., & Petermann, F. (2000). Frequency, comorbidity, and psychosocial impairment of depressive disorders in adolescents. *Journal of Adolescent Research, 15*, 470–481.

Feldman, S. S., Fisher, L., & Seitel, L. (1997). The effect of parents' marital satisfaction on young adults' adaptation: A longitudinal study. *Journal of Research on Adolescence, 7*, 55–80.

Fincham, F. D., Beach, S. R. H., Harold, G. T., & Osborne, L. N. (1997). Marital satisfaction and depression: Different causal relationships for men and women? *Psychological Science, 8*, 351–357.

Formoso, D., Gonzales, N. A., & Aiken, L. S. (2000). Family conflict and children's internalizing and externalizing behaviors: Protective factors. *American Journal of Community Psychology, 28*, 175–179.

Frank, S. J., Poorman, M. O., Van Egeren, L. A., & Field, D. T. (1997). Perceived relationships with parents among adolescent inpatients with depressive preoccupations and depressed mood. *Journal of Child Clinical Psychology, 26*, 205–215.

Franzoi, S. L., Davis, M. H., & Vasquez-Suson, K. A. (1994). Two social worlds: Social correlates and stability of adolescent status groups. *Journal of Personality and Social Psychology, 67*, 462–473.

Friedrich, W., Reams, R., & Jacobs, J. (1988). Sex differences in depression in early adolescents. *Psychological Reports, 62*, 475–481.

Furman, W. (1999). Friends and lovers: The role of peer relationships in adolescent romantic relationships. In W. A. Collins & B. Laursen (Eds.), *Relationships as developmental contexts: The 30th Minnesota Symposium on Child Development* (pp. 133–154). Mahwah, NJ: Lawrence Erlbaum Associates.

Furman, W., & Wehner, E. A. (1993, March). *Adolescent romantic relationships: A developmental perspective.* Paper presented at the Society for Research in Child Development Biennial Meeting, New Orleans.

Furman, W., & Wehner, E. A. (1994). Romantic views: Toward a theory of adolescent romantic relationships. In R. Montmayer, G. R. Adams, & G. P. Gullota (Eds.), *Advances in adolescent development: Volume 6, Relationships during adolescence* (pp. 168–175). Thousand Oaks, CA: Sage.

Gotlib, I. H., & Beach, S. R. H. (1995). A marital/family discord model of depression: Implications for therapeutic intervention. In N. S. Jacobson & A. S. Gurman (Eds.), *Clinical handbook of couple therapy* (pp. 411–436). New York: Guilford.

Gotlib, I. H., & Hammen, C. (1992). *Psychological aspects of depression: Toward a cognitive-interpersonal integration.* Chicester, UK: Wiley.

Gotlib, I. H., Lewinsohn, P. M., & Seeley, J. R. (1998). Consequences of depression during adolescence: Marital status and marital functioning in early adulthood. *Journal of Abnormal Psychology, 107*, 686–690.

Gotlib, I. H., & Whiffen, V. E. (1989). Depression and marital functioning: An examination of specificity and gender differences. *Journal of Abnormal Psychology, 98*, 23–30.

Gray, M. R., & Steinberg, L. (1999). Adolescent romance and the parent–child relationship: A contextual perspective. In W. Furman, B. B. Brown, & C. Feiring

(Eds.), *The development of romantic relationships in adolescence* (pp. 235–265). New York: Cambridge University Press.

Greenberger, E., Chen, C., Tally, S. R., & Dong, Q. (2000). Family, peer, and individual correlates of depressive symptomatology among U.S. and Chinese adolescents. *Journal of Consulting and Clinical Psychology, 68*, 209–219.

Hammen, C. L. (1991). The generation of stress in the course of unipolar depression. *Journal of Abnormal Psychology, 100*, 555–561.

Hatfield, E., Brinton, C., & Cornelius, J. (1989). Passionate love and anxiety in young adolescents. *Motivation and Emotion, 13*, 271–289.

Hautzinger, M., Linden, M., & Hoffman, N. (1982). Distressed couples with and without a depressed partner: An analysis of their verbal interaction. *Journal of Behavior Therapy and Experimental Psychology, 13*, 307–314.

Hazan, C., & Shaver, P. (1987). Romantic love conceptualized as an attachment process. *Journal of Personality and Social Psychology, 52*, 511–524.

Joyner, K., & Udry, R. (2000). You don't bring me anything but down: Adolescent romance and depression. *Journal of Health and Social Behavior, 41*, 369–391.

Karney, B. R. (2001). Depressive symptoms and marital satisfaction in the early years of marriage: The implications of a growth curve analysis. In S. R. H. Beach (Ed.), *Marital and family processes in depression* (pp. 45–68). Washington, DC: American Psychological Association.

Kendler, K. S., Kessler, R. C., Walters, E. E., MacLean, C., Neale, M. C., Heath, A. C., & Eaves, L. J. (1995). Stressful life events, genetic liability, and onset of episode of major depression in women. *American Journal of Psychiatry, 162*, 833–842.

Kessler, R. C., McGonagle, K. A., Zhao, S., Nelson, C. B., Hughes, M., Eshleman, S., Wittchen, H.-U., & Kendler, K. S. (1994). Lifetime and 12-month prevalence of DSM-III-R psychiatric disorders in the United Stated: Results from the National Comorbidity Survey. *Archives of General Psychiatry, 51*, 8–19.

Kinsfogel, K. M., & Grych, J. H. (2004). Interparental conflict and adolescent dating relationships: Integrating cognitive, emotional, and peer influences. *Journal of Family Psychology, 18*, 505–515.

Kreider, R. M., & Fields, J. M. (2001). Number, timing, and duration of marriages and divorces: 1996. *Current Population Reports* (pp. 70–80). U.S. Census Bureau, Washington DC.

Kurdek, L. A. (1998). The nature and predictors of the trajectory of change in marital quality over the first 4 years of marriage for first-married husbands and wives. *Journal of Family Psychology, 12*, 494–510.

Kurdek, L. A. (1999). More differences about gender differences in marriage: A reply to Beach, Davey, and Fincham (1999). *Journal of Family Psychology, 13*, 669–674.

Laible, D. J., Carlo, G., & Raffaelli, M. (2000). The differential relations of parent and peer attachment to adolescent adjustment. *Journal of Youth and Adolescence, 29*, 45–59.

Larson, R. W., Clore, G. L., & Wood, G. A. (1999). The emotions of romantic relationships: Do they wreak havoc on adolescents? In W. Furman, B. Brown, & C. Feiring (Eds.), *The development of romantic relationships in adolescence* (pp. 19–49). New York: Cambridge University Press.

Lasko, D., Field, T., Bendall, D., Yando, R., Scafidi, F., LaGreca, A., & Trapani, L. (1997). Adolescent psychiatric patients' interactions with their mothers. *Adolescence, 32*, 977–988.

Leventhal, T., & Brooks-Gunn, J. (2000). The neighborhoods they live in: The effects of neighborhood residence on child and adolescent outcomes. *Psychological Bulletin, 126*, 309–337.

Levy, M., & Davis, K. (1988). Lovestyles and attachment styles compared: Their relations to each other and to various relationship characteristics. *Journal of Social and Personal Relationships, 5,* 439–471.

Lewinsohn, P. M., & Essau, C. A. (2002). Depression in adolescents. In I. H. Gotlib & C. L. Hammen (Eds.), *Handbook of depression* (pp. 541–559). New York: Guilford.

Lewinsohn, P. M., Roberts, R. E., Seeley, J. R., Rohde, P., Gotlib, I. H., & Hops, H. (1994). Adolescent psychopathology: II. Psychosocial risk factors for depression. *Journal of Abnormal Psychology, 103,* 302, 315.

Lewinsohn, P. M., Rohde, P., Seeley, J. R., Klein, D. N., & Gotlib, I. (2000). Natural course of adolescent major depressive disorder in a community sample: Predictors of recurrence in · young adults. *American Journal of Psychiatry, 157,* 1584–1591.

Lewis, S. F., & Fremouw, W. (2001). Dating violence: A critical review of the literature. *Clinical Psychology Review, 21,* 105–127.

McKeown, R. E., Garrison, C. Z., Jackson, K. L., Cuffe, S. P., Addy, C. L., & Waller, J. L. (1997). Family structure and cohesion, depressive symptoms in adolescents. *Journal of Research on Adolescence, 7,* 267–281.

Monroe, S. M., Rohde, P., Seeley, J. R. (1999). Life events and depression in adolescence: Relationship loss as a prospective risk factor for first onset of major depressive disorder. *Journal of Abnormal Psychology, 108,* 606–614.

Peterson, L., Mullins, L., & Ridley-Johnson, R. (1985). Childhood depression; peer reactions to depression and life stress. *Journal of Abnormal Child Psychology, 13,* 597–609.

Pine, D. S., Cohen, E., Cohen, P., & Brook, J. (1999). Adolescent depressive symptoms as predictors of adult depression: Moodiness or mood disorder? *American Journal of Psychiatry, 156,* 133–135.

Reese-Weber, M., & Bartle-Haring, S. (1998). Conflict resolution styles in family subsystems and adolescent romantic relationships. *Journal of Youth and Adolescence, 27,* 735–752.

Reese-Weber, M., & Marchand, J. F. (2002). Family and individual predictors of late adolescents' romantic relationships. *Journal of Youth and Adolescence, 31,* 197–206.

Reinherz, H. Z., Giaconia, R. M., Pakiz, B., Silverman, A. B., Frost, A. K., & Lefkowitz, E. S. (1993). Psychosocial risks for major depression in late adolescence: a longitudinal community study. *Journal of the American Academy of Child and Adolescent Psychiatry, 32,* 1155–1164.

Roisman, G. I., Madsen, S. D., Henninghausen, K. H., Sroufe, L. A., & Collins, W. A. (2001). The coherence of dyadic behavior across parent–child and romantic relationships as mediated by the internalized representation of experience. *Attachment and Human Development, 3,* 156–172.

Rudolph, K. D., Hammen, C., & Burge, D. (1994). Interpersonal functioning and depressive symptoms in childhood: Addressing the issue of specificity and comorbidity. *Journal of Abnormal Child Psychology, 22,* 355–371.

Sheeber, L., Hops, H., Albert, A., Davis, B., & Andrews, J. (1997). Family support and conflict: Prospective relations to adolescent depression. *Journal of Abnormal Child Psychology, 25,* 333–344.

Sheeber, L., Hops, H., Andrews, J., Alpert, A., & Davis, B. (1998). Interactional processes in families with depressed and nondepressed adolescents: Reinforcements of depressive behavior. *Behaviour Research and Therapy, 36,* 417–427.

Sheeber, L., Hops, H., & Davis, B. (2001). Family processes in adolescent depression. *Clinical Child and Family Psychology Review, 4,* 19–35.

Shulman, S., & Scharf, M. (2000). Adolescent romantic behaviors and perceptions: Age- and gender-related differences, and links with family and peer relationships. *Journal of Research on Adolescence, 10,* 99–118.

Stark, K. D., Humphrey, L. L., Crook, K., & Lewis, K. (1990). Perceived family environments of depressed and anxious children: Child's and maternal figure's perspective. *Journal of Abnormal Child Psychology, 18*, 527–547.

Welsh, D. P., Grello, C. M., & Harper, M. S. (2003). When love hurts: Depression and adolescent romantic relationships. In P. Florsheim (Ed.), *Adolescent romantic relationships and sexual behavior: Theory, research, and practical implications* (pp. 185–211). Mahwah, NJ: Lawrence Erlbaum Associates.

Whiffen, V. E., Kallos-Lilly, V., & MacDonald, B. J. (2001). Depression and attachment in couples. *Cognitive Therapy and Research, 25*, 421–434.

Whisman, M. A. (2001). The association between depression and marital dissatisfaction. In S. R. H. Beach (Ed.), *Marital and family processes in depression: A scientific foundation for clinical practice* (pp. 3–24). Washington, DC: American Psychological Association.

Whisman, M. A., & Bruce, M. L. (1999). Marital dissatisfaction and incidence of major depressive episode in a community sample. *Journal of Abnormal Psychology, 108*, 674–678.

Windle, M. (1994). A study of friendship characteristics and problem behaviors among middle adolescents. *Child Development, 65*, 1764–1777.

Chapter 3

The Consequences of Adolescent Major Depressive Disorder on Young Adults

Peter M. Lewinsohn
Paul Rohde
John R. Seeley
Oregon Research Institute

Daniel N. Klein
State University of New York at Stony Brook

Ian H. Gotlib
Stanford University

On the basis of studies begun during the 1970s, quite a bit has become known about depression during adolescence and childhood (e.g., Fleming & Offord, 1990; Garber, Kriss, Koch, & Lindholm, 1988; Kovacs, 1996; Lewinsohn, Hops, Roberts, Seeley, & Andrews, 1993; McGee et al., 1990). In an effort to contribute to this literature, our group at the Oregon Research Institute has been engaged since the mid-1980s in an extensive program of research on the epidemiology and treatment of adolescent depression. A central component of this effort is the Oregon Adolescent Depression Project (OADP), which is based on a large, randomly selected cohort of high school students who were assessed at two points over a period of 1 year using rigorous diagnostic criteria and structured diagnostic interviews (Lewinsohn et al., 1993). We recently completed a third wave of diagnostic assessments with a subset of participants after they had turned

24 years of age. The goal of this chapter is to summarize findings from the OADP concerning the consequences of adolescent depression on young adult functioning. Although our primary focus in this chapter is to summarize findings that have emerged from the OADP, we relate our data to other pertinent research findings as much as possible.

Our review focuses on the natural course and the consequences of affective disorders during childhood/adolescence. Our research indicates that major depressive disorder (MDD) is the most prevalent form of affective disorder among adolescents (e.g., Lewinsohn et al., 1993). Bipolar disorders (primarily bipolar II and cyclothymia) occur in less than 1% of community adolescents (Lewinsohn, Klein, & Seeley, 1995), whereas lifetime rates of unipolar depression (i.e., MDD and dysthymia) are approximately 20%. Among adolescents with unipolar depression, the vast majority—approximately 80%—experience MDD by itself or in conjunction with a nonaffective disorder (10% experience dysthymia without MDD, and the remaining 10% experience comorbid MDD and dysthymia; see Lewinsohn, Rohde, Seeley, & Hops, 1991; Rohde, Lewinsohn, & Seeley, 1991).

A brief description of the OADP data set is provided next, giving a general overview of the study to date. Methodological details relevant to specific issues are described later in the appropriate section.

DESCRIPTION OF THE OADP DATA SET

Adolescents

The OADP began with a randomly selected sample of 1,709 high school students who completed a diagnostic interview and a wide array of psychosocial measures at entry into the study (Time 1, or T_1) when they were 14 to 18 years of age. Approximately 1 year later (T_2), 1,507 (88%) of the participants returned for a second diagnostic interview. At both assessments, participants were administered a questionnaire designed to measure a comprehensive array of psychosocial constructs either known or hypothesized to be important in the etiology and course of depression.

Average age of the OADP participants at T_1 was 16.6 ($SD = 1.2$). Slightly over half (53%) were female, 91% were White, 12% had repeated a grade in school, 53% were living with both biological parents at the time of the T_1 interview, and an additional 18% were living with a biological parent and stepparent. Most participants resided in households in which one or both parents worked as a minor professional (44%) or professional (31%).

After individuals in the sample reached their 24th birthday, all participants with a history of MDD and other psychopathology at T_2 were invited to participate in a T_3 telephone interview (Rohde, Lewinsohn, & Seeley, 1997), as were an approximately equal number of randomly selected control participants with no history of mental disorder at T_2. Of the 1,101 individuals selected for T_3 interview, 941 (85%) participated: 57% were female, average T_3 age = 24.2 years (SD = 0.6), 89% were White, 34.1% were married, 97% had graduated from high school, and 31% had received a bachelors degree or higher. Women were more likely than men to complete the T_3 assessments (89% vs. 81%); $\chi^2(1, n = 1101) = 13.55, p < .001$. Differences in T_3 participation as a function of other demographics and T_2 diagnostic status were nonsignificant.

Participants at T_1 had been interviewed with a version of the Schedule for Affective Disorders and Schizophrenia in School-Aged Children (K-SADS), which combined features of the epidemiologic version (Orvaschel, Puig-Antich, Chambers, Tabrizi, & Johnson, 1982), and the present episode version included additional items to derive DSM-III diagnoses (American Psychiatric Association, 1987). At T_2 and T_3, participants were interviewed using the Longitudinal Interval Follow-Up Evaluation (Keller et al., 1987), which elicited detailed information about the course of psychiatric symptoms and disorders since the previous interview. T_3 diagnoses were made using DSM-IV (American Psychiatric Association, 1994) criteria.

DSM-IV personality disorders were added to the T_3 assessment. Our experience with the initial T_3 participants indicated that the rates of most personality disorders in our community sample of young adults were extremely low (Lewinsohn, Rohde, Seeley, & Klein, 1997). Therefore, we focused on the two personality disorders that were most frequent and most relevant to our purposes for the remainder of T_3: antisocial and borderline personality disorders, which were assessed with relevant portions of the Personality Disorder Examination (PDE; Loranger, 1988). The PDE results in both categorical diagnoses and dimensional scores (i.e., summation of partial and full symptom criteria), which were dichotomized at the 90th percentile to define elevated dimensional score for the two personality disorders. Interrater reliability of the interviews at all three assessments was high and comparable to what has been found in other studies (e.g., kappas generally greater than .80).

In addition to the diagnostic interview, an extensive battery of psychosocial measures was administered at T_1 and T_2 to all participants. All measures had been previously shown to possess very good psychometric properties (Andrews, Lewinsohn, Hops, & Roberts, 1993). Variables were standardized and scored such that higher values reflected more problematic functioning. Depression symptom level was assessed using the 20-item Center for Epidemiologic Studies—Depression (CES—D) scale (Radloff, 1977; α = .89, T_1-T_2 r = .61). Negative cognitions were assessed using 27 items concerning self-reinforcement, likelihood of future positive events, dysfunctional attitudes, and perceived control over one's life (α = .81, T_1-T_2 r = .61). Attributional style was assessed using the 48-item Kastan Attributional Style Questionnaire for

Children (Kaslow, Tanenbaum, & Seligman, 1978) (α = .63, T_1-T_2 r = .55). Self-esteem was assessed using nine items regarding physical appearance and general self-esteem (α = .81, T_1-T_2 r = .62). Excessive emotional reliance on others was assessed using 10 items regarding the extent to which individuals desire excessive support and approval from others, and are interpersonally sensitive (α = .83, T_1-T_2 r = .54). Self-rated social competence was assessed using 12 items (α = .85, T_1-T_2 r = .64). Coping skills were assessed using 17 items (α = .76, T_1-T_2 r = .55). Social support: friends was assessed using 13 items (α = .81, T_1-T_2 r = .60). Social support: family was assessed using 22 items (α = .86, T_1-T_2 r = .64).

Conflict with parents was assessed using the 45-item Issues Checklist scale (Robin & Weiss, 1980; α = .81, T_1-T_2 r = .51). Daily hassles were assessed using 20 items from the Unpleasant Events Schedule (Lewinsohn, Mermelstein, Alexander, & MacPhillamy, 1985; α = .79, T_1-T_2 r = .55). Major life events were assessed using 11 negative life events to self or significant other (parent, sibling, other relative, close friend) during the past year (α = .78, T_1-T_2 r = .52). Academic problems were assessed using nine items from the questionnaire and T_1 K-SADS interview (e.g., lifetime occurrence of school expulsion or suspension, truancy, repeating a grade in school, most recent grade point average). Physical illness was assessed using 90 items regarding physical symptoms, number of sick days, and physician visits during the past year.

Young adult psychosocial functioning was assessed at T_3 by questionnaire and as part of the diagnostic interview using both dichotomous and continuous measures. Dichotomous measures included current marital status, divorce or separation, being a parent, recent mental health utilization, and current daily smoking. Continuous-type measures consisted of global functioning (DSM Global Assessment of Functioning [GAF]), years of education, weeks unemployed in past year, household income, quality of relationship with family members (α = .88; 10 items; Procidano & Heller, 1983); quality of relationship with friends (α = .88; 10 items; Procidano & Heller, 1983); social network (α = .69; size and frequency of social contact; 3 items; Berkman & Syme, 1979); minor hassles (α = .88; daily hassles during the last 4 weeks, as assessed by 20 items from the Unpleasant Events Schedule; Lewinsohn, Mermelstein, et al., 1985); major events (α = .71; major life events in past 12 months, as assessed by 33 events occurring to the participant, based on the Social Readjustment Rating Scale; Holmes & Rahe, 1967; and the Psychiatric Epidemiology Research Inventory; Dohrenwend, Levav, & Shrout, 1986); physical health (α = .50; four items assessing self-rated health, number of times received treatment in past year, treatment for illness or injury in past year, and chronic medical problems distress); and life satisfaction (α = .89; 15 items; chosen from Andrews & Withey, 1976; Campbell, Converse, & Rodgers, 1976).

Family Members

During the time of the T_3 assessments, lifetime psychiatric information was obtained from the first-degree relatives over the age of 13 (biological parents, full siblings) of the OADP participants in the T_3 assessment. To supplement the direct interviews, informant psychiatric data were collected from OADP probands or another first-degree relative. Our goal was to collect two sources of diagnostic data regarding each family member. Of the 941 probands with T_3 data, family diagnostic data were available for 803 (85%). Direct interviews were obtained on 63% of the family members and two sources of data were obtained for 84% of family members.

Parents and siblings were interviewed using either the Structured Clinical Interview for DSM-IV, nonpatient version (SCID-NP; Spitzer, Williams, Gibbon, & First, 1992) or the K-SADS employed in the T_1 proband assessment, modified for collection of DSM-IV criteria. Family history data were collected using the revised Family Informant Schedule and Criteria (FISC; Mannuzza & Fyer, 1990), based on the Family History Research Diagnostic Criteria (FH-RDC; Endicott, Andreason, & Spitzer, 1978) modified for DSM-IV criteria. Best-estimate diagnoses (Leckman, Sholomskas, Thompson, Belanger, & Weissman, 1982) were derived, blind to proband diagnoses, for relatives using all available data by the four senior diagnosticians on the project (Drs. Rohde, Klein, Lewinsohn, and Nicholas Allen).

Next, we summarize our recent research findings regarding four key issues concerning the natural course of adolescent MDD: (a) the continuity of MDD and other psychopathology from adolescence to young adulthood, (b) the role of familial psychopathology in adolescent MDD, (c) the predictors of MDD recurrence in young adulthood, and (d) the psychosocial functioning of young adults who were depressed in adolescence. We then summarize our findings on bipolar and hypomania disorders, concluding with a brief description of our future research plans.

CONTINUITY OF MDD FROM ADOLESCENCE TO YOUNG ADULTHOOD

In Lewinsohn, Rohde, Klein, and Seeley (1999), we examined whether children and adolescents with a history of MDD were at increased risk for (a) new episodes of MDD in adulthood and (b) other affective and non-affective disorders as adults. Participants with a history of MDD in childhood or adolescence were compared to three groups: (a) participants with other nonaffective disorders prior to age 19 (primarily anxiety, substance use, and disruptive behavior disorders), (b) participants with a history of adjustment disorder with depressed mood prior to age 19, and (c) participants with no history of psychiatric disorder prior to age 19.

We felt that it was important to include adjustment disorder with depressed mood (which we will refer to as *adjustment disorder*) as a comparison group for several reasons. First, as a "near-neighbor" category, it provided a good comparison for MDD, although its relationship to the mood disorders is unclear. Several studies have reported that most youths with adjustment disorder recover quickly, and that their risk of developing other psychiatric disorders is less than or does not differ from psychiatric controls, although it is perhaps greater than that of children without any psychiatric disorder (Kovacs et al., 1984; Kovacs, Gatsonis, Pollock, & Parrone, 1994; Kovacs, Ho, & Pollock, 1995). Conversely, other studies have reported that the majority of children and adolescents with adjustment disorder have poor outcomes, and often develop more severe forms of psychopathology (Andreasen & Hoenk, 1982; Cantwell & Baker, 1989). Finally, adjustment disorder is one of the most common psychiatric diagnoses in adolescents (Greenberg, Rosenfeld, & Ortega, 1995; Newcorn & Strain, 1998).

Our data analytic strategy incorporated a hierarchical classification in which MDD took precedence over adjustment disorder, which in turn took precedence over nonaffective disorder. Participants with a lifetime history of MDD and adjustment disorder were included in the adolescent MDD group. Four groups were examined: (a) participants with adolescent MDD (*n* = 261, 74% were female, 8% had comorbid dysthymia, and 51% had a comorbid nonaffective disorder); (b) participants with adolescent adjustment disorder (*n* = 73, 64% were female, and 36% had a comorbid nonaffective disorder); (c) participants with adolescent nonaffective disorder (*n* = 133, 48% were female, 35% had anxiety disorder, 57% had substance use disorder, 22% had disruptive behavior disorder, and 4% had eating disorder); and (d) participants who had no disorder through age 18 (*n* = 272, 50% female).

Results are summarized in Table 3.1. As can be seen, 45% of participants with adolescent MDD experienced another MDD episode between ages 19 and 23. This was significantly higher than were MDD rates in the nonaffective disorder group and the no-disorder control group. Although the MDD group had a very high rate of recurrence, the rate of MDD incidence in the adjustment disorder group was almost as high, and did not significantly differ from the MDD incidence rate in the adolescent MDD group.

The adolescent MDD group also had an elevated rate of nonaffective disorder compared to the no-disorder group. However, this difference appeared to be due to the presence of comorbid mental disorders in individuals with adolescent MDD. When rates of nonaffective disorder between ages 19 and 24 were examined for the no-disorder group versus individuals with "pure" (noncomorbid) adolescent MDD, differences were nonsignificant (20% vs. 27%, respectively). Thus, it appears that having had an adolescent MDD resulted in a very substantial probability of MDD recur-

TABLE 3.1

Frequency of Diagnosis in Young Adulthood as a Function of Adolescent Diagnostic Group

Diagnosis at Ages 19–23	Adolescent Diagnostic Group				MDD Comparisons
	MDD	*ADJUST*	*NONMOOD*	*ND*	
Percentage MDD	45	34	28	18	MDD > NONMOOD and ND
Percentage ADJUST	8	4	10	8	ns
Percentage NONMOOD	33	31	36	20	MDD > ND
Percentage Any Axis I	62	48	54	38	MDD > ADJUST and ND
Percentage Axis II	3	1	2	1	ns
Percentage elevated antisocial PDE score	10	3	17	3	MDD > ADJUST and ND
Percentage elevated borderline PDE score	10	3	5	1	MDD > ND

Note: MDD = major depressive disorder; ADJUST = adjustment disorder; NONMOOD = nonmood disorder; ND = no disorder; ns = not significant.

From Lewinsohn, P. M., Rohde, P., Klein, D. N., & Seeley, J. R. (1999). Natural course of adolescent major depressive disorder: I. Continuity into young adulthood. *Journal of the American Academy of Child and Adolescent Psychiatry, 38*, 56–63. Copyright © 1999 by Lippincott, Williams, & Wilkins. Adapted with permission.

rence between ages 19 and 24, and if the MDD was accompanied by another mental disorder, it was likely that the person would develop a non-mood disorder during young adulthood.

The adolescent MDD and the nonaffective disorder groups were more likely to have elevated antisocial personality disorder symptoms relative to the adjustment and no-disorder controls. Finally, the MDD group had an elevated rate of borderline personality disorder symptoms compared to no-disorder controls, but did not differ from the other diagnostic groups.

Differences between the comorbid and "pure" adolescent MDD participants regarding the likelihood of future MDD, dysthymia, or adjustment were nonsignificant. However, individuals with comorbid adolescent MDD were more likely than those with pure MDD to develop nonaffective disorder in the future (42% vs. 27%), to develop an Axis II (antisocial or borderline) disorder in the future (5% vs. 0%), and to have elevated scores on both antisocial (17% vs. 2%) and borderline personality dimensions (16% vs. 4%).

Being female increased the likelihood of future MDD (adjusted odds ratio [OR] = 1.7) and adjustment disorder (adjusted OR = 2.1), whereas being male increased the likelihood of future nonaffective disorder (OR = 1.7), Axis II disorder (OR = 6.7), and elevated antisocial personality dimensional scores (OR = 7.4). However, gender did not interact with adolescent diagnostic group in predicting young adult psychopathology, suggesting that the patterns of diagnostic continuity from adolescence to young adulthood were the same for women and men.

To our knowledge, this is the largest study addressing the continuity of MDD from childhood and adolescence to young adulthood currently in the literature. The results of this study document that adolescent MDD confers a high degree of risk for MDD recurrence in young adulthood, as well as an increased probability of future nonaffective disorders (predominantly substance use disorders) and Axis II pathology. Taken in their totality, our results have at least two compelling public health implications. First, given the negative consequences of early-onset MDD, the findings stress the importance of developing effective interventions to prevent the onset of depression during childhood and adolescence (e.g., Mrazek & Haggerty, 1994). Given that prevention attempts with adolescents at risk for depression have shown mixed results (e.g., Clarke et al., 1995; Spence, Sheffield, & Donovan, 2005), a major public health priority should be to redouble these efforts. Second, children and adolescents who have experienced MDD need to be targeted for the prevention of future depressive episodes using techniques that have proven useful for adolescents (e.g., Kaufman, Rohde, Seeley, Clarke, & Stice, 2005). Until empirically validated effective depression prevention interventions are developed, periodic clinical monitoring of at-risk adolescents to detect MDD recurrence is needed.

MDD AND OTHER PSYCHOPATHOLOGY IN THE FAMILY MEMBERS OF OADP PARTICIPANTS

Family studies provide a useful approach to exploring the continuities and discontinuities between MDD in childhood/adolescence and MDD in adulthood. Previous family studies of juvenile MDD have suffered from a number of methodological limitations and yielded inconsistent findings. In Klein, Lewinsohn, Seeley, and Rohde (2001), we reported results from a family study of MDD using OADP participants who completed the T_3 interview. T_3 participants were divided into three groups on the basis of adolescent psychopathology: 268 individuals with a history of adolescent MDD, 110 adolescents with a history of nonmood disorders but no history of MDD through age 18, and 291 adolescents with no history of psychopathology through age 18. As noted earlier, psychopathology in their 2,202 first-degree relatives was assessed with semistructured direct and family history interviews, and best-estimate diagnoses were derived using all available data.

We found that the relatives of adolescents with MDD exhibited significantly elevated rates of MDD, dysthymia, and alcohol abuse/dependence, but not anxiety disorders, drug abuse/dependence, and antisocial and borderline personality disorder. The results thus provide strong evidence for the familial aggregation of adolescent MDD, and also indicate that there is a high degree of specificity in the pattern of familial transmission. The family study data lend support to the validity of the diagnosis of MDD in our adolescent probands (e.g., Feighner et al., 1972), and also to the continuity between adolescent and adult MDD. In addition, we observed a significant and relatively specific pattern of familial aggregation for the broad nonmood disorder categories of anxiety and substance use disorders, supporting the validity and distinctiveness of these other forms of adolescent psychopathology.

In another paper based on the OADP family study (Klein, Lewinsohn, Rohde, Seeley, & Durbin, 2002), data were used to examine whether specific features of the adolescent MDD episode (e.g., severity, recurrence, chronicity, onset age, treatment utilization, melancholia, functional impairment, or suicidal behavior) were associated with elevated rates of MDD in first-degree relatives. Depressed adolescents with a history of recurrent MDD episodes had a particularly elevated rate of MDD in their first-degree relatives, suggesting the hypothesis that recurrence may be a marker for a highly familial form of MDD. At the same time, depressed adolescents with only mild functional impairment had a lower rate of MDD in their first-degree relatives, suggesting that mild impairment may be a marker for a less familial form of MDD. The relatives of depressed adolescents were distinguished from the relatives of no-disorder adolescents by a significantly higher rate of MDD with moderate-severe symptom severity, and the *de-*

pressed relatives of MDD and no-disorder adolescents were distinguished by symptom severity, age of onset, impairment, and treatment, suggesting that genetic studies might restrict the definition of the MDD phenotype to relatives with these features. There was little evidence for the familial aggregation of particular clinical features. Rather than defining discrete subtypes, most of the clinical features examined in this study appear to reflect an underlying dimension of familial liability.

PREDICTORS OF MDD RECURRENCE IN YOUNG ADULTHOOD

Our primary goal in the next report (Lewinsohn, Rohde, Seeley, Klein, & Gotlib, 2000) was to identify the factors in formerly depressed adolescents (i.e., those who had recovered by age 19) that predicted MDD recurrence by young adulthood. The framework that guided our research is based on an integrative, multifactorial model (Lewinsohn, Hoberman, Teri, & Hautzinger, 1985), in which depression is conceptualized as the end result of environmentally initiated changes in behavior, affect, and cognition. The model distinguishes between antecedents (which occur before the onset of depression) and consequences (which are observable during and after an episode of depression). The model also recognizes individual vulnerabilities and protective factors that moderate the impact of antecedent events or consequences on depression incidence and recurrence. Examined vulnerabilities include the presence of psychopathology among family members, being female (which has often been shown to be a depression risk factor), elevated depression symptoms, depressotypic cognitions, excessive emotional reliance, academic problems, and poor physical health. Examined protective factors included self-rated social competence, positive coping skills, and social support from family and friends. Our initial model, like most other current theories of the etiology of depression, did not distinguish between first onset and recurrent episodes of depression, even though the results of various studies (e.g., Lewinsohn, Allen, Seeley, & Gotlib, 1999; Monroe, Rohde, Seeley, & Lewinsohn, 1999; Post, Weiss, & Leverich, 1994) suggested that these two types of episodes may be predicted by different variables.

Based on the often-observed finding that the experience of having an episode of depression increases the likelihood of another episode (e.g., Amenson & Lewinsohn, 1981), clinical aspects of the adolescent MDD episode (e.g., early onset, longer duration, recurrence during adolescence, greater severity, treatment utilization, and suicide attempts) also were hypothesized to lead to recurrence. Comorbid adolescent psychopathology (including daily cigarette use, as a proxy for nicotine dependence) was also hypothesized to be a vulnerability for recurrence. Finally, traits measuring selected young adult personality disorders (i.e., antisocial and borderline personality disorders) were posited to reflect stable characteristics of the person that act as vulnerabilities for MDD recurrence.

This study focused on 274 T_3 participants who had experienced and recovered from an episode of MDD during adolescence, which we defined as before age 19. Based on their subsequent psychiatric outcome, individuals were partitioned into four mutually exclusive groups:

1. Those who experienced no further disorder (ND; $n = 87$).
2. Those who experienced a recurrent episode of MDD with no comorbid mental disorder ($n = 58$).
3. Those who experienced a recurrent MDD that was accompanied by a nonmood disorder (NONMOOD) ($n = 67$).
4. Those who did not experience MDD recurrence during ages 19 through 23 but experienced a NONMOOD ($n = 62$).

Of the 129 participants with NONMOOD during the 19–23 age period, the two most prevalent categories were substance use disorder (present in 77%) and anxiety disorder (present in 34%).

This design allowed us to address three questions: What T_1 variables are general predictors of staying well (Group 1 vs. Groups 2, 3, and 4)? What factors specifically predict MDD recurrence (Groups 1 and 4 vs. Groups 2 and 3)? What factors predict "pure" (i.e., noncomorbid) MDD versus MDD with a co-occurring NONMOOD (Group 2 vs. Group 3)? Results for the three contrasts are summarized in Table 3.2.

Formerly depressed adolescents who developed psychiatric problems during young adulthood were characterized during adolescence by more severe depressive episodes, elevated stress and conflict, and interpersonal dependency; additionally, for males only, by a negative attributional style. These individuals also had an elevated rate of substance use disorder during adolescence and, as young adults, showed traits associated with borderline and antisocial personality disorder. In addition, their parents and siblings were more likely to have experienced both single-episode and recurrent MDD. Excessive emotional reliance is a component of the broader construct of interpersonal dependency (e.g., Hirschfeld et al., 1989), which has been implicated theoretically in the etiology of depression, especially in the psychoanalytic literature (Blatt, Quinlan, Chevron, McDonald, & Zuroff, 1982; Hirschfeld, Klerman, Chodoff, Korchin, & Barrett, 1976). We previously reported that excessive emotional reliance predicted depression onset in adolescents (Lewinsohn et al., 1994) and that it remained elevated after MDD recovery (Rohde, Lewinsohn, & Seeley, 1994). The present results indicate that emotional reliance is also predictive of the recurrence of psychopathology, and of MDD in particular, underscoring both its centrality to depression theory and its potential explanatory breadth to other disorders.

TABLE 3.2

Diagnostic Outcome Group Comparisons

Unique and Independent T1 Predictors*	Additional Significant T1 Predictors
Predictors of not staying well (i.e., developing any disorder)	
Excessive emotional reliance	Conflict with parents
Recurrent adolescent MDD episodes	Daily hassles
Proportion of family members with recurrent MDD	Academic problems
	Longer adolescent MDD duration
Elevated borderline PD symptoms	More severe adolescent episodes
Elevated antisocial PD symptoms	Suicide attempt
	Substance use disorders
	Proportion of family members with MDD
Predictors of MDD recurrence	
Female gender	Excessive emotional reliance
Recurrent adolescent MDD episodes	Longer adolescent MDD duration
Proportion of family members with recurrent MDD	Proportion of family members with MDD
Elevated borderline PD symptoms	
Predictors of comorbid versus pure MDD	
Anxiety disorders	Academic problems
Substance use disorders	Adolescent cigarette use
Elevated antisocial PD symptoms	Oppositional defiant/conduct disorders
	MDD was secondary disorder
	Proportion of family members with nonmood disorders
	Elevated borderline PD symptoms

*Variable was a unique and independent predictor in the summary MLR models.
Adapted with permission from the American Journal of Psychiatry, Copyright © 2000. American Psychiatric Association.

Variables that specifically predicted MDD recurrence included multiple depressive episodes in adolescence, a family history of recurrent MDD, and borderline personality disorder symptomatology; additionally, for females only, increased conflict with parents. Gender was retained in the multivariate solution, but this finding appeared to be due to the fact that formerly depressed male adolescents were most likely to develop pure nonmood disorders in young adulthood (i.e., gender differences between the "pure" MDD and no-disorder controls were nonsignificant). These findings suggest that clinical characteristics, both of the proband and of the first-degree relatives, are among the strongest predictors of MDD recurrence.

There was no evidence that adolescent comorbidity acted as a risk factor for "pure" MDD in young adulthood. The presence of nonmood disorders in adolescence predicted nonmood disorders in young adulthood, generally comorbid with recurrent MDD.

Familial psychopathology was notable in all three contrasts. Most significantly, the proportion of family members with recurrent MDD predicted MDD recurrence in the offspring, with and without nonmood disorder. These findings are consistent with previous research indicating that the presence of MDD in family members dramatically increases the likelihood of MDD recurrence in adults (e.g., Merikangas, Wicki, & Angst, 1994; Weissman et al., 1987). The present results extend previous research by indicating that recurrent depression breeds true from parent to offspring.

Both elevated antisocial and borderline personality disorder symptoms were significant in multiple contrasts. Several adult studies have suggested strong comorbidity between depression and borderline personality disorder and symptomatology (e.g., Akiskal, Hirschfeld, & Yerevanian, 1983; Oldham et al., 1995) and a small number of studies of adult patients have shown that Axis II pathology, especially Cluster B disorders (i.e., antisocial, borderline, narcissistic, and histrionic), increases the likelihood of depression recurrence in treated adult patients (e.g., Ilardi, Craighead, & Evans, 1997; Pfohl, Coryell, Zimmerman, & Stangl, 1987). The present findings on Axis II psychopathology need to be qualified in two respects. First, rates of personality disorders were low, so elevated dimensional scores were generally in the subthreshold range. Second, the Axis II data were obtained at T_3. Therefore, the direction of these associations cannot be determined, although previous research supports the hypothesis that adolescent depression precedes the onset of personality disorder symptoms (Cohen, 1996).

The clinical implications of this study are straightforward. Clinicians are routinely faced with decisions about what to do with young people who have a history of MDD. We found that roughly one quarter of formerly depressed adolescents experienced subsequent pure MDD in young adulthood, one quarter experienced comorbid MDD, one quarter remained free from depression recurrence but experienced a nonmood disorder, and only one quarter remained free of disorder during the assessment period. Earlier and better identification of the most salient risk factors is the first step in avoiding a protracted course of disorder. Our study indicates that depressed female adolescents (especially those who experience high conflict with parents), adolescents with multiple MDD episodes, and those with a family history of recurrent depression are at particularly high risk for depression recurrence. These individuals should be closely monitored or receive continued prophylactic treatment. Future studies need to examine the effects of Axis II psychopathology on the course of MDD and determine whether treatments specifically addressing the personality disorder symptomatology are necessary in impacting the course of depression.

YOUNG ADULT PSYCHOSOCIAL FUNCTIONING OF INDIVIDUALS WHO WERE DEPRESSED IN ADOLESCENCE

The presence of depression during adolescence has been found to be associated with serious negative psychosocial consequences in young adulthood, including impaired academic and occupational functioning, early childbearing, social difficulties and poor peer relationships, lowered life satisfaction, increased adversity, increased treatment utilization, criminal arrests, and reduced global functioning (e.g., Aronen & Soininen, 2000; Bardone, Moffitt, Caspi, Dickson, & Silva, 1996; Devine, Kempton, & Forehand, 1994; Fergusson & Woodward, 2002; Fleming, Boyle, & Offord, 1993; Gotlib & Hammen, 1992; Hammen, 1991; Kandel & Davies, 1986; Kovacs, Akiskal, Gatsonis, & Parrone, 1994; Kovacs & Goldston, 1991; Puig-Antich et al., 1993; Rao et al., 1995; Rao, Weissman, Martin, & Hammond, 1993; Reinherz, Giaconia, Carmola, Wasserman, & Silverman, 1999; Winokur & Tsuang, 1996). In a more recent paper (Lewinsohn, Rohde, Seeley, Klein, & Gotlib, 2003), we focused on the psychosocial functioning of young adults who have experienced an episode of MDD during childhood/adolescence. Six issues were addressed:

1. To what extent is the psychosocial functioning of young adults who experienced an episode of MDD during adolescence impaired relative to those who did not experience adolescent MDD?
2. Are the differences in psychosocial functioning specific to adolescent depression or are they also associated with other forms of adolescent psychopathology?
3. To what extent are the differences in functioning evident only in depressed individuals with comorbid nonmood disorders?
4. Are the differences in young adult functioning detectable even in formerly depressed adolescents who remain free of MDD in young adulthood?
5. Are the differences in functioning detected in young adulthood already evident in adolescence?
6. Do differences remain significant after controlling for current depression level at the time of the young adult assessment?

Young adult psychosocial functioning was assessed either in the mailer questionnaire or as part of the T_3 interview using both dichotomous and continuous measures. Dichotomous measures included current marital status, divorce or separation (assessed only among participants who had been married), parenting, mental health treatment utilization in past year, and current daily cigarette smoking. Continuous measures consisted of DSM global level of functioning, number of years of school completed, number of weeks unemployed in past year, annual household income, quality of relationships with family members, quality of relationships with friends, social network, minor hassles (daily hassles during the last 4 weeks), major events (major life events in past 12 months), physical health (four items assessing self-rated health, chronic medical problems, and recent treatment), and life satisfaction. Eight of these variables had also been assessed at T_1. To control for depression symptoms at the time of the young adult assessment, CES-D scores assessed in the mailer questionnaire preceding T_3 were entered into the analyses.

T_3 participants who completed a mailer questionnaire between the ages of 23 and 25 formed the sample for this study, of which 319 had experienced an episode of MDD by age 19 (175 with a lifetime comorbid adolescent nonmood disorder), 208 participants had had an adolescent nonmood disorder (without MDD), and the remaining 324 had experienced no mental disorder by age 19.

Without adjusting for any of the covariates, almost all of the measures of young adult functioning were found to be associated with adolescent MDD (results are summarized in Table 3.3). Given the pervasive effects of depression, it was somewhat surprising that four of the young adult functioning measures were unrelated to adolescent MDD, even at the unadjusted level: income level, quality of relationships with friends, marital status, and divorce/separation. After controlling for the presence of adolescent nonmood disorder and demographics, five additional variables became nonsignificant: years of education, recent unemployment, physical health, parenting status, and daily smoking. These associations appeared to be to due to adolescent demographic factors or the presence of nonmood disorders in adolescence.

Two variables (global functioning levels and recent mental health treatment utilization) appeared to be driven by the presence of MDD recurrence in young adulthood. One third of the formerly depressed adolescents who experienced MDD recurrence sought and received mental health treatment, as opposed to 17.5% of the formerly depressed who did not relapse. This result is understandable—people seek treatment for current psychopathology. The remaining five variables were associated with adolescent MDD, controlling for adolescent psychopathology or disorders during the young adult period (i.e., 19–23 years of age), and appeared to cluster in the relatively specific domains of relationship quality and environmental adversity. All associations, however, became nonsignificant after controlling for either adolescent (T_1) level of the measure or current depression level at the time of the young adult assessment.

Only one variable in young adulthood appeared to be uniquely associated with adolescent MDD: life satisfaction. Thus, many of the impair-

TABLE 3.3

Relationships Between Young Adult Functioning and a History
of Adolescent MDD

Measures of functioning at age 24 that were related to adolescent MDD

Due to demographic factors or presence of comorbid adolescent psychopathology

Being a parent Years of education
Recent unemployment level
Poor physical health
Daily cigarette smoking

Due to MDD recurrence in young adulthood

Global functioning (GAF)
Recent mental health treatment utilization

Accounted for by T1 level of the functioning measure or current depression levels

Quality of relationships with family
Small social network
Minor hassles
Major events
Low life satisfaction

Measures of functioning at age 24 that were unrelated to adolescent MDD

Current marital status
Divorce or separation
Household income
Quality of relationships with friends

From Lewinsohn, P. M., Rohde, P., Seeley, J. R., Klein, D. N., & Gotlib, I. (2003). Psychosocial functioning of young adults who have experienced and recovered from major depressive disorder during adolescence. *Journal of Abnormal Psychology, 112,* 353–363. Copyright © 2003 by the American Psychological Association. Adapted with permission.

ments in young adulthood are associated with the occurrence of adolescent psychopathology more broadly.

In conclusion, we should note that although we can say with confidence that young adults with a history of adolescent MDD showed numerous signs of functional impairment, we cannot determine the causal chain of events. All of the functioning deficits apparent in young adulthood could be due to factors other than adolescent depression, including genetic factors, prenatal and perinatal complications, early childhood experiences (e.g., physical and sexual abuse), or cultural/societal factors, including limited opportunities, discrimination, or socioeconomic status.

Impact of Adolescent MDD on Martial Status and Functioning

Gotlib, Lewinsohn, and Seeley (1998) examined the associations between adolescent MDD and marital status and functioning in greater detail. We found a significant three-way interaction among MDD history, age, and gender. For the young women, the main effect for age was significant. As would be expected, a greater proportion of older than younger women had married (43% of the 24- to 26-year-olds were married vs. 32% of the 19- to 23-year-olds). However, the interaction of MDD history and age significantly improved the model. Among the younger women, a significantly greater proportion of those with a history of MDD (40%) were married, compared to those without a history of MDD (29%). In the male sample, the interaction of MDD history and age was not significant. Therefore, the study seems to show that the younger female subjects with a history of MDD were more likely to be married. Apparently, if the woman did not marry early, then a history of MDD did not make a significant difference.

The fact that adolescent depression is associated with increased likelihood of early marriage for young women is consistent with similar gender findings reported by Forthofer, Markman, Cox, Stanley, and Kessler (1996). This results is also consistent with the finding that depressed individuals are elevated on interpersonal dependence, which may increase the need to have a partner, and conflictual relationships with parents, which may hasten early leaving of the family of origin (e.g., Quinton & Rutter, 1988). The effect appeared to be specific to depression. When diagnosed depression was controlled statistically, neither history of a nonaffective disorder nor lifetime comorbidity of depression and a nonaffective disorder predicted participant marital status.

In addition to marital status, marital adjustment was assessed by: (a) the Dyadic Adjustment Scale (Spanier, 1976), a very well-known measures of general marital adjustment; (b) the perceived criticism scale (Hooley & Teasdale, 1989), which assesses how critical participants perceive their spouses to be of them (two items), and how upset participants are in the face of criticism (two items); and (c) marital disagreement, assessed with 10 items developed by McGonagle, Kessler, and Gotlib (1993) to determine conflict style and resolution of marital disagreements.

Four models were examined that predicted marital adjustment. In the models predicting DAS scores, high scores (indicative of good marital adjustment) were associated with being female, a shorter length of marriage, lower CES-D scores (i.e., less current depression), being Caucasian, and with not having a history of adolescent MDD. Higher perceived criticism scores was associated with being male and with higher CES-D scores. In addition, becoming upset in the face of spousal criticism was associated with higher CES-D scores.

These results replicated the general finding in the literature of a concurrent association between marital status and current depression (which we assessed with the CES-D). More important, they also demonstrated that, independent of current symptoms, depression during adolescence significantly predicted subsequent diminished marital satisfaction and, for male participants, elevations in marital disagreements. Again, these effects were specific to adolescent depression. The fact that currently and formerly depressed young people report more marital dissatisfaction and disagreements is consistent with research suggesting that depressed individuals have problematic social behaviors that accompany depression (e.g., Gotlib & Robinson, 1982; Youngren & Lewinsohn, 1980).

COURSE OF BIPOLAR SPECTRUM DISORDERS

We recently summarized our program of research on bipolar disorder (Lewinsohn, Seeley, & Klein, 2003). It is currently accepted that the classical form of bipolar disorder (BD; Kraepelin, 1921/1976) can be manifested in children and adolescents. There is also consensus that, with relatively minor modifications, the DSM-III-R and DSM-IV criteria for BD can be used with children and adolescents. Studies of the epidemiology of BD in adults (Angst, 1988; Kessler, Rubinow, Holmes, Abelson, & Zhao, 1997) have indicated that the lifetime prevalence of BD ranges from 3% to 6% across a variety of countries and cultures (Weissman et al., 1996). Although there are no data from community samples on the prevalence of what has been called *prepubertal, juvenile,* and *pediatric BD,* it may be relatively common in clinically referred children (e.g., Biederman et al., 2004; Wozniak et al., 1995). Juvenile BD typically is characterized by high rates of rapid cycling (e.g., more than 364 cycles per year) and very high rates of comorbidity with attention deficit hyperactivity disorder (ADHD; Biederman et al., 2004; Geller et al., 2000) and conduct disorder (Biederman et al., 1997, 2004). Prepubertal BD differs in presentation from adolescent BD in showing dysphoric mania, irritability, aggressiveness, and the absence of clear-cut episodes of which good premorbid adjustment follow. Juvenile BD appears to be an extremely chronic condition, resulting in severe impairment, emotional lability, and impulsivity (e.g., Carlson, 1995).

Our OADP study suggests that the lifetime prevalence of bipolar disorders (predominantly bipolar II and cyclothymia) was approximately 1%. An additional 5.7% of the sample reported having experienced the core manic symptom (i.e., a distinct period of abnormally and persistently elevated, expansive, or irritable mood), even though they never met criteria for bipolar disorder. The mean age of onset of the first affective episode for the 18 bipolar cases through T_2 was 11.8 years (range = 7 to 15). In the majority of cases, the first episode was depression rather than mania.

There were six new cases of BD from ages 19 through 23. Three of these cases had a history of major depressive disorder (MDD) prior to age 19. However, they comprised only 1% of the adolescents with MDD in our sample, which is a much lower rate of "switching" than the 20%–30% reported in previous studies of MDD in patient samples (e.g., Geller, Fox, & Clark, 1994; Strober, Lampert, Schmidt, & Morrell, 1993). MDD before age 19 did not significantly predict the onset of BD during period of ages 19–23.

Adolescents with BD and subsyndromal BD had high rates of comorbidity. Both groups had high lifetime rates of anxiety (32%, 33% vs. 8% for the controls) and disruptive behavior disorders (19%, 22% vs. 7% for the controls). In addition, adolescents with BD and subsyndromal BD had significantly elevated rates of substance use disorders (22%, 24% vs. 10% for the controls). It is important to note that although comorbidities with ADHD (8%, 11% vs. 3%) and CD (8%, 3% vs. 3%) were significantly elevated, they were substantially below those reported by Biederman et al. (1997) and Geller et al. (2000) for prepubertal case BD. Regarding suicidal behavior, the BD group had a higher rate of suicide attempt (44%) compared to those with MDD (22%), the subsyndromal BD (18%), and no-disorder controls (1.2%).

Family studies provide an important means of testing the validity of diagnostic constructs and exploring the links between disorders. Therefore, we used the family study data to explore the validity of a diagnosis of BD in adolescents, and the relationship between full and subsyndromal BD. The first-degree relatives of adolescents with BD exhibited significantly higher rates of MDD (43%) and subsyndromal BD (4%) than did the first-degree relatives of adolescents with no history of mental disorder through age 18 (27% and 1%, respectively). In addition, the first-degree relatives of adolescents with subsyndromal BD had significantly higher rates of BD and MDD than did the relatives of never mentally ill adolescents. Interestingly, there were also significantly higher rates of anxiety disorders in the relatives of adolescents with bipolar and subsyndromal BD than in the relatives of adolescents with no history of psychopathology. However, the groups of relatives did not differ on rates of alcohol and/or drug use disorders.

In conclusion, our data provide support for the existence of a bipolar spectrum, which extends from classic bipolar I disorder to bipolar II (hypomanic) disorders to subsyndromal, milder forms of the disorder. With early detection and remediation, the many adverse consequences associated with BD, such as suicidal behavior, may be prevented. Given the pernicious course of prepubertal and adolescent BD, such efforts should be a high public health priority. An implication for clinical practice is that clinicians need to be sensitive not only to the presence of the full-blown BD syndrome, but also to the milder and less easily perceived manifestations of this disorder.

FUTURE DIRECTIONS FOR THE OADP

Our work with the OADP sample continues. Currently, we are conducting a fourth wave of diagnostic interviews (T_4) with participants at 30 years of age. We will continue to follow the course and consequences of adolescent MDD.

Given that our participants are now young adults, many of them have become parents. We are interested in how their psychiatric history as adolescents may impact their parenting status and parenting behavior, and more important, the functioning of their children. In addition, given that we interviewed the parents of OADP participants, we will have extensive data on three generations of individuals, which will allow us to examine the familial transmission of psychopathology in children. To our knowledge, there has been no previous study in which detailed prospective information has been available to examine individual differences in parents' psychiatric history prior to and following the birth of a child. We believe that this project will have substantial public health implications.

Finally, we are expanding our research beyond depression. A major focus of the T_4 assessments will be on the course and consequences of substance use disorders, which had a very high incidence rate in the T_2–T_3 period. In addition, we have become interested in the onset, phenomenology, and course of eating disorders from adolescence into young adulthood.

We believe the OADP has provided extremely valuable information regarding adolescent and young adult depression. We look forward to continuing these lines of research.

REFERENCES

Akiskal, H. S., Hirschfeld, R. M. A., & Yerevanian, B. I. (1983). The relationship of personality to affective disorders. *Archives of General Psychiatry, 40*, 801–810.

Amenson, C. S., & Lewinsohn, P. M. (1981). An investigation into the observed sex difference in prevalence of unipolar depression. *Journal of Abnormal Psychology, 90*, 1–13.

American Psychiatric Association. (1987). *Diagnostic and statistical manual of mental disorders, III-R*. Washington, DC: Author.

American Psychiatric Association. (1994). *Diagnostic and statistical manual of mental disorders* (4th ed.). Washington, DC: Author.

Andreasen, N. C., & Hoenk, P. R. (1982). The predictive value of adjustment disorders: A follow-up study. *American Journal of Psychiatry, 139*, 584–590.

Andrews, F. M., & Withey, S. B. (1976). *Social indicators of well-being: Americans' perceptions of life quality*. New York: Plenum.

Andrews, J. A., Lewinsohn, P. M., Hops, H., & Roberts, R. E. (1993). Psychometric properties of scales for the measurement of psychosocial variables associated with depression in adolescence. *Psychological Reports, 73*, 1019–1046.

Angst, J. (1988). Clinical course of affective disorders. In T. Helgason & R. J. Daly (Eds.), *Depressive illness: Prediction of course and outcome* (pp. 1–44). Heidelberg: Springer-Verlag.

Aronen, E. T., & Soininen, M. (2000). Childhood depressive symptoms predict psychiatric problems in young adults. *Canadian Journal of Psychiatry, 45,* 465–470.

Bardone, A. M., Moffitt, T. E., Caspi, A., Dickson, N., & Silva, P. A. (1996). Adult mental health and social outcomes of adolescent girls with depression and conduct disorder. *Development and Psychopathology, 8,* 811–829.

Berkman, L. F., & Syme, S. L. (1979). Social networks, host resistance, and mortality: A nine-year follow-up study of Alameda County residents. *American Journal of Epidemiology, 109*(2), 186–204.

Biederman, J., Faraone, S. V., Hatch, M., Mennin, D., Taylor, A., & George, P. (1997). Conduct disorder with and without mania in a referred sample of ADHD children. *Journal of Affective Disorders, 44,* 177–188.

Biederman, J., Faraone, S. V., Wozniak, J., Mick, E., Kwon, A., & Aleardi, M. (2004). Further evidence of unique developmental phenotypic correlates of pediatric bipolar disorder: Findings from a large sample of clinically referred preadolescent children assessed over the last 7 years. *Journal of Affective Disorders, 82S,* S45–S58.

Blatt, S., Quinlan, D., Chevron, E., McDonald, C., & Zuroff, D. (1982). Dependency and self-criticism: Psychological dimensions of depression. *Journal of Consulting and Clinical Psychology, 50,* 113–124.

Campbell, A., Converse, P. E., & Rodgers, W. L. (1976). *The quality of American life.* New York: Russell Sage Foundation.

Cantwell, D. P., & Baker, L. (1989). Stability and natural history of DSM-III childhood diagnoses. *Journal of the American Academy of Child and Adolescent Psychiatry, 28,* 691–700.

Carlson, G. A. (1995). Identifying prepubertal mania. *Journal of the American Academy of Child and Adolescent Psychiatry, 34*(6), 750–753.

Clarke, G. N., Hawkins, W., Murphy, M., Sheeber, L. B., Lewinsohn, P. M., & Seeley, J. R. (1995). Targeted prevention of unipolar depressive disorder in an at-risk sample of high school adolescents: A randomized trial of a group cognitive intervention. *Journal of the American Academy of Child and Adolescent Psychiatry, 34,* 312–321.

Cohen, P. (1996). Childhood risks for young adult symptoms of personality disorder: Method and substance. *Multivariate Behavioral Research, 31,* 121–148.

Devine, D., Kempton, T., & Forehand, R. (1994). Adolescent depressed mood and young adult functioning: A longitudinal study. *Journal of Abnormal Child Psychology, 22*(5), 629–640.

Dohrenwend, B. P., Levav, I., & Shrout, P. E. (1986). Screening scales from the Psychiatric Epidemiology Research Interview (PERI). In M. M. Weissman, J. K. Myers, & C. Ross (Eds.), *Community surveys of psychiatric disorders* (pp. 349–375). New Brunswick, NJ: Rutgers University Press.

Endicott, J., Andreason, N., & Spitzer, R. L. (1978). *Family history: Research diagnostic criteria.* New York: Biometrics Research.

Feighner, J. P., Robins, E., Guze, S. B., Woodruff, R. A., Winokur, G., & Muñoz, R. F. (1972). Diagnostic criteria for use in psychiatric research. *Archives of General Psychiatry, 26,* 57–63.

Fergusson, D. M., & Woodward, L. J. (2002). Mental health, educational, and social role outcomes of adolescents with depression. *Archives of General Psychiatry, 59,* 225–231.

Fleming, J. E., Boyle, M. H., & Offord, D. R. (1993). The outcome of adolescent depression in the Ontario child health study follow-up. *Journal of the American Academy of Child and Adolescent Psychiatry, 32,* 28–33.

Fleming, J. E., & Offord, D. R. (1990). Epidemiology of childhood depressive disorders: A critical review. *Journal of the American Academy of Child and Adolescent Psychiatry, 29*, 571–580.

Forthofer, M. S., Markman, H. J., Cox, M., Stanley, S., & Kessler, R. C. (1996). Associations between marital distress and work loss in a national sample. *Journal of Marriage and the Family, 58*, 597–605.

Garber, J., Kriss, M. R., Koch, M., & Lindholm, L. (1988). Recurrent depression in adolescents: A follow-up study. *Journal of the American Academy of Child and Adolescent Psychiatry, 27*, 49–54.

Geller, B., Fox, L. W., & Clark, K. A. (1994). Rate and predictors of prepubertal bipolarity during follow-up of 6- to 12-year-old depressed children. *Journal of the American Academy of Child and Adolescent Psychiatry, 33*, 461–468.

Geller, B., Zimerman, B., Williams, M., Bolhofner, K., Craney, J. L., DelBello, M. P., & Soutullo, C. A. (2000). Diagnostic characteristics of 93 cases of a prepubertal and early adolescent bipolar disorder phenotype by gender, puberty and comorbid attention deficit hyperactivity disorder. *Journal of Child and Adolescent Psychopharmacology, 10*, 157–164.

Gotlib, I. H., & Hammen, C. (1992). *Psychological aspects of depression: Toward an interpersonal integration.* New York: Wiley.

Gotlib, I. H., Lewinsohn, P. M., & Seeley, J. R. (1998). Consequences of depression during adolescence: Marital status and marital functioning in early adulthood. *Journal of Abnormal Psychology, 107*, 686–690.

Gotlib, I. H., & Robinson, L. A. (1982). Responses to depressed individuals: Discrepancies between self-report and observer-rated behavior. *Journal of Abnormal Psychology, 91*, 231–240.

Greenberg, W. M., Rosenfeld, D. N., & Ortega, E. A. (1995). Adjustment disorder as an admission diagnosis. *American Journal of Psychiatry, 152*(3), 459–461.

Hammen, C. (1991). The generation of stress in the course of unipolar depression. *Journal of Abnormal Psychology, 100*, 555–561.

Hirschfeld, R. M. A., Klerman, G. L., Chodoff, P., Korchin, S., & Barrett, J. (1976). Dependency—self-esteem—clinical depression. *Journal of the American Academy of Psychoanalysis, 4*, 373–388.

Hirschfeld, R. M. A., Klerman, G. L., Lavori, P., Keller, M. B., Griffith, P., & Coryell, W. (1989). Premorbid personality assessments of first onset of major depression. *Archives of General Psychiatry, 46*, 345–350.

Holmes, T. H., & Rahe, R. H. (1967). The social readjustment rating scale. *Psychosomatic Medicine, 11*, 213–218.

Hooley, J. M., & Teasdale, J. D. (1989). Predictors of relapse in unipolar depressives: Expressed emotion, marital distress, and perceived criticism. *Journal of Abnormal Psychology, 98*, 229–235.

Ilardi, S. S., Craighead, W. E., & Evans, D. D. (1997). Modeling relapse in unipolar depression: The effects of dysfunctional cognitions and personality disorders. *Journal of Consulting and Clinical Psychology, 65*, 381–391.

Kandel, D. B., & Davies, M. (1986). Adult sequelae of adolescent depressive symptoms. *Archives of General Psychiatry, 43*, 255–262.

Kaslow, N., Tanenbaum, R. L., & Seligman, M. E. P. (1978). *The KASTAN: A children's attributional style questionnaire.* Unpublished manuscript.

Kaufman, N. K., Rohde, P., Seeley, J. R., Clarke, G. N., & Stice, E. (2005). Potential mediators of cognitive-behavioral therapy for adolescents with comorbid major depression and conduct disorder. *Journal of Consulting and Clinical Psychology, 73*, 38–46.

Keller, M. B., Lavori, P. W., Friedman, B., Nielsen, E., Endicott, J., & McDonald-Scott, P. A. (1987). The Longitudinal Interval Follow-up Evaluation: A comprehensive method for assessing outcome in prospective longitudinal studies. *Archives of General Psychiatry, 44,* 540–548.

Kessler, R. C., Rubinow, D. R., Holmes, C., Abelson, J. M., & Zhao, S. (1997). The epidemiology of DSM-III-R bipolar I disorder in a general population survey. *Psychological Medicine, 27,* 1079–1089.

Klein, D. N., Lewinsohn, P. M., Rohde, P., Seeley, J. R., & Durbin, C. E. (2002). Clinical features of major depressive disorder in adolescents and their relatives: Impact on familial aggregation, implications for phenotype definition, and specificity of transmission. *Journal of Abnormal Psychology, 111,* 98–106.

Klein, D. N., Lewinsohn, P. M., Seeley, J. R., & Rohde, P. (2001). A family study of major depressive disorder in a community sample of adolescents. *Archives of General Psychiatry, 58,* 13–20.

Kovacs, M. (1996). Presentation and course of major depressive disorder during childhood and later years of the life span. *Journal of the American Academy of Child and Adolescent Psychiatry, 35,* 705–715.

Kovacs, M., Akiskal, H. S., Gatsonis, C., & Parrone, P. L. (1994). Childhood-onset dysthymic disorder: Clinical features and prospective naturalistic outcome. *Archives of General Psychiatry, 51,* 365–374.

Kovacs, M., Feinberg, T. L., Crouse-Novack, M. A., Paulauskas, S. L., Pollock, M., & Finkelstein, R. (1984). Depressive disorders in childhood. II: A longitudinal study of the risk for a subsequent major depression. *Archives of General Psychiatry, 41,* 643–649.

Kovacs, M., Gatsonis, C., Pollock, M., & Parrone, P. L. (1994). A controlled prospective study of DSM-III adjustment disorder in childhood: Short-term prognosis and long-term predictive validity. *Archives of General Psychiatry, 51*(7), 535–541.

Kovacs, M., & Goldston, D. (1991). Cognitive and social cognitive development of depressed children and adolescents. *Journal of the American Academy of Child and Adolescent Psychiatry, 30,* 388–392.

Kovacs, M., Ho, V., & Pollock, M. H. (1995). Criterion and predictive validity of the diagnosis of adjustment disorder: A prospective study of youths with new-onset insulin-dependent diabetes mellitus. *American Journal of Psychiatry, 152,* 523–528.

Kraepelin, E. (1921/1976). Manic-depressive insanity and paranoia (R. M. Barclay, Trans.). New York: Arno.

Leckman, J. F., Sholomskas, D., Thompson, D., Belanger, A., & Weissman, M. M. (1982). Best estimate of lifetime psychiatric diagnosis: A methodological study. *Archives of General Psychiatry, 39,* 879–883.

Lewinsohn, P. M., Allen, N. B., Seeley, J. R., & Gotlib, I. H. (1999). First onset versus recurrence of depression: Differential processes of psychosocial risk. *Journal of Abnormal Psychology, 108,* 483–489.

Lewinsohn, P. M., Hoberman, H., Teri, L., & Hautzinger, M. (1985). An integrative theory of depression. In S. Reiss & R. Bootzin (Eds.), *Theoretical issues in behavior therapy* (pp. 331–359). New York: Academic Press.

Lewinsohn, P. M., Hops, H., Roberts, R. E., Seeley, J. R., & Andrews, J. A. (1993). Adolescent psychopathology: I. Prevalence and incidence of depression and other DSM-III-R disorders in high school students. *Journal of Abnormal Psychology, 102,* 133–144.

Lewinsohn, P. M., Klein, D. N., & Seeley, J. R. (1995). Bipolar disorders in a community sample of older adolescents: Prevalence, phenomenology, comorbidity, and course. *Journal of the American Academy of Child and Adolescent Psychiatry, 34,* 454–463.

Lewinsohn, P. M., Mermelstein, R. M., Alexander, C., & MacPhillamy, D. (1985). The Unpleasant Events Schedule: A scale for the measurement of aversive events. *Journal of Clinical Psychology, 41*, 483–498.

Lewinsohn, P. M., Roberts, R. E., Seeley, J. R., Rohde, P., Gotlib, I. H., & Hops, H. (1994). Adolescent psychopathology: II. Psychosocial risk factors for depression. *Journal of Abnormal Psychology, 103*, 302–315.

Lewinsohn, P. M., Rohde, P., Klein, D. N., & Seeley, J. R. (1999). Natural course of adolescent major depressive disorder: I. Continuity into young adulthood. *Journal of the American Academy of Child and Adolescent Psychiatry, 38*, 56–63.

Lewinsohn, P. M., Rohde, P., Seeley, J. R., & Hops, H. (1991). Comorbidity of unipolar depression: I. Major depression with dysthymia. *Journal of Abnormal Psychology, 100*(2), 205–213.

Lewinsohn, P. M., Rohde, P., Seeley, J. R., & Klein, D. N. (1997). Axis II psychopathology as a function of Axis I disorders in childhood and adolescence. *Journal of the American Academy of Child and Adolescent Psychiatry, 36*, 1752–1759.

Lewinsohn, P. M., Rohde, P., Seeley, J. R., Klein, D. N., & Gotlib, I. H. (2000). Natural course of adolescent major depressive disorder in a community sample: Predictors of recurrence in young adults. *American Journal of Psychiatry, 157*, 1584–1591.

Lewinsohn, P. M., Rohde, P., Seeley, J. R., Klein, D. N., & Gotlib, I. (2003). Psychosocial functioning of young adults who have experienced and recovered from major depressive disorder during adolescence. *Journal of Abnormal Psychology, 112*, 353–363.

Lewinsohn, P. M., Seeley, J. R., & Klein, D. N. (2003). Bipolar disorder in adolescents: Epidemiology and suicidal behavior. In B. Geller & M. DelBello (Eds.), *Bipolar disorder in childhood and early adolescence* (pp. 7–24). New York: Guilford.

Loranger, A. W. (1988). *Personality disorder examination (PDE) manual.* Yonkers, NY: DV Communications.

Mannuzza, S., & Fyer, A. J. (1990). *Family informant schedule and criteria (FISC)* (rev. ed.). New York: Anxiety Disorders Clinic, New York State Psychiatric Institute.

McGee, R., Feehan, M., Williams, S., Partridge, F., Silva, P. A., & Kelly, J. (1990). DSM-III disorders in a large sample of adolescents. *Journal of the American Academy of Child and Adolescent Psychiatry, 29*, 611–619.

McGonagle, K. A., Kessler, R. C., & Gotlib, I. H. (1993). The effects of marital disagreement style, frequency, and outcome on marital disruption. *Journal of Social and Personal Relationships, 10*, 385–404.

Merikangas, K. R., Wicki, W., & Angst, J. (1994). Heterogeneity of depression: Classification of depressive subtypes by longitudinal course. *British Journal of Psychiatry, 164*, 342–348.

Monroe, S. M., Rohde, P., Seeley, J. R., & Lewinsohn, P. M. (1999). Life events and depression in adolescence: Relationship loss as a prospective risk factor for first onset of major depressive disorder. *Journal of Abnormal Psychology, 108*, 606–614.

Mrazek, P. J., & Haggerty, R. J. (1994). *Reducing risks for mental disorders: Frontiers for preventive intervention research.* Washington, DC: National Academy Press.

Newcorn, J. H., & Strain, J. (1998). Adjustment disorder in children and adolescents. *Journal of the American Academy of Child and Adolescent Psychiatry, 31*, 318–326.

Oldham, J. M., Skodol, A. E., Kellman, H. D., Hyler, S. E., Doidge, N., Rosnick, L., & Gallagher, P. E. (1995). Comorbidity of Axis I and Axis II disorders. *American Journal of Psychiatry, 152*, 571–578.

Orvaschel, H., Puig-Antich, J., Chambers, W. J., Tabrizi, M. A., & Johnson, R. (1982). Retrospective assessment of prepubertal major depression with the Kiddie-SADS-E. *Journal of the American Academy of Child Psychiatry, 21*, 392–397.

Pfohl, B., Coryell, W., Zimmerman, M., & Stangl, D. (1987). Prognostic validity of self-report and interview measures of personality disorder in depressed inpatients. *Journal of Clinical Psychiatry, 48*, 468–472.

Post, R. M., Weiss, S. B., & Leverich, G. S. (1994). Recurrent affective disorder: Roots in developmental neurobiology and illness progression based on changes in gene expression. *Development and Psychopathology, 6*, 781–813.

Procidano, M. E., & Heller, K. (1983). Measures of perceived social support from friends and from family: Three validation studies. *American Journal of Community Psychology, 11*, 1–24.

Puig-Antich, J., Kaufman, J., Ryan, N., Williamson, D. E., Dahl, R. E., Lukens, E., Todak, G., Ambrosini, P., Rabinovich, H., & Nelson, B. (1993). The psychosocial functioning and family environment of depressed adolescents. *Journal of the American Academy of Child and Adolescent Psychiatry, 32*, 244–253.

Quinton, D., & Rutter, M. (1988). *Parenting breakdown: The making and breaking of intergenerational links.* Avebury, UK: Gower.

Radloff, L. S. (1977). The CES-D Scale: A self-report depression scale for research in the general population. *Applied Psychological Measurement, 1*, 385–401.

Rao, U., Ryan, N. D., Birmaher, B., Dahl, R. E., Williamson, D. E., Kaufman, J., Rao, R., & Nelson, B. (1995). Unipolar depression in adolescents: Clinical outcomes in adulthood. *Journal of the American Academy of Child Psychiatry, 34*, 566–578.

Rao, U., Weissman, M. M., Martin, J. A., & Hammond, R. W. (1993). Childhood depression and risk of suicide: A preliminary report of a longitudinal study. *Journal of the American Academy of Child and Adolescent Psychiatry, 32*, 21–27.

Reinherz, H., Giaconia, R. M., Carmola, A. M., Wasserman, M. W., & Silverman, A. B. (1999). Major depression in young adulthood: Risks and impairments. *Journal of Abnormal Psychology, 108*, 500–510.

Robin, A. L., & Weiss, J. G. (1980). Criterion-related validity of behavioral and self-report measures of problem-solving communication skills in distressed and nondistressed parent–adolescent dyads. *Behavioral Assessment, 2*, 339–352.

Rohde, P., Lewinsohn, P. M., & Seeley, J. R. (1991). Comorbidity of unipolar depression: II Comorbidity with other mental disorders in adolescents and adults. *Journal of Abnormal Psychology, 100*, 214–222.

Rohde, P., Lewinsohn, P. M., & Seeley, J. R. (1994). Are adolescents changed by an episode of major depression? *Journal of the American Academy of Child and Adolescent Psychiatry, 33*, 1289–1298.

Rohde, P., Lewinsohn, P. M., & Seeley, J. R. (1997). Comparability of telephone and face-to-face interviews assessing Axis I and II disorders. *American Journal of Psychiatry, 154*, 1593–1598.

Spanier, G. B. (1976). Measuring dyadic adjustment: New scales for assessing the quality of marriage and similar dyads. *Journal of Marriage and the Family, 38*, 15–28.

Spence, S. H., Sheffield, J. K., & Donovan, C. L. (2005). Long-term outcome of a school-based, universal approach to prevention of depression in adolescents. *Journal of Consulting and Clinical Psychology, 73*, 160–167.

Spitzer, R. L., Williams, J. B. W., Gibbon, M., & First, M. B. (1992). The Structured Clinical Interview for DSM-III-R (SCID): I. History, rationale, and description. *Archives of General Psychiatry, 49*, 624–629.

Strober, M., Lampert, C., Schmidt, S., & Morrell, W. (1993). The course of major depressive disorder in adolescents: I. Recovery and risk of manic switching in a follow-up of psychotic and nonpsychotic subtypes. *Journal of the American Academy of Child and Adolescent Psychiatry, 32*, 34–42.

Weissman, M. M., Bland, R. C., Canino, G. J., Faravelli, C., Greenwald, S., Hwu, H. G., Joyce, P. R., Karam, E. G., Lee, C. K., Lellouch, J., Lépine, J. P., Newman, S. C., Rubio-Stipec, M., Wells, J. E., Wickramaratne, P. J., Wittchen, H. U., & Yeh, E. K. (1996). Cross-national epidemiology of major depression and bipolar disorder. *Journal of the American Medical Association, 276*(4), 293–299.

Weissman, M. M., Gammon, G. D., John, K., Merikangas, K. R., Warner, V., Prusoff, B. A., & Sholomskas, D. (1987). Children of depressed parents: Increased psychopathology and early onset of major depression. *Archives of General Psychiatry, 44*, 847–853.

Winokur, G., & Tsuang, M. T. (1996). *The natural history of mania, depression, and schizophrenia.* Washington, DC: American Psychiatric Press.

Wozniak, J., Biederman, J., Kiely, K., Ablon, S., Faraone, S. V., Mundy, E., & Mennin, D. (1995). Mania-like symptoms suggestive of childhood-onset bipolar disorder in clinically referred children. *Journal of the American Academy of Child and Adolescent Psychiatry, 34*, 867–876.

Youngren, M., & Lewinsohn, P. M. (1980). The functional relation between depression and problematic interpersonal behavior. *Journal of Abnormal Psychology, 89*, 333–341.

view and annual interviews at 1, 2, 3, 4, and 5 years. For each follow-up, in addition to interviews, packets of questionnaires were mailed and returned. Also, at each follow-up permission was obtained to recruit the woman's "best friend" and if available, a steady boyfriend—to complete questionnaires about their relationship and characteristics of the subject. The majority of follow-up interviews were conducted by telephone, when possible using the same interviewer who had been following the subject over time.

Measures

Each interview included a Structured Diagnostic Interview for DSM-III-R (SCID; Spitzer, Williams, Gibbon, & First, 1990). The initial interview evaluated lifetime history of disorders, and subsequent follow-up SCID interviews covered the interval since the previous interview. At one follow-up, the SCID II covering Axis II disorders was included. Interviews for chronic stress and functioning, and episodic life events, were also conducted initially and at each follow-up, using methods previously developed by our group (e.g., Hammen et al., 1987). These measures yielded interviewer ratings of ongoing stress/functioning in the following domains: close friend, social life, romantic relationship, family, school, work, and health, as well as episodic life events scored for objective severity by an independent rating team.

Numerous questionnaires were also included, covering topics such as attachment cognitions and social competence, BDI, relationship satisfaction, and others as noted in subsequent sections.

DEPRESSION OUTCOMES OVER FOLLOW-UP

The rates of diagnosable depressive disorders were relatively high (Rao, Hammen, & Daley, 1999). Prior to the start of the study, 31% of the women had reported a diagnosable major depressive episode or dysthymic disorder, mostly occurring around ages 15 and 16. These figures are consistent with rates reported by Lewinsohn, Hops, Roberts, Seeley, and Andrews (1993) for similar-aged adolescent women. At the time of the first interview, 7% of the women were currently in an episode of major depressive disorder (MDD) or dysthymic disorder, and several other women reported current anxiety, eating, or substance use disorders.

Confirming that, for young women, the transition to adulthood is a high-risk period for development of depression, 47% of the women retained in the follow-up had one or more episodes of MDD during the study. This figure included both first onsets and recurrences, and the first-onset rate for never-depressed women during the ages of 18 and 22 was 37%. For the entire sample, the first 2 years of the follow-up after high school graduation were associated with the highest risk for depressive episodes. Overall, the rates of significant depression were high, although relatively consistent with continuing follow-ups from the Oregon Adolescent Depression Study (Lewinsohn et al., 1993: Lewinsohn, Rohde, Klein, & Seeley, 1999).

INTERPERSONAL PREDICTORS OF DEPRESSION

Interpersonal factors are important precipitants of depression. Consistent with our diathesis-stress framework, we predicted that women who have cognitions about their close relationships that suggest vulnerability in attachment, and who experience stressful life events of an interpersonal content, will be likely to become depressed (Hammen et al., 1995). Based on Bowlby's attachment hypothesis that working models (cognitive representations) of relationships that are formed in early childhood with the caretaker will have enduring effects on one's attitudes about close relationships with others, we administered the Revised Adult Attachment Scale (RAAS; Collins & Read, 1990) to measure adult attachment cognitions. Controlling for initial symptoms, we found that the combination of RAAS cognitions about relationships and interpersonal stressful life events predicted subsequent symptomatology. The subscale—anxiety about abandonment or not being loved—was especially significant in interaction with interpersonal stressors when predicting increases in depression symptoms.

Interpersonal stressors are potent precipitants of depression, as the previous study indicated—and this may be especially true of those with previous dysfunctional beliefs that make them vulnerable. Another crucial issue concerning interpersonal life events, however, is that they typically occur in part because of the subject's actions or characteristics. Hence, an argument with an important friend, a breakup with a romantic partner, or a fight with a parent are events that occur in part because of the subject. In prior work, we have noted that women with depression histories do not randomly experience events that are at least in part dependent on their behaviors or characteristics; rather, they have relatively higher rates of such dependent events than do comparisons such as medically ill or never-ill women (Hammen, 1991b). We called this process "stress generation," and tested whether it would be observed in the high school transition sample.

Fig. 4.1 is based on data reported by Daley et al. (1997), and demonstrates that the tendency to experience higher rates of "dependent" events in the subsequent year was indeed higher among those who had previous depressive disorders, compared with those who had nondepressive disorders or who had no disorders. Dependent events are largely interpersonal in content. In contrast, there were no differences among the groups in "independent" or fateful events whose occurrence was outside the person's control. Thus, the stress generation hypothesis may be extended beyond a clinical sample (Hammen, 1991b) to a community sample of women. It should be noted, however, that among the group of women with comorbid depression and other nondepressive disorders, rates of interpersonal conflict life events were especially high. In both stress generation studies noted, the stressful life events did not typically occur during a depressive episode, and therefore may not be due to the effects of depression itself. More recent research has evaluated this claim using a longitudinal framework. Depressed women and non-disordered controls were followed up at 1 year and 10 years. There was no difference between the groups in independent stressors, but the depressed group experienced more dependent stressors at the 1-year follow-up. Notably, the depressed group also experienced more dependent interpersonal stressors at the 10-year follow-up (Chun, Cronkite, & Moos, 2004). We hypothesize, in keeping with a relational pathology perspective, that underlying and enduring social dysfunction contributes to the future occurrence of interpersonal stressors—a topic about which more is said later in the chapter.

A singular implication of the generation of dependent (largely interpersonal) life events is that such events are highly likely to precipitate depressive episodes, especially in those persons at risk due to vulnerability factors. Davila, Hammen, Burge, Paley, and Daley (1995) examined the predictive effects of interpersonal stress on subsequent depression over a longitudinal period. We found that a measure combining interpersonal chronic stress and interpersonal conflict events (dependent at least in part

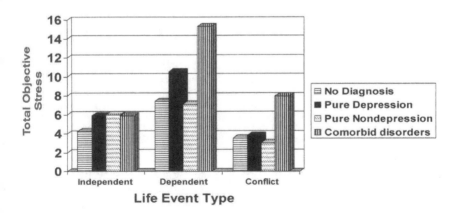

FIG. 4.1. Total objective stress ratings of Year 2 episodic events according to Year 1 diagnoses. Data from Daley et al. (1997). Predictors of the generation of episodic stress: A longitudinal study of late adolescent women. *Journal of Abnormal Psychology, 106*, 251–259. Copyright © 1997 by the American Psychological Association. Adapted with permission.

on the person) was a significant predictor of subsequent depression, controlling for initial symptoms. One important implication of "stress generation" concerns recurrence of depression. We speculate that the transaction between the depressed person and the environment creates a stressful context in which negative interpersonal events occur that precipitate new episodes of depression, creating a vicious cycle with high likelihood of recurring depression.

INTERPERSONAL CONSEQUENCES AND CORRELATES OF DEPRESSION

Based on research that has clearly indicated that depression is often associated with marital discord and disruption (e.g., Gotlib & Hammen, 1992), we predicted that young women with depression histories would be likely to experience difficulties in their dating relationships. Rao et al. (1999) examined the relationships between amount of depression (proportion of time spent in major depressive episodes over the 5-year period) and the women's functioning at the end of the study. We found that among the domains of role functioning, the two that were most strongly impacted by depression over the prior years were school and romantic relationship functioning. Significant negative correlations were observed between amount of depression and level of functioning rated by the interviewers at the end of the 5-year period (r-values $= -.23$ and $-.28$ for school and romantic relationships, respectively). Moreover, ratings by the boyfriends also reflected their relative dissatisfaction; the greater the women's prior depression in 5 years, the less relationship satisfaction their boyfriends reported ($r = -.31$, $p < .05$). Interestingly, the women's reports of their own relationship satisfaction were unrelated to their prior depression experiences. Also, highly tellingly, measures of the Modified Conflict Tactics Scale (MCTS; Neidig & Friedman, 1984) indicated significant correlations between the amount of the women's prior depression and their boyfriends' use of psychological coercion ($r = .23$, $p < .05$) and physical coercion ($r = .34$, $p < .01$).

A clue as to the partners' reported relative dissatisfaction comes from observations of actual quality of interaction. We recruited a small group ($n = 30$) of women with ongoing relationships and their partners to participate in a 10-minute interaction task to discuss a self-selected topic on which they disagreed (Cohen & Hammen, 1999). Four scores based on the women's behavior were coded from the videotaped interaction tasks, rated blind as to depression history: negative affect, negative content, positive affect, and positive content. There were no associations between negative affect and content and the women's depression history. However, number of prior episodes of depression and worst self-report BDI scores were significantly negatively correlated with positive affect. It appeared, therefore, that even when not currently depressed, women with histories of more depression displayed less positive affect—smiling, nodding, affectionate touching, and making eye contact—in their partner interactions. Other clues about possibly dysfunctional interaction styles are noted in the following section on suspected mechanisms of relational pathology.

MECHANISMS OF RELATIONAL PATHOLOGY

Thus far, we have noted that results from the study indicate high rates of depression that appeared to be predicted, and presumably precipitated, by negative interpersonal life events, and associated with relatively negative interpersonal consequences, including more romantic relationship dysfunction, partner dissatisfaction, and generation of dependent (mostly interpersonal) life events. A question remains: What are the nature and origin of possible interpersonal difficulties?

To date, we have addressed the issues in several ways, although we do not claim to have evidence that the dysfunctional characteristics existed prior to depression, or that they are specific to depression. However, we explored the general question to learn more about interpersonal functioning, and we hypothesized that relationship difficulties would be associated with maladaptive cognitions and interpersonal problem-solving capabilities. We reasoned that such deficits would eventually cause disruption and conflict in important relationships creating stressful life events, thus precipitating depressive reactions.

One of the first efforts was to determine whether young women who had deficits in interpersonal problem-solving skills would be at risk for development of depression. In the Hammen (1991b) study, women who had been in treatment for depression showed higher rates of dependent life events, and their subcategories of interpersonal and conflict events, compared with medically ill, bipolar, and nonill women. The levels of conflict events over a 1-year period were especially noteworthy and suggested the possibility that these women either were unable to avoid the conflict or were unable to resolve it satisfactorily before it became a major negative life event. Thus, we hypothesized that interpersonal problem-solving skills might be part of the reason for the women's high levels of conflict.

Accordingly, Davila et al. (1995) developed a measure of interpersonal problem solving using procedures similar to Schultz, Yeates, and Selman (1989) in their interpersonal negotiation strategies interview. Participants were presented with several scenarios representing interpersonal situations involving potential conflicts. Specific probes were used to elicit participants' ability to identify the problem (and recognition of the mutuality of the problem), generation of solutions (and ability to solve the problem in a way that takes into account the needs of both parties), and consequential thinking (ability to foresee and articulate consequences). Scores on problem identification, solution generation, and recognition of consequences were combined for a total IPS score. A structural equation model analysis confirmed the hypothesis that quality of interpersonal problem-solving predicted extent of later interpersonal stress, that in turn predicted the worst depressive experience (if any) during a 1-year period. Thus, the study provided preliminary evidence that social problem-solving skills predicted subsequent occurrence of interpersonal stress, which in turn predicted depressive symptoms. However, the composite score used in the analyses did not allow more precise understanding of specific deficits in problem solving.

Other methods were used to attempt to clarify interpersonal characteristics of the women and their association with stress generation. A measure of interpersonal competence, the Interpersonal Competence Questionnaire (ICQ; Buhrmester, Furman, Wittenberg, & Reis, 1988), assessed subjects' self-perceived competence in five interpersonal tasks: initiating relationships, asserting displeasure with others, disclosing personal information, providing emotional support and advice, and dealing with interpersonal conflict. Daley and Hammen (2002) found that self-reported overall ICQ scores were significantly negatively correlated with participants' mean BDI scores over 5 years ($r = -.39, p < .001$), and also with their boyfriends' report of the subjects' interpersonal competence ($r = -.28, p < .05$).

Several studies examined predictors of stress generation. Perceived competence (ICQ) was a significant predictor of chronic interpersonal stress 1 year later, controlling for initial symptoms and initial chronic stress (Herzberg et al., 1998). Specifically, participants who perceived that they provided less emotional support for others were those with the most increased chronic interpersonal stress. Similarly, Nelson, Hammen, Daley, Burge, and Davila (2001) noted that need for control, a subscale of the autonomy scale of the sociotropy-autonomy measure (Beck, Epstein, Harrison, & Emery, 1983) predicted chronic interpersonal stress 18 months later, controlling for initial interpersonal stress and symptoms. Daley et al. (1997) had also found that autonomy, but not sociotropy, predicted future interpersonal and conflict episodic life events. Daley et al. (1997) additionally determined that psychopathology and chronic interpersonal stress made independent contributions to the prediction of later interpersonal episodic stress.

Taken together, these studies suggest several patterns concerning the generation of stressful events and chronic stress. One is that there is an apparent link between self- and other-perceived interpersonal competence and depression. Furthermore, individuals who have lower levels of observed skill in resolving interpersonal disputes generate more stress. Another is that personality attributes such as need for control (autonomy) and low emotional support for others contribute to increases in interpersonal discord and reduced quality of social relationships. Also, these effects can occur even when initial symptoms are controlled, suggesting that although symptomatology may contribute to stress generation, other factors are also involved. Finally, as the Daley et al. (1997) study suggested, quality of interpersonal relationships predicts future occurrence of stressful life events, indicating that individuals not only create stressors through their own characteristics and behaviors but, once in adverse situations, the chronic conditions themselves contribute to an increased likelihood of future stressful life events.

In addition to skills related to interpersonal problem solving and social competence, another area of investigation concerns attachment-related cognitions. We speculated that cognitions about relationships with others that reflect negative expectations of others' availability and dependability, and comfort with closeness, may represent dysfunctional cognitions serving as vulnerability factors for depression. Several of our studies indicated that relatively negative attachment cognitions on the RAAS predicted future increases in depression, especially in interaction with initial symptoms (e.g., Burge et al., 1997)—although negative attachment cognitions were not specific to depression changes—and also predicted changes in other symptoms, such as anxiety, eating disorders, and substance abuse.

Relatively insecure attachment cognitions were shown to be associated with social support: Those persons with more insecure attachment beliefs about parents and peers were significantly more likely to report less perceived and enacted social support (Herzberg et al., 1999). As Herzberg et al. (1999) noted, relationships lacking in emotionally supportive transactions may be a feature of insecurely attached individuals, following the continuity hypothesis of Sroufe and Fleeson (1986), who predicted that individuals will seek close relationships that replicate the emotional qualities of the original attachment dyad.

Daley and Hammen (2002) further explored the idea that depression in young women may be associated with selection into unsupportive relationships. Several studies had suggested that depressed women are more likely to marry men who themselves evidence psychopathology (e.g., Hammen, 1991a; Mathews & Reus, 2001) or who otherwise provide problematic marital material. Additionally, women's depressive symptoms have been shown to be predictive of both physical and psychological aggression from their male partners (Kim & Capaldi, 2004). Although the vast majority of women in the present study were not married, nor did we have data on their partners' possible psychological diagnoses, we were able to explore the quality of relationships with the romantic partner and the woman's best friend, to determine whether "assortative pairing" (differential association with symptomatic friends and partners) would be observed.

Table 4.1 presents correlations among several features of the relationships and women's mean level of depression (BDI) over the 5 years (Daley

& Hammen, 2002). There was more strain in both these relationships among relatively more depressed women. Also, subjects' reports of friend emotional support were unrelated to their depression level, but friends' reports of emotional support were higher for the more depressed women. This pattern suggests that friends of depressed women felt that they provided more support to the women than the subjects themselves perceived. Moreover, both the subjects and their romantic partners reported less emotional support for the subjects the more depressed they were. Thus, depression in the women was associated with less support by their partners but more support by their best friends (although the subjects did not perceive the support). Finally, Table 4.1 indicates support for an element of "assortative pairing," showing significant associations between the extent of the subjects' depression and personality pathology in their friends and partners. In analyses testing a mediational model of romantic partners' emotional support over a prospective period, Daley and Hammen (2002) found that the relatively depressed women paired with partners who had Axis II symptoms, particularly Cluster A (which includes characteristics such as interpersonally aloof, guarded, restricted in affect, and lacking empathy), which predicted less emotional support. In the generally non-clinical range of psychopathology, such patterns may also reflect partners' "dismissive" or avoidant attachment style. Whether the partners' unsupportive emotional behaviors may have developed as a result of the negative effects of the woman's depression, or whether such partners were "selected" by women with insecure attachments, cannot be determined in the present study. By either pathway, however, the patterns portend a pernicious and problematic course of relationship functioning, and one likely to eventuate in conflict or dissolution that may trigger further depression in the woman.

There are numerous other candidates to pursue for clarifying the mechanisms by which interpersonal processes may be involved in depression. These analyses suggest fertile ground for further research, but many questions remain.

CONCLUSION

Fig. 4.2 presents a graphic representation of several elements that we have emphasized in the work described herein, as well as continuing work on depression in other samples not presented. The figure is meant to summarize a complex approach to depression. It is essentially an intergenerational model of interpersonal vulnerability, with dysfunctional cognitions and skills mediating the impact of adverse family conditions on the development of interpersonal experiences that portend depression (or recurrence). The figure is intended to present some of the relevant variables in an interpersonal model, but it is not expected to be a complete model, nor

TABLE 4.1

Zero-Order Correlations Between Participants' Depressive Symptoms
and the Relationship Variables

Relationship Variable	r With Participant BDI
Interviewer rating of chronic stress[a]	
Best friendship stress	.33***
Romantic relationship stress	.47***
Emotional support, friendship[b]	
Participant's report	.00
Friend's report	.26*
Emotional support, romantic[c]	
Participant's report	−.36**
Partner's report	−.31*
Best friend's self-reported symptomatology	
Cluster A symptoms[d]	.40***
Cluster B symptoms[d]	.10
Cluster C symptoms[d]	.11
Depression[e]	.18†
Romantic partner's self-reported symptomatology	
Cluster A symptoms[f]	.35**
Cluster B symptoms[f]	.46***
Cluster C symptoms[f]	.49***
Depression[g]	.18

Note: BDI = Beck Depression Inventory
[a]$n = 138$, [b]$n = 84$, [c]$n = 48$, [d]$n = 76$, [e]$n = 91$, [f]$n = 51$, [g]$n = 60$.
†$p < .09$, *$p \leq .05$, **$p \leq .01$, ***$p \leq .001$, all two-tailed.
From Daley, S., & Hammen, C. (2002). Symptoms of depression and close relationships in late adolescence: Perspectives from dysphoric young women, their best friends, and their romantic partners. *Journal of Consulting and Clinical Psychology, 70*, 129–141. Copyright © 2002 by the American Psychological Association. Adapted with permission.

do we anticipate that the associations among the key ingredients necessarily operate only as shown. This is a work in progress, and the goal of presenting the diagram is mainly to capture the complexity of transactional diathesis-stress processes that emphasize interpersonal causal features of depression in women.

The study of interpersonal processes in depressive disorders has accelerated in recent years, spurred at least in part by significant and consistent evidence of high rates of depression emerging in young women during ad-

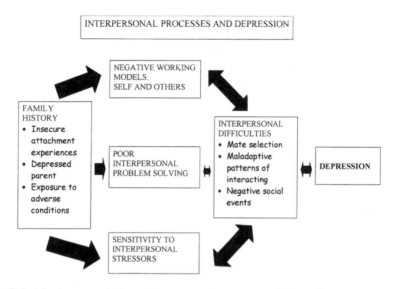

FIG. 4.2. A representation of interpersonal processes and depression outcomes.

olescence at a time of considerable change in social development and transitions, and evidence of highly problematic family environments observed among those with depressive disorders. Such findings have drawn attention to the role played by interpersonal events and circumstances as precipitants and consequences of depression. Additionally, researchers have increasingly come to view depression as a recurrent if not chronic mental health problem, such that the need for understanding factors that contribute to its continuation is a pressing issue. Research described in this chapter suggests some of the ways in which depression and the interpersonal context of the individual's life interact in ways that, over time, predict recurring depression.

At the same time, however, researchers have come to appreciate that depression is heterogeneous not only in its presentation, but also in its etiological roots. Therefore, it is important to emphasize that the research discussed in this chapter is entirely based on women, and its generality to adolescent males and young men with depression needs to be pursued. Similarly, we do not intend to imply that interpersonal processes are salient in all instances of female depression, and we acknowledge that an interpersonal perspective is only one approach.

Having acknowledged caveats, we nonetheless believe that all depressions have the potential for serious interpersonal consequences, and that the contexts in which they occur may contribute to recurrences, regardless of the initial etiological agents. A transactional perspective, in which the individual and the environment affect each other, would seem to be universally applicable in understanding the chronic or recurrent nature of depression and its effects on others. There is much remaining to be done to pursue several critically important issues: the role of interpersonal factors as vulnerability and causal ingredients for initial depression; the integration of social variables into complex biopsychosocial models of depressive disorders; and determination of the specificity, if any, of interpersonal factors for depressive outcomes.

REFERENCES

Beck, A. T., Epstein, N., Harrison, R., & Emery, G. (1983). *Development of the Sociotropy-Autonomy Scale: A measure of personality factors in psychopathology.* Unpublished manuscript, University of Pennsylvania, Philadelphia.

Buhrmester, D., Furman, W., Wittenberg, M. T., & Reis, H. T. (1988). Five domains of interpersonal competence in peer relationships. *Journal of Personality and Social Psychology, 55,* 991–1008.

Burge, D., Hammen, C., Davila, J., Daley, S., Paley, B., Lindberg, N., Herzberg, D., & Rudolph, K. (1997). The relationship between attachment cognitions and psychological adjustment in late adolescent women. *Development and Psychopathology, 9,* 151–168.

Chun, C-A., Cronkite, R. C., & Moos, R. H. (2004). Stress generation in depressed patients and community controls. *Journal of Social and Clinical Psychology, 23,* 390–412.

Cohen, A., & Hammen, C. (1999). *Effects of previous depression on current interactions in romantic relationships among young women.* Unpublished manuscript, University of California, Los Angeles.

Collins, N. L., & Read, S. J. (1990). Adult attachment, working models, and relationship quality in dating couples. *Journal of Personality and Social Psychology, 58,* 644–663.

Daley, S., & Hammen, C. (2002). Symptoms of depression and close relationships in late adolescence: Perspectives from dysphoric young women, their best friends, and their romantic partners. *Journal of Consulting and Clinical Psychology, 70,* 129–141.

Daley, S., Hammen, C., Burge, D., Davila, J., Paley, B., Lindberg, N., & Herzberg, D. (1997). Predictors of the generation of episodic stress: A longitudinal study of late adolescent women. *Journal of Abnormal Psychology, 106,* 251–259.

Davila, J., Hammen, C., Burge, D., Paley, B., & Daley, S. (1995). Poor interpersonal problem-solving as a mechanism of stress generation in depression among adolescent women. *Journal of Abnormal Psychology, 104,* 592–600.

Gotlib, I., & Hammen, C. (1992). *Psychological aspects of depression: Toward cognitive and interpersonal integration.* Chicester, UK: Wiley.

Hammen, C. (1991a). *Depression runs in families: The social context of risk and resilience in children of depressed mothers.* New York: Springer-Verlag.

Hammen, C. (1991b). The generation of stress in the course of unipolar depression. *Journal of Abnormal Psychology, 100,* 555–561.

Hammen, C., Adrian, C., Gordon, D., Burge, D., Jaenicke, C., & Hiroto, D. (1987). Children of depressed mothers: Maternal strain and symptom predictors of dysfunction. *Journal of Abnormal Psychology, 96,* 190–198.

Hammen, C., Burge, D., Daley, S., Davila, J., Paley, B., & Rudolph, K. (1995). Interpersonal attachment cognitions and prediction of symptomatic responses to interpersonal stress. *Journal of Abnormal Psychology, 104,* 436–443.

Herzberg, D., Hammen, C., Burge, D., Daley, S., Davila, J., & Lindberg, N. (1998). Social competence as a predictor of chronic interpersonal stress. *Personal Relationships, 5,* 207–218.

Herzberg, D., Hammen, C., Burge, D., Daley, S., Davila, J., & Lindberg, N. (1999). Attachment cognitions predict perceived and enacted social support during late adolescence. *Journal of Adolescent Research, 14,* 387–404.

Kim, H. K., & Capaldi, D. M. (2004). The association of antisocial behavior and depressive symptoms between partners and risk for aggression in romantic relationships. *Journal of Family Psychology, 18,* 82–96.

Lewinsohn, P. M., Hops, H., Roberts, R. E., Seeley, J. R., & Andrews, J. A. (1993). Adolescent psychopathology: I. Prevalence and incidence of depression and other DSM-III-R disorders in high school students. *Journal of Abnormal Psychology, 102,* 133–144.

Lewinsohn, P. M., Rohde, P., Klein, D. M., & Seeley, J. R. (1999). Natural course of adolescent major depressive disorder: I. Continuity into young adulthood. *Journal of the American Academy of Child and Adolescent Psychiatry, 38,* 56–63.

Lyons-Ruth, K. (1995). Broadening our conceptual frameworks: Can we reintroduce relational strategies and implicit representational systems to the study of psychopathology? *Developmental Psychology, 31,* 432–436.

Mathews, C. A., & Reus, V. I. (2001). Assortative mating in the affective disorders: A systematic review and meta-analysis. *Comprehensive Psychiatry, 42,* 257–262.

Neidig, P. H., & Friedman, D. H. (1984). *Spouse abuse: A treatment program for couples.* Champaign, IL: Research Press.

Nelson, D., Hammen, C., Daley, S., Burge, D., & Davila, J. (2001). Sociotropic and autonomous personality styles: Contributions to chronic life stress. *Cognitive Therapy and Research, 25,* 61–76.

Rao, U., Hammen, C., & Daley, S. (1999). Continuity of depression during the transition to adulthood: A 5-year longitudinal study of young women. *Journal of the American Academy of Child and Adolescent Psychiatry, 38,* 908–915.

Schultz, L. H., Yeates, K. O., & Selman, R. L. (1989). *The Interpersonal Negotiation Strategies (INS) Interview: A scoring manual.* Cambridge, MA: Harvard Graduate School of Education, The Group for the Study of Interpersonal Development.

Spitzer, R. L., Williams, J. B. W., Gibbon, M., & First, M. B. (1990). *User's guide for the structured clinical interview for DSM-III-R: SCID.* Washington, DC: American Psychiatric Press.

Sroufe, L. A., & Fleeson, J. (1986). Attachment and the construction of relationships. In W. Hartup & Z. Rubin (Eds.), *Relationships and development* (pp. 51–71). Hillsdale, NJ: Lawrence Erlbaum Associates.

Chapter 5

Cognitive Vulnerability to Depression: Current Status and Developmental Origins[1]

Lyn Y. Abramson
University of Wisconsin, Madison

Lauren B. Alloy
Temple University

COGNITIVE VULNERABILITY HYPOTHESIS OF DEPRESSION

Imagine the following scenario. Two women are fired from their jobs at the same firm. One woman becomes upset and mildly discouraged for a couple of days and then picks herself up and begins searching the want ads for a new job. In contrast, the other woman develops a serious episode of depression lasting for months and never tries to find a new job. Why are some people vulnerable to depression whereas others never seem to become depressed? According to the cognitive theories of depression, the way people typically interpret or explain events in their lives—their cognitive styles—importantly affects their vulnerability to depression. Thus, as a complement to work emphasizing biological or genetic risk for depression, the hopelessness theory (Abramson et al., 2002; Abramson, Metalsky, & Alloy, 1989) and Beck's theory (Beck, 1967, 1987; Clark, Beck, & Alford, 1999) highlight cognitive risk for depression.

[1]The research reviewed in this chapter was supported by National Institute of Mental Health Grants MH 43866 to Lyn Y. Abramson and MH 48216 to Lauren B. Alloy.

For example, according to the hopelessness theory (Abramson et al., 1989), people who characteristically attribute negative life events to stable causes (likely to persist over time) and global causes (likely to affect many areas of life), infer that further negative consequences will follow from a current negative life event, and believe that the occurrence of a negative event in their lives means that they are fundamentally flawed or worthless are hypothesized to be more likely to develop episodes of depression—particularly the subtype of "hopelessness depression" (HD)—when they confront negative life events than are people who don't exhibit these inferential styles. The logic here is that people who exhibit this hypothesized depressogenic inferential style should be more likely to make negative inferences about the cause, consequences, and self-implications of any particular negative life event they confront, thereby increasing the likelihood that they will develop hopelessness and, in turn, the symptoms of depression, particularly HD.

In Beck's theory (Beck, 1967, 1987; Clark et al., 1999), negative self-schemata revolving around themes of inadequacy, failure, loss, and worthlessness are hypothesized to provide cognitive vulnerability to depressive symptoms. Such negative self-schemata often are represented as a set of dysfunctional attitudes or self-worth contingencies, such as "If I fail partly, it is as bad as being a complete failure" or "I am nothing if a person I love doesn't love me." When they encounter negative life events that impinge on their cognitive vulnerability, individuals exhibiting such negative self-schemata or dysfunctional attitudes are hypothesized to develop negatively biased construals of the self (low self-esteem), world, and future (hopelessness), and, in turn, depressive symptoms. Thus, both the hopelessness theory and Beck's theory can be conceptualized as vulnerability-stress theories in which negative inferential styles provide cognitive vulnerability to depression through their effect on the interpretation or processing of personally relevant negative life events.

TESTING THE COGNITIVE VULNERABILITY HYPOTHESIS: THE BEHAVIORAL HIGH-RISK DESIGN

A powerful strategy for testing the cognitive vulnerability hypothesis is the "behavioral high-risk design" (e.g., Depue et al., 1981). Similarly to the genetic high-risk paradigm, the behavioral high-risk design involves studying participants who do not currently have the disorder of interest but who are hypothesized to be at high or low risk for developing it. In contrast to the genetic high-risk paradigm, in the behavioral high-risk study, individuals are selected on the basis of hypothesized psychological, rather than genetic, vulnerability or invulnerability to the disorder. Thus, to test the cognitive vulnerability hypotheses of depression, one would want to select nondepressed people who were at high versus low risk for depression based on the presence versus absence of the hypothesized depressogenic cognitive styles. One would then compare these cognitively high- and low-risk groups on their likelihood of exhibiting depression both in the past (in a retrospective version of the design) and the future (in a prospective version of the design). The prospective version of the design is superior to the retrospective version because the cognitive "vulnerability" that is assessed in the latter might actually be a *scar* of a prior depressive episode (Rohde, Lewinsohn, & Seeley, 1991) rather than a *causal* factor in that prior episode (Gotlib & Abramson, 1999).

The results of studies that have used methods less optimal than the behavioral high-risk design to test the cognitive vulnerability hypothesis of depression have been equivocal (see Barnett & Gotlib, 1988, for a review). In contrast, studies using or approximating a behavioral high-risk design have obtained considerable support for the cognitive vulnerability hypothesis of depression. For example, using a retrospective behavioral high-risk design, Alloy, Lipman, and Abramson (1992) tested the attributional vulnerability hypothesis of the hopelessness theory for clinically significant depression. In this study, currently nondepressed college students who either did or did not exhibit attributional vulnerability for depression with low self-esteem were compared on the likelihood that they had experienced major depressive disorder, as well as the hypothesized subtype of HD, over the past 2 years. Consistent with the cognitive vulnerability hypothesis, attributionally vulnerable students were more likely to have exhibited major depressive disorder and the syndrome of HD over the previous 2 years, and to have experienced a greater number of episodes of these disorders, than were attributionally invulnerable students. Moreover, studies that have used variants of the prospective behavioral high-risk design consistently have found that people who exhibit the hypothesized cognitive vulnerability are more likely to develop depressive moods and/or depressive symptoms when they experience negative life events than are individuals who do not show this vulnerability (Alloy & Clements, 1998; Alloy, Just, & Panzarella, 1997; Metalsky, Halberstadt, & Abramson, 1987; Metalsky & Joiner, 1992; Metalsky, Joiner, Hardin, & Abramson, 1993; Nolen-Hoeksema, Girgus, & Seligman, 1992).

THE TEMPLE–WISCONSIN COGNITIVE VULNERABILITY TO DEPRESSION (CVD) PROJECT

The Temple–Wisconsin Cognitive Vulnerability to Depression (CVD) Project was a collaborative, two-site study that used a prospective behavioral high-risk design to test the cognitive vulnerability and other etiological hypotheses of hopelessness and Beck's theories of depression for both depressive symptoms and clinically significant depressive episodes. In the CVD Project, first-year college students at either high or low cognitive risk for depression who were nondepressed and had no other current Axis I psychopathology at the outset of the study were followed every 6 weeks for 2½ years with self-report and structured interview assessments of stressful life events, cognitions, and symptoms and diagnosable episodes of psychopathology. The participants then were followed for an additional 3 years, with assessments occurring every 4 months.

Because the cognitively high-risk (HR) participants were required to score in the highest quartile on measures of the cognitive vulnerabilities featured in both the hopelessness theory (Cognitive Style Questionnaire [CSQ]; Alloy et al., 2000) and Beck's theory (expanded Dysfunctional Attitude Scale [DAS]; Weissman & Beck, 1978), and the cognitively low risk (LR) participants were required to score in the lowest quartile on both of these measures, the CVD Project provided a broad test of a "generic" cognitive vulnerability hypothesis. A strength of this study is that the two sites permitted a built-in assessment of replicability of results. Whereas the University of Wisconsin sample had a high representation of Caucasian individuals from rural, farming, small town, and suburban backgrounds, the Temple University sample was more urban, with a high representation of minority (largely African Americans) and lower socioeconomic participants. Importantly, all of the results reported in this chapter replicated across the two sites.

COGNITIVE VULNERABILITY AND THE PREDICTION OF DEPRESSION AND SUICIDALITY

The CVD Project behavioral high-risk design allowed for retrospective and prospective tests of the cognitive vulnerability hypothesis. We now review findings on the predictive validity of the hypothesized negative cognitive styles for depressive disorders and suicidality.

Based on the cognitive vulnerability hypothesis and evidence that attributional styles exhibit some stability over the life span (Burns & Seligman, 1989), Alloy et al. (2000) examined the lifetime prevalence rates of DSM-III-R and RDC depressive disorders, the syndrome of HD, and other Axis I disorders in HR versus LR participants. Consistent with the cognitive vulnerability hypothesis, Alloy et al. (2000) found that the HR group showed greater lifetime prevalence than did the LR group of major depressive disorder (DSM and RDC) and HD, as well as marginally higher rates of RDC minor depression. Moreover, these HR-LR differences were specific to depressive disorders. The groups did not differ on lifetime prevalence rates of anxiety disorders, alcohol and drug abuse, or other Axis I disorders.

In a follow-up to the Alloy et al. (2000) study, Haeffel et al. (2003) used a new sample of unselected undergraduates to examine the unique associations between negative inferential styles and dysfunctional attitudes and lifetime history of depressive and other disorders. Haeffel et al. noted that negative inferential styles were more strongly and consistently associated with lifetime history of major depressive disorder and HD than were dysfunctional attitudes, suggesting that negative inferential styles, as assessed by the CSQ, may have been a particularly potent component of the "generic" cognitive vulnerability effect in Alloy et al.'s (2000) study using CVD Project data.

Although suggestive, an important limitation of the retrospective tests of the cognitive vulnerability hypothesis is that the findings are as supportive of the alternative hypothesis that negative cognitive styles are a consequence or "scar" left by the past experience of depression (see Lewinsohn, Steinmetz, Larson, & Franklin, 1981) as they are of the hypothesis that negative cognitive styles provide vulnerability to depression. Thus, data from the prospective portion of the CVD Project provide a more crucial test of the cognitive vulnerability hypothesis. Results from the first 2.5 years of follow-up in the CVD Project indicate that negative cognitive styles did indeed predict prospectively both first onsets and recurrences of depressive disorders (Abramson et al., 1999; Alloy et al., 1999, in press). Alloy et al. (in press) reported that among participants with no prior history of depression, and controlling for current depressive symptoms at the outset of the prospective follow-up, HR individuals were more likely than were LR individuals to experience a first lifetime onset of major depressive disorder, minor depression, and HD. These findings provide especially strong support for the cognitive vulnerability hypothesis because they are based on a truly prospective test, uncontaminated by prior history of depression.

What about those participants who, although nondepressed at the outset of the CVD Project, did have a prior history of clinically significant depression? This subsample allows a test of whether the cognitive vulnerability hypothesis holds for recurrences of depression, which is particularly important given that depression often is recurrent (e.g., Judd, 1997). Consistent with the cognitive vulnerability hypothesis, HR participants with a past history of clinically significant depression were more likely than were LR participants with previous depression to develop recurrences of depressive episodes during the follow-up. Thus, the CVD Project findings suggest that, at least in part, similar cognitive vulnerabilities may play a role in risk for both the first and subsequent episodes of depressive disorders.

Finally, HR participants also were more likely than were LR participants to exhibit suicidality, on a continuum from suicidal ideation to suicidal behavior, during the initial prospective follow-up (Abramson et al., 1998). Fortunately, no participants died by suicide.

These findings provide the first demonstration that the hypothesized cognitive vulnerabilities do indeed confer risk for both first onsets and recurrences of full-blown, clinically significant depressive disorders, the hypothesized subtype of HD, and suicidality. These results refute the criticism that the cognitive theories of depression apply only to mild depression. Moreover, the results also provide support for the hypothesis that the specific subtype of HD exists in nature and conforms to theoretical description.

Lewinsohn, Joiner, and Rohde (2001) reported that both dysfunctional attitudes (at the level of a statistical trend) and attributional styles interacted with stress to predict major depressive disorder among adolescents over a 1-year interval. Interestingly, the form of the interaction between cognitive vulnerability and stress differed for attributional styles and dysfunctional attitudes. Specifically, attributional style had its largest effect on depression under lower levels of stress, whereas it had little impact on depression under higher levels of stress.

This result for attributional style is intriguing because it supports the *titration* model of vulnerability-stress relations discussed in the original statement of the hopelessness theory (Abramson et al., 1989; Abramson, Alloy, & Hogan, 1997; see also Monroe & Simons, 1991). According to the titration model of the cognitive vulnerability-stress interaction, lower "doses" of stress are sufficient to trigger depression in cognitively vulnerable individuals, whereas higher doses of stress are required to precipitate depression in nonvulnerable individuals. At lower levels of stress only cognitively vulnerable individuals may become depressed, whereas at very high levels of stress both cognitively vulnerable and nonvulnerable individuals alike may become depressed. In contrast to the titration model, it typically has been assumed that the vulnerability-stress model featured in both hopelessness theory and Beck's theory is a *synergistic* interaction in which only cognitively vulnerable individuals who experience high levels of stress develop depression. Lewinsohn et al.'s (2001) results for dysfunctional attitudes, as well as the results of a number of prior studies (e.g., Metalsky & Joiner, 1992), conform to this synergistic interaction model. An exciting direction for future research is to specify more precisely how cognitive vulnerability and stress combine to produce depression.

DEVELOPMENTAL ORIGINS OF COGNITIVE VULNERABILITY TO DEPRESSION

Given mounting evidence that negative cognitive styles do confer vulnerability for depression and suicidality, as indicated by the CVD Project findings, then it is important to understand the antecedents of these negative cognitive styles. What are the developmental origins of cognitive vulnerability to depression? Reviews of the developmental antecedents of depression and cognitive vulnerability to depression (e.g., Garber & Flynn, 1998; Gibb, 2002; Goodman & Gotlib, 1999; Haines, Metalsky, Cardamone, & Joiner, 1999; Rose & Abramson, 1992) suggest that genetic, neurochemical, social learning, and early traumatic processes all contribute to the development of negative cognitive styles that, in turn, increase risk for depression. In the CVD Project, we focused on exploring the social learning and early traumatic factors that may contribute to the development of cognitive vulnerabilities and risk for depression. Specifically, we examined the role of modeling of parents' cognitive styles, direct learning from parents' inferential feedback regarding the causes and consequences of negative events in their child's life, negative parenting practices, early childhood life events in general, and childhood maltreatment experiences in particular in the potential development of cognitive vulnerability among our CVD Project participants.

Modeling of Parents' Cognitive Styles and Parental Inferential Feedback

Social learning may play a role in the development of cognitive vulnerability to depression. Two such social learning mechanisms are modeling of parents' negative cognitive styles for events in the parents' lives and incorporating negative inferential feedback from parents regarding the causes and consequences of negative life events in their child's life.

Children may learn their cognitive styles in part by observing and modeling the attributions and inferences their parents make when negative events happen to the parents (Abramson et al., 1999; Alloy et al., 1999; Garber & Flynn, 1998; Haines et al., 1999). If the modeling hypothesis is correct, then children's cognitive styles should correlate with those of their mothers or fathers. Studies of modeling of cognitive styles have obtained mixed results, with some studies finding a relationship between mothers'—but not fathers'—and children's attributional styles (Seligman et al., 1984) and negative cognitions (Stark, Schmidt, & Joiner, 1996), and others showing no association between parents' and their offspring's cognitive styles (Garber & Flynn, 2001; Kaslow, Rehm, Pollack, & Siegel, 1988; Oliver & Berger, 1992; Turk & Bry, 1992).

Alloy et al. (2001) tested the modeling hypothesis using CVD Project data and discerned that mothers of HR participants had significantly more dysfunctional attitudes and marginally more negative inferential styles than did mothers of LR participants, controlling statistically for the mothers' levels of depressive symptoms. In contrast, there were no risk group differences in fathers' dysfunctional attitudes or inferential styles. Thus, to the extent that modeling of parents' cognitive styles contributes to the development of cognitive vulnerability to depression in offspring, the CVD Project findings combined with those from other studies suggest that it is mothers' cognitive styles that are modeled. If mothers are the primary caretakers of their children, as is likely, then the greater similarity of offspring's cognitive styles to those of their mothers than of their fathers could be the result of greater exposure to mothers during the formative years.

Another way in which children may learn their cognitive styles is through inferential feedback from their parents. Parents may communicate their own inferences about the causes and consequences of negative events in their child's life such that the child develops an inferential style consistent with the parental feedback. If the feedback hypothesis is correct, then offspring's inferential styles should correlate with the typical attributional and consequence feedback they received from their parents. Prior studies, although small in number, consistently support the parental feedback hypothesis for attributional styles (Fincham & Cain, 1986; Garber & Flynn, 2001; Turk & Bry, 1992). In addition, Dweck, Davidson, Nelson, and Enna (1978) showed that children's attributions for academic performance outcomes are influenced by the attributional feedback they receive from their teachers.

Alloy et al. (2001) tested the parental inferential feedback hypothesis using CVD Project data. They examined the inferential feedback styles of the parents of the HR and LR participants as reported by both the parents and the participants on the Parental Attributions for Children's Events Questionnaire (PACE; Alloy et al., 2001). The PACE contains 12 hypothetical negative events. Following each event, there are four attributional statements presented in random order that parents might communicate to their child:

1. Internal, stable, global (ISG).
2. External, stable, global (ESG).
3. Internal, unstable, specific (IUS).
4. External, unstable, specific (EUS).

These are followed by two consequence statements, positive versus negative. HR and LR participants rated the likelihood that their mothers and fathers would say each attribution and each consequence statement to their child when he or she was growing. Parents, in turn, rated the likelihood that they themselves would do so.

Alloy and colleagues (2001) found that according to both participants' and their parents' reports on the PACE, both mothers and fathers of HR individuals provided more stable, global attributional feedback for negative events in their child's life than did mothers and fathers of LR individuals. In addition, mothers of HR participants also provided more negative consequence feedback for negative events in their child's life than did mothers of LR participants, according to both respondents' reports; so did fathers of HR participants, according to the participants' reports. Most, but not all, of these associations were maintained when the depressive symptom levels of the respondent were controlled statistically. Thus, negative cognitive styles among offspring were associated with negative inferential feedback from parents. Indeed, the association of participants' cognitive risk status with negative inferential feedback from their parents was stronger than the association of their cognitive risk with their parents' cognitive styles.

Also using CVD Project data, Crossfield, Alloy, Abramson, and Gibb (2002) noted that maternal inferential feedback moderated the relationship between parents' reports of their children's negative childhood life events and cognitive risk status. Specifically, high levels of negative childhood events in interaction with negative maternal inferential feedback were associated with participants' HR status. Thus, the CVD Project findings suggest that parents might contribute to the development of negative cognitive styles and vulnerability to depression in their children, not so much by modeling negative inferences for events in their own lives, but more by communicating negative attributional and consequence feedback to their children for negative events in the children's lives.

Parenting Styles

Parents may contribute to the development of cognitive vulnerability to depression in their children not only by providing negative inferential feedback for stressful events in their children's lives, but also by engaging in generally negative parenting practices. Numerous studies have found that parenting characterized by lack of warmth and caring and by negative psychological control (criticism, intrusiveness, and guilt induction)—a pattern referred to as "affectionless control" by Parker (1983)—is associated with both depression and negative cognitive styles in offspring (Brewin, Firth-Cozens, Furnham, & McManus, 1992; Garber & Flynn, 2001; Goodman, Adamson, Riniti, & Cole, 1994; Ingram & Ritter, 2000; Jaenicke et al., 1987; Koestner, Zuroff, & Powers, 1991; Litovsky & Dusek, 1985; Parker, 1983, 1993; Radke-Yarrow, Belmont, Nottelmann, & Bottomly, 1990; Randolph & Dykman, 1998; Stark et al., 1996; Whisman & Kwon, 1992; Whisman & McGarvey, 1995; but see Oliver & Berger, 1992, for an exception). In the CVD Project, Alloy et al. (2001) further explored the negative parenting hypothesis by examining the parenting behaviors of cognitively HR and LR participants' parents, as reported by both the participants and their parents on the Children's Report of Parental Behavior Inventory (CRPBI; Schaeffer, 1965). The CRPBI yields scores on three dimensions of parenting: emotional warmth or acceptance, psychological control, and lax discipline.

Consistent with the lack of emotional warmth part of the "affectionless control" pattern, Alloy et al. (2001) noted that the fathers of HR participants exhibited less warmth and acceptance than did fathers of LR participants, as reported by both the participants and their fathers. Based on the fathers' reports, this relationship remained significant even when the fathers' levels of depressive symptoms were statistically controlled, suggesting that the association between fathers' lack of warmth and their offspring's negative cognitive styles cannot be attributed to fathers' depressed mood or reporting biases that may arise from depressed mood. There were no risk group differences, however, for fathers' levels of psychological or lax control or for mothers' parenting on any of the dimensions. The relationship between fathers' lack of acceptance and their sons' or daughters' cognitive vulnerability indicates that despite the predominance of mothers as primary caretakers, fathers too may be important in their offspring's development of positive versus negative cognitive styles.

History of Childhood Maltreatment

In extending the etiological chain of the hopelessness theory, Rose and Abramson (1992) proposed a developmental pathway by which negative events in childhood, particularly childhood maltreatment, may contribute to the development of negative cognitive styles, which, in turn, increase individuals' vulnerability to developing hopelessness and both symptoms and episodes of depression. Specifically, Rose and Abramson (1992) suggested that when a negative event such as maltreatment occurs, children initially attempt to explain its occurrence in a way that will maintain their sense of hopefulness that the event will not recur (hopefulness-inducing attributions). For example, if a child's father beats him or her, the child may initially explain the maltreatment by saying it happened because his or her dad was in a bad mood that day (external, unstable, specific). If the maltreatment is chronic or widespread, however, the child's hopefulness-inducing attributions will meet with repeated disconfirmation and the child may begin to make hopelessness-inducing attributions. For example, the child may begin to explain the maltreatment by thinking, "I'm such a bad kid, I deserve all the bad things that happen to me" (internal, stable, global). Over time, these types of causal attributions may generalize to other negative life events, crystallizing into a negative cognitive style.

Rose and Abramson (1992) predicted that childhood emotional maltreatment should be more likely to contribute to the development of negative cognitive styles than should either childhood physical or sexual maltreatment. This is because, with emotional maltreatment, the depressotypic cognitions (e.g., "You're so stupid, you'll never amount to anything") are directly supplied to the child by the abuser. In contrast, with physical or sexual maltreatment, the child must supply his or her own attributions and has an opportunity to make more benign interpretations.

In a qualitative and quantitative review of studies examining the relation between childhood maltreatment and cognitive vulnerability to depression, Gibb (2002) found that a history of both sexual and emotional maltreatment, but not physical maltreatment, were associated with negative cognitive styles. We more fully explored the validity of Rose and Abramson's maltreatment model based on CVD Project participants' reports of their histories of childhood (prior to age 15) emotional, physical, and sexual maltreatment on the Life Experiences Questionnaire (LEQ; Gibb et al., 2001). The LEQ was modeled on Cicchetti's (1989) Child Maltreatment Interview, and consistent with the suggestions of Brewin, Andrews, and Gotlib (1993), the LEQ assessed a broad range of specific events rather than asking individuals for global estimates of maltreatment. Examples of childhood emotional maltreatment assessed included humiliation, rejection, extortion, and teasing. Examples of physical maltreatment assessed included being hit with an object or fist, being choked, and being the victim of deliberate physical pain. Finally, examples of sexual maltreatment assessed included unwanted exposure to pornography, exhibitionism, fondling, and attempted and completed rape.

Consistent with Rose and Abramson's hypothesis that childhood emotional maltreatment would be more strongly related to negative cognitive styles than would either childhood physical or sexual maltreatment, Gibb et al. (2001) noted that HR individuals reported more emotional, but not physical or sexual, maltreatment than did LR individuals, even after their depressive symptom levels and the effects of the other two forms of maltreatment were statistically controlled.

Despite the strengths of this study, a number of questions remained. First, was the association of childhood emotional maltreatment with negative cognitive styles due to the maltreatment itself or to some as yet unaccounted for third variable, such as genetic influences or negative family environment more generally? A behavior geneticist might suggest that developmental maltreatment by parents does not actually contribute directly to the formation of cognitive vulnerability to depression in their offspring. Instead, it may be that the genes that maltreating parents pass on to their offspring contribute both to the parents abusing their offspring and to the formation of cognitive vulnerability in the offspring. To address this issue, Gibb, Abramson, and Alloy (2004) also examined the relationship between maltreatment by nonrelatives (i.e., peers, nonfamily adults, strangers, and boyfriends/girlfriends) during development and cognitive vulnerability to depression in adulthood with the CVD Project data. Gibb et al. (2004) discerned that even when parental variables such as parental history of psychopathology and maltreatment by parents were statistically controlled, emotional maltreatment by nonrelatives still was significantly associated with cognitive vulnerability.

It was also unclear from the CVD Project findings whether the relations between childhood emotional maltreatment and negative cognitive styles and depression were due to specific behavioral experiences, participants' interpretation of their experiences (i.e., global beliefs that they were maltreated in childhood), or both. To address this ambiguity, Gibb, Alloy, and Abramson (2003) assessed an unselected sample of undergraduates' histories of childhood emotional, physical, and sexual maltreatment in two ways. First, on the LEQ, participants were asked if they had experienced a broad range of specific behaviors considered to constitute maltreatment. Second, participants were asked more globally if they believed they had been emotionally, physically, and/or sexually maltreated as children. Gibb, Alloy, and Abramson (2003) found that reported specific instances of childhood emotional maltreatment remained significantly related to participants' dysfunctional attitudes, even after their global reports of childhood emotional maltreatment were statistically controlled. In combination, therefore, these additional studies support the hypothesis that the relation between reported childhood emotional maltreatment and negative cognitive styles is attributable to the actual experience of emotionally abusive behaviors and not due to purely genetic influences, general negative family environment, or global reporting biases.

A second question that remained regarding the CVD Project findings on the role of maltreatment was whether a childhood history of emotional maltreatment is related to negative inferential styles, dysfunctional attitudes, or both. Given that cognitive risk status in the CVD Project was based on both negative inferential styles and dysfunctional attitudes, it is difficult to tease apart their separate associations with emotional maltreatment. Two follow-up studies conducted with unselected samples of undergraduates indicated that reported levels of childhood emotional maltreatment were related to both negative inferential styles (Gibb, Alloy, Abramson, & Marx, 2003) and dysfunctional attitudes (Gibb, Alloy, & Abramson, 2003).

Another issue is the process by which childhood emotional maltreatment contributes to the development of negative cognitive styles. That is, although the CVD Project findings supported Rose and Abramson's (1992) hypothesis that levels of emotional maltreatment would be significantly related to individuals' cognitive styles, the study did not evaluate their hypothesis that inferences about specific maltreatment experiences would mediate this relation. To test this hypothesis, Gibb, Alloy, Abramson, and Marx (2003) conducted a cross-sectional evaluation of a sample of unselected undergraduates' reports of childhood maltreatment, inferences for specific maltreatment experiences, inferential styles, levels of hopelessness, and symptoms of HD. Gibb, Alloy, Abramson, and Marx (2003) noted that participants' inferences for specific experiences of emotional maltreatment fully mediated the relation between childhood emotional maltreatment and participants' inferential styles.

Of course, all of these findings regarding the role of childhood emotional maltreatment in the development of negative cognitive styles are based on cross-sectional or retrospective reports of participants. Thus, a final issue left unanswered by the CVD Project findings and our related studies is whether emotional maltreatment actually contributes causally to the formation of negative cognitive styles. As a first step in providing support for a causal role of emotional maltreatment in the development of negative cognitive styles, Gibb et al. (in press) conducted a prospective study of the development of negative attributional styles in fourth- and fifth-grade children. Gibb et al. (in press) and Gibb and Alloy (under review) examined the role of emotional maltreatment, as well as other factors, in predicting change in attributional style and depressive symptoms in fourth and fifth graders over a 6-month period. Emotional maltreatment occurring during the 6-month follow-up, as well as emotional maltreatment occurring in the 6 months prior to Time 1, predicted change in children's attributional styles over the follow-up (Gibb et al., in press). Only emotional maltreatment occurring during the 6-month follow-up predicted change in children's depressive symptoms over the follow-up (Gibb & Alloy, under review). The more emotional maltreatment a child experienced, the more negative his or her attributional style became and the more depressive symptoms he or she developed over the follow-up. The Gibb et al. (in press) and Gibb and Alloy (under review) findings suggest that emotional maltreatment may be predictive of and, at least, show temporal precedence with respect to the development of some negative cognitive styles and depressive symptoms.

CONCLUSION: THE CONTINUUM OF EMOTIONAL FEEDBACK IN THE DEVELOPMENT OF COGNITIVE VULNERABILITY TO DEPRESSION

To summarize, three main developmental factors were associated with negative cognitive styles and vulnerability to depression in the CVD Project: a history of childhood emotional maltreatment, negative inferential feedback from parents regarding the causes and consequences of negative events in their child's life, and parenting characterized by low emotional warmth. These three developmental variables may be seen as falling on a continuum of emotional feedback (Alloy et al., 2001). For example, low emotional acceptance or warmth as measured by the CRPBI (e.g., "Tells me how much he loves me" or "Gives me a lot of care and attention" rated as "not like" one's parent) and negative inferential feedback as assessed on the PACE (e.g., "Of course you weren't invited. You aren't easy to get along with"; "Now you'll be identified as an outcast and people won't invite you to other parties either") could be viewed as milder ends of a continuum that also includes outright emotional abuse (e.g., humiliation, rejection, extortion, and teasing) at the more severe end.

Thus, emotional criticism and rejection from significant others, such as parents, teachers, and peers, may provide a psychological environment that promotes the development of depressogenic cognitions whether it is expressed indirectly through provision of negative inferential feedback or lack of affection or directly through explicitly abusive language (Alloy et al., 2001; Garber & Flynn, 1998). The findings from the CVD Project and related studies reviewed herein suggest that the old childhood adage "Sticks and stones may break my bones, but words will never hurt me" may be patently untrue (Gibb et al., in press). Negative emotional feedback, ranging from lack of warmth and negative inferential communications to psychological abuse, may be particularly virulent in promoting cognitive vulnerability to depression.

As we indicated at the outset, with the exception of the studies by Gibb et al. (in press) and Gibb and Alloy (under review), the developmentally relevant findings from the CVD Project are retrospective. Thus, they may be seen as providing a conceptual and empirical basis for further investigations of the development of cognitive vulnerability to depression. Future studies, particularly prospective studies beginning earlier in childhood, should target this potential continuum of emotional feedback (ranging from mildly negative parenting practices and feedback to emotional abuse) as an important contributor to the development of cognitive vulnerability to depression and to depression itself.

REFERENCES

Abramson, L. Y., Alloy, L. B., Hankin, B. L., Haeffel, G. J., MacCoon, D. G., & Gibb, B. E. (2002). Cognitive vulnerability-stress models of depression in a self-regulatory and psychobiological context. In I. H. Gotlib & C. L. Hammen (Eds.), *Handbook of depression* (pp. 268–294). New York: Guilford.

Abramson, L. Y., Alloy, L. B., & Hogan, M. E. (1997). Cognitive/personality subtypes of depression: Theories in search of disorders. *Cognitive Therapy and Research, 21*, 247–265.

Abramson, L. Y., Alloy, L. B., Hogan, M. E., Whitehouse, W. G., Cornette, M., Akhavan, S., & Chiara, A. (1998). Suicidality and cognitive vulnerability to depression among college students: A prospective study. *Journal of Adolescence, 21*, 157–171.

Abramson, L. Y., Alloy, L. B., Hogan, M. E., Whitehouse, W. G., Donovan, P., Rose, D. T., Panzarella, C., & Raniere, D. (1999). Cognitive vulnerability to depression: Theory and evidence. *Journal of Cognitive Psychotherapy: An International Quarterly, 13*, 5–20.

Abramson, L. Y., Metalsky, G. I., & Alloy, L. B. (1989). Hopelessness depression: A theory-based subtype of depression. *Psychological Review, 96*, 358–372.

Alloy, L. B., Abramson, L. Y., Hogan, M. E., Whitehouse, W. G., Rose, D. T., Robinson, M. S., Kim, R., & Lapkin, J. B. (2000). The Temple–Wisconsin Cognitive Vulnerability to Depression (CVD) Project: Lifetime history of Axis I psychopathology in individuals at high and low cognitive risk for depression. *Journal of Abnormal Psychology, 109*, 403–418.

Alloy, L. B., Abramson, L. Y., Tashman, N. A., Berrebbi, D. S., Hogan, M. E., Whitehouse, W. G., Crossfield, A. G., & Morocco, A. (2001). Developmental origins of cognitive vulnerability to depression: Parenting, cognitive, and inferential feedback styles of the parents of individuals at high and low cognitive risk for depression. *Cognitive Therapy and Research, 25*, 397–423.

Alloy, L. B., Abramson, L. Y., Whitehouse, W. G., Hogan, M. E., Panzarella, C., & Rose, D. T. (in press). Prospective incidence of first onsets and recurrences of depression in individuals at high and low cognitive risk for depression. *Journal of Abnormal Psychology,*

Alloy, L. B., Abramson, L. Y., Whitehouse, W. G., Hogan, M. E., Tashman, N. A., Steinberg, D. L., Rose, D. T., & Donovan, P. (1999). Depressogenic cognitive styles: Predictive validity, information processing and personality characteristics, and developmental origins. *Behaviour Research and Therapy, 37*, 503–531.

Alloy, L. B., & Clements, C. M. (1998). Hopelessness theory of depression: Tests of the symptom component. *Cognitive Therapy and Research, 22*, 303–335.

Alloy, L. B., Just, N., & Panzarella, C. (1997). Attributional style, daily life events, and hopelessness depression: Subtype validation by prospective variability and specificity of symptoms. *Cognitive Therapy and Research, 21*, 321–344.

Alloy, L. B., Lipman, A. J., & Abramson, L. Y. (1992). Attributional style as a vulnerability factor for depression: Validation by past history of mood disorders. *Cognitive Therapy and Research, 16*, 391–407.

Barnett, P. A., & Gotlib, I. H. (1988). Psychosocial functioning and depression: Distinguishing among antecedents, concomitants, and consequences. *Psychological Bulletin, 104*, 97–126.

Beck, A. T. (1967). *Depression: Clinical, experimental, and theoretical aspects.* New York: Harper & Row.

Beck, A. T. (1987). Cognitive models of depression. *Journal of Cognitive Psychotherapy: An International Quarterly, 1*, 5–37.

Brewin, C. R., Andrews, B., & Gotlib, I. H. (1993). Psychopathology and early experience: A reappraisal of retrospective reports. *Psychological Bulletin, 113*, 82–98.

Brewin, C. R., Firth-Cozens, J., Furnham, A., & McManus, I. C. (1992). Self-criticism in adulthood and recalled childhood experience. *Journal of Abnormal Psychology, 101*, 561–566.

Burns, M. O., & Seligman, M. E. P. (1989). Explanatory style across the life span: Evidence for stability over 52 years. *Journal of Personality and Social Psychology, 56*, 471–477.

Cicchetti, D. (1989). *Maltreatment Classification Interview.* Rochester, NY: University of Rochester, Mount Hope Family Center.

Clark, D. A., Beck, A. T., & Alford, B. A. (1999). *Scientific foundations of cognitive theory and therapy of depression.* New York: Wiley.

Crossfield, A. G., Alloy, L. B., Abramson, L. Y., & Gibb, B. E. (2002). The development of depressogenic cognitive styles: The role of negative childhood life events and parental inferential feedback. *Journal of Cognitive Psychotherapy: An International Quarterly, 16*, 487–502.

Depue, R. A., Slater, J., Wolfstetter-Kausch, H., Klein, D., Goplerud, E., & Farr, D. (1981). A behavioral paradigm for identifying persons at risk for bipolar depressive disorder: A conceptual framework and five validation studies [Monograph]. *Journal of Abnormal Psychology, 90*, 381–437.

Dweck, C. S., Davidson, W., Nelson, S., & Enna, B. (1978). Sex differences in learned helplessness: II. The contingencies of evaluative feedback in the classroom and III. An experimental analysis. *Developmental Psychology, 14*, 268–276.

Fincham, F. D., & Cain, K. M. (1986). Learned helplessness in humans: A developmental analysis. *Developmental Review, 6*, 301–333.

Garber, J., & Flynn, C. (1998). Origins of the depressive cognitive style. In D. Routh & R. J. DeRubeis (Eds.), *The science of clinical psychology: Evidence of a century's progress* (pp. 53–93). Washington, DC: American Psychological Association.

Garber, J., & Flynn, C. (2001). Predictors of depressive cognitions in young adolescents. *Cognitive Therapy and Research, 25,* 353–376.

Gibb, B. E. (2002). Childhood maltreatment and negative cognitive styles: A quantitative and qualitative review. *Clinical Psychology Review, 22,* 223–246.

Gibb, B. E., Abramson, L. Y., & Alloy, L. B. (2004). Emotional maltreatment from parents, verbal peer victimization, and cognitive vulnerability to depression. *Cognitive Therapy and Research, 28,* 1–21.

Gibb, B. E., & Alloy, L. B. (under review). *A prospective test of the hopelessness theory of depression in children.* Manuscript under editorial review.

Gibb, B. E., Alloy, L. B., & Abramson, L. Y. (2003). Global reports of childhood maltreatment versus recall of specific maltreatment experiences: Relationships with dysfunctional attitudes and depressive symptoms. *Cognition and Emotion, 17,* 903–915.

Gibb, B. E., Alloy, L. B., Abramson, L. Y., & Marx, B. P. (2003). Childhood maltreatment and maltreatment-specific inferences: A test of Rose and Abramson's (1992) extension of the hopelessness theory. *Cognition and Emotion, 17,* 917–931.

Gibb, B. E., Alloy, L. B., Abramson, L. Y., Rose, D. T., Whitehouse, W. G., Donovan, P., Hogan, M. E., Cronholm, J., & Tierney, S. (2001). History of childhood maltreatment, negative cognitive styles, and episodes of depression in adulthood. *Cognitive Therapy and Research, 25,* 425–446.

Gibb, B. E., Alloy, L. B., Walshaw, P. D., Comer, J. S., Chang, G. H., & Villari, A. G. (in press). Predictors of attributional style change in children. *Journal of Abnormal Child Psychology,*

Goodman, S. H., Adamson, L. B., Riniti, J., & Cole, S. (1994). Mothers' expressed attitudes: Associations with maternal depression and children's self-esteem and psychopathology. *Journal of the American Academy of Child and Adolescent Psychiatry, 33,* 1265–1274.

Goodman, S. H., & Gotlib, I. H. (1999). Risk for psychopathology in the children of depressed mothers: A developmental model for understanding mechanisms of transmission. *Psychological Review, 106,* 458–490.

Gotlib, I. H., & Abramson, L. Y. (1999). Attributional theories of emotion. In T. Dalgleish & M. Power (Eds.), *Handbook of cognition and emotion* (pp. 613–636). Chicester, UK: Wiley.

Haeffel, G. J., Abramson, L. Y., Voelz, Z. R., Metalsky, G. I., Halberstadt, L., Dykman, B. M., Donovan, P., Hogan, M. E., Hankin, B. L., & Alloy, L. B. (2003). Cognitive vulnerability to depression and lifetime history of Axis I psychopathology: A comparison of negative cognitive styles (CSQ) and dysfunctional attitudes (DAS). *Journal of Cognitive Psychotherapy: An International Quarterly, 17,* 3–22.

Haines, B. A., Metalsky, G. I., Cardamone, A. L., & Joiner, T. (1999). Interpersonal and cognitive pathways into the origins of attributional style: A developmental perspective. In T. Joiner & J. C. Coyne (Eds.), *The interactional nature of depression* (pp. 65–92). Washington, DC: American Psychological Association.

Ingram, R. E., & Ritter, J. (2000). Vulnerability to depression: Cognitive reactivity and parental bonding in high-risk individuals. *Journal of Abnormal Psychology, 109,* 588–596.

Jaenicke, C., Hammen, C., Zupan, B., Hiroto, D., Gordon, D., Adrian, C., & Burge, D. (1987). Cognitive vulnerability in children at risk for depression. *Journal of Abnormal Child Psychology, 15,* 559–572.

Judd, L. L. (1997). The clinical course of unipolar major depressive disorders. *Archives of General Psychiatry, 54,* 989–991.

Kaslow, N. J., Rehm, L. P., Pollack, S. L., & Siegel, A. W. (1988). Attributional style and self-control behavior in depressed and nondepressed children and their parents. *Journal of Abnormal Child Psychology, 16*, 163–175.

Koestner, R., Zuroff, D. C., & Powers, T. A. (1991). Family origins of adolescent self-criticism and its continuity into adulthood. *Journal of Abnormal Psychology, 100*, 191–197.

Lewinsohn, P. M., Joiner, T. E., & Rohde, P. (2001). Evaluation of cognitive diathesis-stress models in predicting major depressive disorder in adolescents. *Journal of Abnormal Psychology, 110*, 203–215.

Lewinsohn, P. M., Steinmetz, J., Larson, D., & Franklin, J. (1981). Depression related cognitions: Antecedents or consequences? *Journal of Abnormal Psychology, 90*, 213–219.

Litovsky, V. G., & Dusek, J. B. (1985). Perceptions of child rearing and self-concept development during the early adolescent year. *Journal of Youth and Adolescence, 14*, 373–387.

Metalsky, G. I., Halberstadt, L. J., & Abramson, L. Y. (1987). Vulnerability to depressive mood reactions: Toward a more powerful test of the diathesis-stress and causal mediation components of the reformulated theory of depression. *Journal of Personality and Social Psychology, 52*, 386–393.

Metalsky, G. I., & Joiner, T. E. (1992). Vulnerability to depressive symptomatology: A prospective test of the diathesis-stress and causal mediation components of the hopelessness theory of depression. *Journal of Personality and Social Psychology, 63*, 667–675.

Metalsky, G. I., Joiner, T. E., Hardin, T. S., & Abramson, L. Y. (1993). Depressive reactions to failure in a naturalistic setting: A test of the hopelessness and self-esteem theories of depression. *Journal of Abnormal Psychology, 102*, 101–109.

Monroe, S. M., & Simons, A. D. (1991). Diathesis-stress theories in the context of life stress research: Implications for the depressive disorders. *Psychological Bulletin, 110*, 406–425.

Nolen-Hoeksema, S., Girgus, J. S., & Seligman, M. E. P. (1992). Predictors and consequences of childhood depressive symptoms: A 5-year longitudinal study. *Journal of Abnormal Psychology, 101*, 405–422.

Oliver, J. M., & Berger, L. S. (1992). Depression, parent–offspring relationships, and cognitive vulnerability. *Journal of Social Behavior and Personality, 7*, 415–428.

Parker, G. (1983). Parental "affectionless control" as an antecedent to adult depression. *Archives of General Psychiatry, 34*, 138–147.

Parker, G. (1993). Parental rearing style: Examining for links with personality vulnerability factors for depression. *Social Psychiatry and Psychiatric Epidemiology, 28*, 97–100.

Radke-Yarrow, M., Belmont, B., Nottelmann, E., & Bottomly, L. (1990). Young children's self-conceptions: Origins in the natural discourse of depressed and normal mothers and their children. In D. Cicchetti & M. Beeghly (Eds.), *The self in transition: Infancy to childhood* (pp. 345–361). Chicago: University of Chicago Press.

Randolph, J. J., & Dykman, B. M. (1998). Perceptions of parenting and depression-proneness in the offspring: Dysfunctional attitudes as a mediating mechanism. *Cognitive Therapy and Research, 22*, 377–400.

Rohde, P., Lewinsohn, P. M., & Seeley, J. R. (1991). Are people changed by the experience of having an episode of depression? A further test of the scar hypothesis. *Journal of Abnormal Psychology, 99*, 264–271.

Rose, D. T., & Abramson, L. Y. (1992). Developmental predictors of depressive cognitive style: Research and theory. In D. Cicchetti & S. L. Toth (Eds.), *Rochester symposium on developmental psychopathology* (Vol. 4, pp. 323–349). Hillsdale, NJ: Lawrence Erlbaum Associates.

Schaeffer, E. F. (1965). Children's report of parental behavior: An inventory. *Child Development, 36*, 413–424.

Seligman, M. E. P., Peterson, C., Kaslow, N. J., Tanenbaum, R. L., Alloy, L. B., & Abramson, L. Y. (1984). Attributional style and depressive symptoms among children. *Journal of Abnormal Psychology, 93*, 235–238.

Stark, K. D., Schmidt, K. L., & Joiner, T. E. (1996). Cognitive triad: Relationship to depressive symptoms, parents' cognitive triad, and perceived parental messages. *Journal of Abnormal Child Psychology, 24*, 615–631.

Turk, E., & Bry, B. (1992). Adolescents' and parents' explanatory styles and parents' causal explanations about their adolescents. *Cognitive Therapy and Research, 16*, 349–357.

Weissman, A., & Beck, A. T. (1978). *Development and validation of the Dysfunctional Attitudes Scale: A preliminary investigation.* Paper presented at the meeting of the American Educational Research Association, Toronto.

Whisman, M. A., & Kwon, P. (1992). Parental representations, cognitive distortions, and mild depression. *Cognitive Therapy and Research, 16*, 557–568.

Whisman, M. A., & McGarvey, A. L. (1995). Attachment, depressotypic cognitions, and dysphoria. *Cognitive Therapy and Research, 19*, 633–650.

Chapter 6

Depression and the Response of Others: A Social-Cognitive Interpersonal Process Model

William P. Sacco
University of South Florida

Christine A. Vaughan
University of South Florida

In the mid-1970s, several important publications indicated that interpersonal processes could play an important role in the development, maintenance, and exacerbation of depression. These studies showed, for example, that the interpersonal behaviors of depressed individuals differed from those of nondepressed persons (Forrest & Hokanson, 1975), and that other people responded more negatively to depressed persons—typically experiencing more negative affective reactions and a desire to avoid future contact with the depressed person (Coyne, 1976). Subsequent research reinforced these findings and suggested that "intrapersonal" theories of depression, such as cognitive and attributional formulations (Abramson, Seligman, & Teasdale, 1978; Beck, 1967), did not adequately account for the role that the interpersonal environment played in the development and manifestation of depressive symptoms (Sacco & Hokanson, 1978, 1982). Although a plethora of studies have since demonstrated the importance of interpersonal aspects of depression (Joiner, 2000; Joiner & Coyne, 1999; Segrin & Dillard, 1992), debates about the relative contribution of interpersonal versus intrapersonal factors continue (Coyne & Gotlib, 1983; Lau, Gemar, & Segal, 2000).

The model described in this chapter integrates interpersonal and cognitive factors, while simultaneously attempting to describe and explain social-cognitive processes involved in depressogenic transactions between depressed and nondepressed others (Sacco, 1999; Sacco & Nicholson, 1999). The model thus offers a potentially useful conceptual framework for organizing and understanding a diverse array of findings on interpersonal and cognitive aspects of depression. In the material that follows, we describe the social-cognitive interpersonal process model and supporting evidence. Some key questions that the model addresses are: How do others perceive the depressed person? How do others explain the depressed person's successes, failures, and personal problems? To what extent are perceptions and attributions about the depressed person biased? How are others' social-cognitive responses related to affective and behavioral reactions to depressed individuals? Do negative perceptions and attributions about the depressed person change after symptoms remit? Do depressed individuals accurately perceive how others view and respond to them? Do these social-cognitive processes play a role in the development, maintenance, or exacerbation of depression?

BACKGROUND

Despite considerable evidence that others' responses to depressed (and depression-prone) persons may influence the development and course of depression, theory and research have paid little attention to questions such as those just posed. This lack of attention has occurred despite substantial advances in the study of social cognition (Wyer & Srull, 1994) and, in particular, cognition in close relationships (Berscheid, 1994; Bradbury & Fincham, 1990; Clark, Helgeson, Mickelson, & Pataki, 1994; Fletcher & Fincham, 1991). Depression researchers have also largely overlooked the vast body of theory and research on the influence of affect on social judgment (Clore, Schwarz, & Conway, 1994; Forgas, 1995). In an attempt to enhance our understanding of interpersonal aspects of depression, the present model applies this literature to the conceptualization of depressogenic interpersonal processes. Relevant theory and research from social cognition (e.g., attributions and trait representations), marital/relationship satisfaction, cognition and affect, and perceptions of others' appraisals are also included. The model is intended to be integrative and heuristic. Although most applicable to the role that interpersonal processes may play in the maintenance or worsening of depression, the model can also be applied to our understanding of the development of depression.

A SOCIAL-COGNITIVE INTERPERSONAL PROCESS MODEL

Fig. 6.1 illustrates the model. Variables in the non-shaded circles depict the hypothesized cognitive, affective, and behavioral responses of individuals interacting with a depressed (or depression-prone) target. Variables in the shaded circles portray the depressed target's responses. The model posits that, in response to depressive displays (e.g., reassurance seeking, self-denigration), others will develop negatively biased mental representations of the depressed target (trait perceptions, attributions) and concomitantly experience negative affective reactions (e.g., anger, depressed mood). These negative social-cognitive and affective reactions result in relationship dissatisfaction and negative behavioral responses toward the depressed target. Negative behavioral reactions may take various forms, such as greater criticism, argumentativeness, withdrawal, nongenuine support, and rejection. These behaviors, when detected, lead to the perception of negative appraisals and loss of support, which in turn adversely influences the target's self-esteem, mood, and behavior. Perceptions of negative appraisal and reduced support are thus posited to be the most proximal cause of depressive reactions.

Adopting a transactional perspective, the model assumes a bidirectional process whereby both the depressed target and others influence interpersonal outcomes. Others' negative reactions are partly due to the depressed target's aversive social behavior (e.g., Joiner, Metalsky, Katz & Beach, 1999; Segrin & Abramson, 1994) and partly due to autonomous cognitive and affective processes that serve to perpetuate a negatively biased mental construction of the depressed person (Carlston & Skowronski, 1994; Forgas, 1995). The depressed person's reactions (e.g., increased reassurance seeking) reinforce others' negative view and their tendency to react negatively to the depressed person, which results in greater depressive displays, thereby maintaining the depressogenic interpersonal process (Rudolph, Hammen, & Burge, 1997).

The model focuses on two social-cognitive constructs—person schema and attributions—and associated affective reactions. Others are expected to develop a negatively valenced schema of the depressed person; that is, a mental model of the depressed person's traits, interests, and values. As a memory structure, the person schema organizes abstract and concrete information about the target that will influence (i.e., bias) target-related information processing (Fiske, 1995; Murray, Holmes, & Griffin, 1996). Others' attributions about the causes of depressed, versus nondepressed, people's failures and problems are expected to be more dispositional (e.g., internal, global, stable, controllable) and to evoke judgments of greater blame, intent, and selfish motivation, suggesting a negative attributional bias toward the depressed target (Sacco, Dumont, & Dow, 1993; Sacco & Dunn, 1990). Negatively biased attributions and a negatively valenced per-

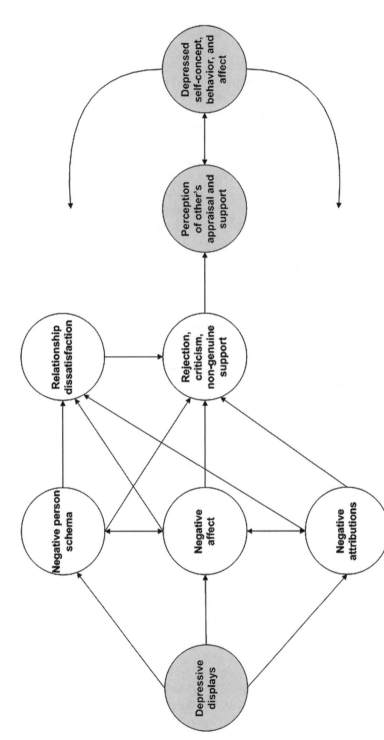

FIG. 6.1.   A social-cognitive model of interpersonal processes in depression. Note: Open circles depict others' responses. Shaded circles depict depressed target's responses.

son schema are posited to evoke and exaggerate negative affective reactions to the depressed person. Consistent with a vast body of research that has demonstrated a reciprocal relationship between social judgment and affect (Forgas, 1995), negative affective reactions are also expected to foster negative social cognitions about the depressed person (Murray & Sacco, 1998; Sacco & Murray, 1997).

Research has repeatedly found that others are less satisfied in relationships with depressed, relative to nondepressed, persons (Hammen & Brennan, 2002; Whisman, 2001), and that others more often reject, criticize, or display nongenuine support in response to depressed persons (e.g., Coyne, 1976; Sacco, Milana, & Dunn, 1988). Attributions, schematic representations, and affect are expected to contribute independently to (i.e., mediate) relationship dissatisfaction and negative behavioral reactions to depressed persons.

Although the model suggests that depressed people detect with some accuracy the reduced support and negative appraisals exhibited by others, a depressogenic self-schema also predisposes them to interpret others' reactions in a negative light (Sacco & Beck, 1995). Perceived negative reactions are expected to depress the target's mood and, concurrently, activate a self-relevant negative cognitive network that alters interpretations and responses to subsequent interpersonal stimuli (Sacco & Nicholson, 1999; Segal & Ingram, 1994). Thus, a basic tenet of cognitive models of depression is integrated into the model.

Finally, several additional points about the explanatory range of the model are worth noting but cannot be fully addressed in this chapter. First, as suggested earlier, the social-cognitive model does not assume that negative appraisals and withdrawal of support will invariably lead to depression. These negative social reactions must be detected and, when they are, their likelihood of producing depressive symptoms may be moderated by a variety of factors. Moderating variables could include cognitive vulnerabilities such as dysfunctional attitudes (Sacco & Beck, 1995), attributional style (Abramson, Metalsky, & Alloy, 1989), vulnerable self-esteem (Roberts & Monroe, 1992), or the tendency to ruminate in response to interpersonal stress (Nolen-Hoeksema, Parker, & Larson, 1994). Noncognitive factors such as extra-relationship social support (Barnett & Gotlib, 1988) or a genetic-biological diathesis may also function as moderators. Second, although the model was originally intended to account for the role that social interactions play in maintaining depressive symptoms, evidence suggests that similar interpersonal processes may be involved in other psychological disorders (Chambless & Steketee, 1999; Davila & Bradbury, 1998; Sacco & Murray, 1997, 2003; Sacco & Nicholson, 1999). Third, although not emphasized, the model suggests that reactions to depressed targets are likely to be influenced by factors that promote negative affect in the other; for examples, when the other is depression prone (Tenzer, Murray,

Vaughan, & Sacco, in press) or is experiencing significant life stressors (Burge & Hammen, 1991; Dumas & Serketich, 1994), or when the parent of a depressed child is maritally distressed (Erel & Burman, 1995). Such occurrences may be likely in relationships involving depressed persons (Hammen, 2000).

COMPARING THE SOCIAL-COGNITIVE MODEL WITH TRADITIONAL COGNITIVE AND INTERPERSONAL CONCEPTUALIZATIONS

Consider, for example, how the model conceptualizes a provocative finding by Hooley and Teasdale (1989)—that the best single predictor of depression relapse was the depressed patient's response to a single item: "How critical is your spouse of you?" Perceived criticism surpassed marital distress and expressed emotion in predicting relapse. At first glance, one may be tempted to conclude that spousal criticism causes higher relapse rates. However, closer inspection reveals a more complicated picture. As suggested by cognitive models of depression (Sacco & Beck, 1995), those most prone to relapse may be more inclined to experience cognitive distortions that lead to perceiving criticism that does not exist. Traditional interpersonal approaches suggest another interpretation: Spousal criticism of relapse-prone patients is greater because such patients display more aversive interpersonal behaviors (Coyne, 1976; Joiner et al., 1999).

The social-cognitive interpersonal process model, however, incorporates both the cognitive and traditional interpersonal perspective, while also taking into account the potentially critical role of the nondepressed other's social-cognitive responses. Applied to Hooley and Teasdale's (1989) finding, the model suggests that greater spousal criticism occurs partly in reaction to aversive interpersonal behaviors by relapse-prone patients, and partly as a result of a negatively biased view of relapse-prone patients that develops from repeated exposure to these aversive interpersonal behaviors. Additionally, the relapse-prone patient's negative self-schema heightens the tendency to perceive spousal criticism. Perceived criticism, in turn, activates negatively valenced self-relevant cognitions that foster depressed affect and behavior. Consistent with Hooley and Teasdale (1989), perceived criticism is posited as the most proximal cause of depressive relapse. In summary, we suggest that traditional cognitive and interpersonal conceptualizations accurately describe important components of depressogenic psychological processes, but that the broader, integrative conceptualization offered by the social-cognitive model provides a more complete account.

PRIMARY HYPOTHESES AND SUPPORTING EVIDENCE

The model's primary hypotheses and supporting evidence are presented in this section.

Hypothesis: Others develop a negative schema of the depressed person that influences attention, encoding, and retrieval of information about the depressed person; as such, these negative schemas will result in faster but often biased perceptions, interpretations, and judgments about the depressed person

A wealth of evidence shows that depressed people are perceived more negatively than are nondepressed persons (Sacco, 1999). In an early study, participants were asked to review a depression inventory presumably completed by another student with whom they would be interacting, and then asked to rate the student on 23 traits. The depressed student was rated more negatively than was the nondepressed student on 22 of the traits (Hall & Sacco, 1983). Therapists rated role players enacting a depressed, compared with a nondepressed, "client" more negatively on 19 of the same 23 trait descriptors (Jenkins-Hall & Sacco, 1991). These studies and subsequent replications (e.g., Nicholson & Sacco, 1999) suggest that others hold negative stereotypes of depressed people that bias perceptions and interpersonal reactions to unfamiliar depressed persons (Cane & Gotlib, 1985).

Of greater significance, people in close relationships with the depressed person also exhibit evidence of a negative schema. Mothers of children with more depressive symptoms rate their children more negatively on a wide range of traits (Sacco, Johnson, & Tenzer, 1993; Tenzer et al., in press). Well spouses evaluate depressed spouses less favorably than do spouses of nondepressed partners (Hautzinger, Linden, & Hoffman, 1982; Horesh & Fennig, 2000; Sacco, Dumont, et al., 1993). Similarly, depressed roommates are held in lower esteem than are nondepressed roommates (Joiner & Metalsky, 1995).

Is the negative view of the depressed person biased, as suggested by the model, or could negative trait ratings of depressed people simply reflect actual behavioral differences (i.e., an unbiased translation of the depressed person's behavior into trait descriptors)?[1] Early evidence of bias

---

[1] Negatively biased perceptions can refer to a tendency to view another person negatively, regardless of the accuracy of those perceptions; that is, biased perceptions can also be accurate (Kenny & Acitelli, 2001). Negative bias can also imply distorted and inaccurate perceptions; that is, errors in judgment. The social-cognitive model posits that a negative person schema of the depressed person increases the probability of *distorted* and *inaccurate* perceptions of the depressed target. Although the accuracy of schematic perceptions can often be ascertained, the accuracy of causal and responsibility attributions is very difficult, if not impossible, to determine. Therefore, the model does not speak to the accuracy of such attributional biases toward depressed persons.

was provided in the study of therapist ratings reported earlier (Jenkins-Hall & Sacco, 1991). Therapists rated depressed "clients" more negatively on the traits "bad–good" and "dirty–clean." Viewing depressed clients as less "good" than nondepressed clients is pejorative, and suggests the possibility of a negative bias. However, more striking evidence of bias was provided by the finding that depressed "clients" were perceived as *dirtier* than the nondepressed "clients," even though the *same actors* played both roles.

Several subsequent studies provide additional evidence of bias. Three studies looked for bias by including traits that were reasonable descriptors of depression (e.g., pessimistic) *and* traits that were irrelevant to depression (e.g., well read, shallow). It was assumed that bias would be exhibited if respondents rated the depressed target negatively on *both* sets of traits, because there is no reason to expect that depressed people actually behave in a way that warrants more negative ratings on traits unrelated to depression. If no bias existed, respondents should rate the depressed target more negatively on only those traits that pertain to depression. Results showed that husbands rated depressed, relative to nondepressed, wives more negatively on both depression-relevant *and* -irrelevant traits (Sacco, Dumont, et al., 1993). More recently, a similarly designed study conducted with mothers of depressed children obtained parallel findings: Children with more depressive symptoms were rated more negatively by their mothers on traits that were relevant to depression *and* on traits that were unrelated to depression (Tenzer, Sacco, & Vaughan, 2002). Further evidence of a negatively biased schema was provided by a laboratory study that measured trait perceptions of depressed versus nondepressed partners (actually confederates) who performed either poorly or well on an interactive task. Participants formed impressions of their partner based on responses to a depression and interest inventory, and were led to believe they were evaluating the performance of a coparticipant on an attention and memory task. Despite equivalent task performance and the absence of behavioral differences, depressed partners were rated more negatively on a broad array of personality traits, regardless of whether the traits were related or unrelated to depression or whether the traits were related or unrelated to task performance (Nicholson & Sacco, 1999).

One potential criticism of these studies is the exclusive reliance on self-report measures to measure schematic content. In recent years, self-report measures have been criticized for their ostensible lack of construct validity (Gotlib & Neubauer, 2000), given that schematic processing, by definition, is largely governed by processes outside of conscious awareness. Although this concern is valid, research has shown that explicit measures of trait perceptions (i.e., trait ratings) do correspond significantly with measures indicative of schematic information processing (Fuhrman & Funder, 1995; Murray, 1998).

How do these observations about others' perceptions of depressed people fit with contemporary theory and research on social cognition, and what are their implications for our understanding of interpersonal processes in depression? Research has amply demonstrated that behavioral observations automatically and unconsciously result in trait inferences that are stored in memory (Carlston & Skowronski, 1994; Maass, Colombo, Colombo, & Sherman, 2001; Van Overwalle, Drenth, & Marsman, 1999). Srull and Wyer (1989) also argued that these personality inferences involve both trait encoding and general valuative impressions, with evidence that behavioral perceptions are organized around a valuative concept rather than a descriptive one. Consistent with their assertion, evidence suggests that knowledge about a person rarely exists without evaluative connotations (Murray et al., 1996; Scott, Fuhrman, & Wyer, 1991), and that evaluative judgments may be a largely unconditional automatic response (Bargh, Chaiken, Raymond, & Hymes, 1996; Jarvis & Petty, 1996). Stored trait and valuative representations influence subsequent processing of information about the other, resulting in faster but often biased perceptions, interpretations, judgments, and recall (Berscheid, 1994; Carlston & Skowronski, 1994; Park, 1986; Scott et al., 1991; Smith & Zarate, 1992; Wyer & Carlston, 1994). Schemas thus allow for heuristical processing, whereby less cognitive effort is required to make judgments and decisions because the preexisting information contained in the schema directs attention to information consistent to the schema, often to the exclusion of information inconsistent to the schema.

People in the depressed person's social network who have formed a negative schema of the depressed person, then, are more likely to attend to and encode information that is consistent with their negative conception of the depressed person. Particularly problematic for depressed individuals is evidence that, compared with positive information, negative information is more easily noticed by others (Pratto & John, 1991), exerts a greater influence on evaluative judgments than does positive information (Ito, Larsen, Smith, & Cacioppo, 1998), and is more likely to be remembered when attributed to the person (versus the situation; Ybarra & Stephan, 1996).

The formation of negative schemas about depressed people has several important implications. Negative schematic processing about the depressed person is likely to influence cognitions, affective reactions, and behavior displayed toward the depressed person, which in turn is likely to affect the depressed person's self-concept and depressive symptoms. Additionally, given that schemas are resistant to change (Sacco, 1999), the negative schemas held by others in the depressed person's social environment could continue to operate even after the depressed person has recovered. Indeed, it is hypothesized that others' negative schemas of the depressed person serve to maintain and perpetuate the depressed person's symptoms, thereby making recovery more difficult to achieve and making relapse more likely even when recovery does occur. A protracted period of symptom remission may be necessary for others to integrate new information into their schema of the formerly depressed person.

Hypothesis: Others explain the behaviors of the depressed person in relatively negative ways

Depression researchers have focused on the nature and impact of self-attributions made by depressed people. In contrast, the social-cognitive model proposes that others' attributions about depressed people are relatively more negative and thus result in more negative affective and behavioral reactions to the depressed target. Specifically, the model posits that others are prone to attribute the depressed person's failures and personal problems to causes that are more internal, stable, global, and controllable relative to attributions about nondepressed persons.

Although this hypothesis has seldom been examined, the available evidence is supportive. In an experiment conducted by Yarkin, Harvey, and Bloxom (1981), participants were told that their partner was happy and emotionally fulfilled, lonely and depressed, or were not given any information. The person with whom participants interacted was a confederate trained to minimize the cues indicative of his/her psychological well-being and to act the same way in all conditions. Participants made more negative attributions and fewer positive attributions about the "depressed" target. In a subsequent interaction, participants exhibited more negative social behaviors toward the "depressed" target, and the valence of their attributions corresponded with the valence of their social behavior. Another experiment found that the failures and personal problems of a hypothetical depressed, versus nondepressed, person were attributed to more dispositional factors (i.e., more internal, stable, global, and controllable). In contrast, the depressed person's successes were attributed to more situational factors (Sacco & Dunn, 1990). Studies of married couples have produced similar findings. Spouses of individuals who were depressed or higher in negative affectivity made more negative attributions about the depressed mate's failures and negative marital behaviors (Karney, Bradbury, Fincham, & Sullivan, 1994; Sacco, Dumont, et al., 1993; Senchak & Leonard, 1993).

One question that has arisen in conducting research on social cognition pertains to the utility of attributions as a construct that is separate and distinct from that of person schema. On what grounds should attributions be considered independent of trait representations, and is there evidence to support this assertion? According to Cantor and Kihlstrom (1987), attributions encompass rules involved in social inference and judgment (also termed *procedural social knowledge*), whereas a person schema consists of declarative social knowledge. Furthermore, making inferences about the target's traits, which comprise the person schema of the target, is a process that has been shown to occur automatically. In contrast, generating an explanation for the target's behavior requires greater cognitive effort and does not occur as readily or frequently as does the formation of trait inferences (Gilbert & Malone, 1995; Gilbert, Pelham, & Krull, 1988; Maass et al., 2001). Consistent with this perspective, attributions and trait perceptions, although correlated, have been shown to explain unique variance in others' responses to targets (e.g., Sacco, Dumont, et al., 1993; Sacco & Murray, 1997, 2003).

Hypothesis: Social cognition about the depressed person influences affect, and affect influences social cognition

Interpersonal interactions with depressed persons are often aversive to others, typically inducing negative affect such as anger, anxiety, and depression (Gotlib & Hammen, 1992; Segrin & Dillard, 1992). A major component of the social-cognitive model is the bidirectional causal relationship between social-cognitive and affective responses to the depressed person. That social-cognition influences affective reactions has been well documented (Murray & Sacco, 1998; Sacco & Beck, 1995). In addition, however, ample evidence shows that, regardless of its cause, affect influences social cognition (Clore et al., 1994; Dolan, 2002; Forgas, 1995). People in good moods tend to view (and act) positively toward others; those in negative moods tend to show the opposite pattern.

The link between causal attributions and affective reactions has been amply demonstrated in both the marital distress (Fincham, Beach, & Nelson, 1987; Fincham & O'Leary, 1983) and parenting (see Dix, 1991; Miller, 1995 for reviews) literature. Consistent with the social-cognitive model, Sacco and Dunn (1990) found that attributions about a depressed target's behavior mediated the relationship between the target's depression and affective reactions to the target.

Nonattributional cognitions about depressed people have seldom been examined with respect to their influence on others' affective reactions. The social-cognitive model asserts that a negative schema of the depressed target plays a causal role in others' negative affective reactions. Sacco, Dumont, et al. (1993) compared the trait perceptions (an indicant of person schema) and affective reactions of husbands of depressed wives with those of husbands of nondepressed wives. Husbands of depressed wives evidenced more negative trait perceptions and more negative affective reactions to their wives than did the husbands of nondepressed wives. The valence of trait perceptions corresponded to the valence of the affective reactions. Similarly, Benazon (2000) noted that spouses' appraisals (i.e., trait perceptions) of their depressed partners were significantly correlated with spouses' affect and negative affectivity as measured by the Level of Expressed Emotion scale (LEE; Cole & Kazarian, 1988). Studies of mother–child dyads have yielded comparable results. The valence of mothers' trait ratings of their children matched the valence of affective reactions to their child (Sacco, Johnson, et al., 1993; Tenzer & Sacco, 2002b).

The data just cited provide correlational evidence consistent with the model's hypothesis that a negative schema influences affective reactions to depressed people. Using an experimental design, Nicholson and Sacco (1999) found that participants rated a depressed target (confederate) more negatively on a list of traits and responded with more negative affect to the depressed target than did participants responding to a nondepressed target. The valence of trait perceptions significantly correlated with valence of affective reactions. Of particular relevance to the model, trait perceptions fully mediated the relationship between the target's depressive symptoms and the participant's affective reactions to the depressed target. In another experiment, Murray and Sacco (1998) randomly assigned mothers to generate a list of negative or positive trait characteristics of their child (i.e., a social-cognitive activation procedure). Mothers who generated positive characteristics of their child experienced a subsequent lift in their mood, regardless of whether their preexisting schema of the child was positively or negatively valenced. However, for mothers assigned to generate negative characteristics of their child, only those with a preexisting negative schema experienced a decrement in mood. This finding corroborates the notion of a person schema as influencing situation-specific cognitions about a target person, and suggests that the person schema creates a cognitive context that will influence affective reactions to the target.

The Murray and Sacco (1998) study also provided support for the model's assertion that an observer's affect directly influences social cognition and judgments about a depressed target. Their social-cognitive activation procedure produced a change in the mothers' trait perceptions of her child; that is, those in the positive activation condition rated their child more positively, whereas those in the negative activation condition rated their child more negatively. This finding raised an important theoretical question. Were postactivation trait ratings due to having just brought to mind the valenced child-relevant information (i.e., the social-cognitive activation procedure), or did the corresponding mood change produce a change in the participants' trait perceptions? Results indicated that after the effects of preactivation mood and the cognitive activation condition were controlled, postactivation mood still contributed significantly to postactivation trait ratings. Thus, the results supported the bidirectional relationship between social cognition and affect posited by the model. Affective reactions caused by activating valenced social cognitions about the child further shifted the view of the child in the direction of the valence of the affective state. According to the model, this reciprocal relationship could yield a self-perpetuating feedback loop that would serve to either deteriorate or enhance the view of the child, particularly if repeated negative interactions occurred.

In summary, a good deal of data supports the model's contention that there is a reciprocal relationship between social-cognitive and affective reactions to depressed persons. Well-documented negative affective reactions to depressed persons can be explained by others' negative social cognitions about the depressed person. Negative affect—whether induced by negative cognitions about the depressed or by factors unrelated to the depressed person—will serve to exacerbate negative social judgments about the depressed person. Because negative affect, regardless of its source, can foster negative cognitions about the depressed person, the model also suggests that factors such as the other's level of depression (Brody & Forehand, 1986; Dumas & Serketich, 1994; Tenzer et al., in press), level of environmental stress (Burge & Hammen, 1991; Dumas & Serketich, 1994), and marital distress (Erel & Burman, 1995) will contribute to negative social-cognitive and affective reactions to the depressed target.

Hypothesis: Relationship dissatisfaction in those involved with the depressed person is mediated by negative schematic representations and attributions about the depressed person as well as affective state

The quality of relationships with depressed people tends to be compromised. Marriages with a depressed spouse are characterized by relationship distress (Davila, 2001; Hammen & Brennan, 2002; O'Mahen, Beach, & Banawan, 2001; Whisman, 2001). The divorce rate for couples with a formerly depressed spouse is nine times greater than the rate for the general population at a 1- to 3-year follow-up (Merikangas, 1984). Evidence supports a reciprocal relationship between depression and marital satisfaction; depression can cause marital dissatisfaction, and marital distress can cause depression (Barnett & Gotlib, 1988; Gotlib & Hammen, 1992; Ulrich-Jakubowski, Russell, & O'Hara, 1988). Similar findings appear in other relationships. Mothers of depressed, relative to nondepressed, children report being less satisfied with the mother–child relationship (Tenzer et al., in press). In undergraduate dating couples, the relationship satisfaction of the female partners was inversely related to the males' self-reported depressive symptoms (Katz, Beach, & Joiner, 1999), and women's depressive symptoms were inversely correlated with their boyfriends' ratings of their interpersonal competence, suggesting lower relationship satisfaction among the boyfriends (Daley & Hammen, 2002).

Because the disruption of attachments and loss of social support are likely to contribute to the onset, maintenance, and worsening of depression, a better understanding of the processes underlying relationship dis-satisfaction is desirable. From a social-cognitive perspective, others' negative schemata of the depressed person, negative affective reactions to the depressed person, and negative attributions made about the depressed person's behavior *independently* contribute to relationship dissatisfaction and mediate the association between depression and relationship dissatis-faction (Sacco, 1999).

Evidence of a robust association between attributions and relationship satisfaction has been amply documented in the literature on marital satis-faction, where it has been shown that spouses who attribute their partners' negative behaviors to causes that are internal, global, and stable, and who blame their partners for negative behaviors, tend to report lower marital satisfaction (Bradbury & Fincham, 1990; Karney & Bradbury, 2000). Lon-gitudinal data support the notion that attributions play a causal role in af-fecting marital distress (Fincham & Bradbury, 1987). In contrast to the proposal that depressed people gravitate toward marital partners who view them negatively (Joiner, 2001; cf. Sacco & Phares, 2001), evidence sug-gests that negative attributions about others are not due to a stable prop-erty of the person making the attributions, but rather are a result of what has been "learned from their ongoing experiences in the relationship" (Karney & Bradbury, 2000, p. 306).

Mirroring the data on marital dyads, the link between attributions and relationship satisfaction has been observed in mother–child dyads. Moth-ers' dispositional causal attributions for their children's negative behaviors have been found to predict lower relationship satisfaction (Sacco & Murray, 1997, 2003; Tenzer et al., Study 2, in press).

Although attributions have received the bulk of attention in the rela-tionship distress literature, trait representations (an operationalization of person schema) also predict relationship satisfaction. The valence of moth-ers' trait representations of children who varied in level of psychopath-ology has been strongly linked to mother–child relationship satisfaction (Sacco & Murray, 1997, 2003; Tenzer et al., in press). The same link has been documented for spouses of depressed wives (Benazon, 2000; Sacco, Dumont, et al., 1993). Statistical analyses have also shown that negative spousal or maternal trait conceptions are not simply a reflection of rela-tionship dissatisfaction (Benazon, 2000; Sacco & Murray, 1997).

Evidence also suggests that attributions, trait representations, and af-fective reactions function as mediators of relationship satisfaction. In a study of married couples, husbands' attributions and trait representa-tions fully mediated the association between their wives' history of de-pression and the husbands' marital satisfaction (Sacco, Dumont, et al., 1993). More recently, studies have found that the association between child disorder and mothers' relationship dissatisfaction was fully medi-ated by trait conceptions of the children and partially mediated by attributions about the children's behaviors (Sacco & Murray, 1997, 2003). In another study, the association between children's depression level and mothers' relationship satisfaction was fully mediated by mothers' trait representations and attributions (Tenzer & Sacco, 2002b). These studies thus indicate that the link between target depression and others' relationship dissatisfaction can be largely accounted for by others' trait perceptions and attributions about the depressed target. It is worth noting, however, that several studies found that trait perceptions accounted for significantly more variance in relationship satisfaction than did attributions, and that trait perceptions account for more of the association between target psychopathology and others' relationship dissatisfaction (e.g., Sacco & Murray, 2003, Tenzer et al., in press).

Given the strong interrelationship between social cognition and affect, it is important to consider the independent influence that affect, in addition to social cognition, may exert on the relationship satisfaction of people involved with individuals with psychological disorders. In several studies, negative affect continued to account for a significant portion of the variance in marital satisfaction after attributions were controlled (Fincham, Beach, & Bradbury, 1989, Study 2; Senchak & Leonard, 1993; cf. Karney, Bradbury, Fincham, & Sullivan, 1994). After controlling for trait conceptions and attributions, affect contributed independently to the relationship dissatisfaction observed in mothers of children with a nonspecific psychological disorder (Sacco & Murray, 1997), in mothers of children with more severe symptoms of ADHD (Sacco & Murray, 2003), and in mothers of relatively depressed children (Tenzer & Sacco, 2002b).

In summary, these studies suggest that a substantial amount of variance in relationship dissatisfaction found in others who interact with depressed persons can be explained by the independent and additive effects of others' negative trait perceptions of the depressed person, others' dispositional attributions about the depressed person's failures and personal problems, and other's affective reactions to the depressed person.

Hypothesis: Behavioral responses to a depressed person are mediated by negative schematic representations and attributions about the depressed person as well as affective state

One of the most robust findings in the depression literature is that depressed people elicit negative behavioral responses from others. Depressed people are rejected more than are nondepressed persons (Segrin & Abramson, 1994) and have smaller and less supportive social networks (Gotlib & Hammen, 1992). Marital dyads with a depressed spouse are more prone to displays of conflict, negativity, and hostility (Gotlib & Beach, 1995). Numerous studies indicate that lack of support and negative interpersonal interactions play a major role in the development, maintenance, and worsening of depression. For example, a review of seven studies of depression relapse revealed that depressed people with a family member classified as high in expressed emotion (EE) were 13.2 times more likely to relapse (Coiro & Gottesman, 1996). Expressed emotion consists of criticism, emotional overinvolvement, and hostility directed at an affectively ill family member.

Evidence indicates that negative behavioral reactions to the depressed are mediated by others' negative social cognition and affect. In a study described earlier, confederates described as depressed (vs. happy), but who acted in an ambiguous manner, received more negative attributions and less positive attributions, were liked less, and, during a subsequent interaction, elicited more negative social responses (e.g., others sat further away, made less eye contact, had more negatively valenced conversations, and spoke less). Valence of attributions was related to valence of social behavior (Yarkin et al., 1981).

The negative schemata that others commonly form of depressed people should foster negative expectations about interpersonal interactions with depressed people, thereby adversely influencing the valence of behavior directed toward the depressed person (Darley & Fazio, 1980; Miller & Turnbull, 1986; Rosenthal, 1994). Consistent with this conceptualization, Sacco, Milana, and Dunn (1985) found, through path analysis, that others expected depressed (vs. nondepressed) targets to place greater interpersonal demands on them, which resulted in a stronger desire to avoid interacting with the depressed person (see also Joiner & Metalsky, 1995; Sacco & Dunn, 1990). In another study, depressed targets were less likely than were nondepressed targets to be chosen as a future work team member, even though they had received the same unsatisfactory score on a memory test as had nondepressed targets. Rejection of the depressed target was fully mediated by participants' trait representations of the target (Nicholson, 1997). Finally, in a direct test of the model's predictions, a study found that mothers of relatively depressed children reported more negative trait perceptions of the child, more negative affective reactions to the child, and exhibited less positive and more negative behavior during interactions with the child. Negative trait perceptions of and affective reactions to the child were associated with more negative and less positive verbal behaviors during mother–child interactions. Most important, the association between child depression and maternal behavior was accounted for by the mother's trait perceptions of and affective reactions to the child, indicating that social cognition and affective reactions mediated the association between child depression and negative maternal behavior (Tenzer & Sacco, 2002a).

Attributions have also been linked to interpersonal behaviors. Spouses who make negative attributions regarding their partners' behavior display more negatively valenced and fewer positively valenced behaviors during interactions with their spouses (Bradbury & Fincham, 1992). Parents' attributions for their children's behavior have also been shown to predict parenting behavior (Dix, 1991; Miller, 1995). Of greater relevance to the proposed mediational role of social cognition, however, is the finding that participants' attributions about a hypothetical depressed target impacted their affective reactions to the target, which in turn predicted social rejection (Sacco & Dunn, 1990).

Hypothesis: The depressed individual accurately perceives others as being less supportive and as appraising him or her more negatively; however, negatively biased information processing commonly found among depressed individuals also influences the perception of appraisals and support

The model assumes that depressed people are reasonably accurate in detecting others' negative reactions, but that the depressed person's bias toward perceiving, remembering, and ruminating about others' negative responses accentuates the negative impact of others' rejection and negative appraisals. A good deal of evidence indicates that depressed people perceive their interpersonal environments more negatively than do nondepressed controls. Depressed individuals report that their social networks are smaller, less supportive, and of poorer quality than do nondepressed persons (Gotlib & Hammen, 1992). Retrospective descriptions by depressed (vs. nondepressed) adults of their family environments are more negative (Gerlsma, Emmelkamp, & Arrindell, 1990). Laboratory studies show that depressed people perceive greater interpersonal rejection (e.g., Dobson, 1989; Segrin, 1993; Strack & Coyne, 1983).

To what extent are these perceptions accurate? Gotlib and Hammen's (1992) review of perceived social support and quality of close relationships suggested that the depressed person's negative perceptions are not distorted. A review of depressed mothers' perceptions of behavioral problems in their children reached a similar conclusion (Richters, 1992). A large-scale longitudinal study of determinants of perceived support among married couples concluded that perceived support is determined strongly by actual interpersonal transactions, moderately by the perceiver's biased negative outlook, and only weakly by the perceiver's anxiety and depression (Vinokur, Schul, & Caplan, 1987). Independent sources of information (e.g., siblings, relatives, longtime friends) about depressed persons' parents corroborate depressed patients' perceptions that their parents were more rejecting than were parents of nondepressed persons (Crook, Raskin, & Eliot, 1981). One study found that relatively depressed young women perceived their boyfriends as providing less emotional support, which the boyfriends corroborated (Daley & Hammen, 2002). A review of the accuracy of retrospective assessments (Brewin, Andrews, &

Gotlib, 1993) concluded that concerns over the unreliability of retrospective reports are exaggerated.

However, Kenny and Depaulo's (1993) review of the person perception literature indicated that self-appraisals are highly correlated with the valence of interpersonal perceptions. That is, depressed and low-self-esteem individuals are more likely to perceive that others view them negatively. Kenny and DePaulo (1993) posited that the influence of the self-concept on social perceptions occurs because targets observe their own behavior during social interactions as they attempt to discern what impression others are forming of them. Those persons who already have formed negative views of themselves are more prone to evaluate their social behavior and thus their impression on others as negative. Thus, as suggested by the model, the negative self-schema of the depressed person is likely to account for a substantial portion of the variance in his or her perceptions of others' appraisals.

Hypothesis: The perception of negative appraisals and reduced support adversely influence the target's depression level

The model posits that perceptions of negative appraisal and reduced support are the most proximal cause of depressive reactions. Numerous studies have documented an association between others' negative interpersonal reactions (e.g., rejection) and depressive symptoms. However, fewer studies have examined the critical role of the depressed target's *perceptions* of others' reactions. Studies that have explicitly done so indicate that perceptions of others' appraisals are indeed an important predictor of the target's psychological symptoms. A study of daily fluctuations in depressive symptoms found that interpersonal stress (e.g., feeling hurt, upset, rejected, or disappointed by someone; having an argument or conflict with someone) preceded the onset of dysphoric reactions by 1 day (Stader & Hokanson, 1998). Depressed college students with recent-onset major depressive episodes relapsed more frequently when they perceived reduced social support and believed that their parents had engaged in harsh disciplinary tactics during their childhoods (Nezlek, Hampton, & Shean, 2000). A recent study found that mothers' negative trait perceptions of their child predicted more negative affective reactions to the child; less positive and more negative maternal behavioral reactions to the child; and greater child depression (Tenzer et al., Study 2, in press). Most important to the present discussion, however, was the finding that the association between negative trait perceptions and child depression was fully mediated by the child's perceptions of the mother's appraisals of them (Tenzer et al., 2002).

Several longitudinal studies have shown that perceiving the interpersonal environment as unsupportive or critical predicts a slower recovery from depression, greater relapse, or an increase in symptoms of depression (Holahan, Moos, Holahan, & Cronkite, 2000; Hooley & Teasdale, 1989; I. W. Miller et al., 1992; Joiner, 1995; McLeod, Kessler, & Landis, 1992; Swindle, Cronkite, & Moos, 1989). For example, Billings and Moos (1985) found that perceived quality of significant relationships correlated with the rate of recovery from depression. As noted earlier, Hooley and Teasdale (1989) found that perceived criticism accounted for more variance in relapse than did the nondepressed spouses' marital distress and expressed emotion (e.g., critical remarks). In addition, after perceived criticism was controlled, expressed emotion no longer significantly contributed to relapse rate. This result is consistent with the model's hypothesis that perceived criticism mediates the effect of spouses' critical behaviors on relapse, and is thus a proximal cause of depression. Finally, a prospective study found that students with roommates who viewed them negatively developed more depressive symptoms, but only when the targets were interested in the roommates' negative feedback (Joiner, 1995). To the extent that "interest" serves as a proxy for "detecting" behavioral evidence of the roommates' negative evaluations, this result supports the model's hypothesis.

Hypothesis: The social-cognitive processes described in the proposed model contribute to the development of depression (i.e., a negative self-concept, depressed mood and behavior)

The material thus far has focused on how the model may aid in our understanding of interpersonal processes involved in the maintenance, worsening, and relapse of depression. However, the model can also be applied to the *development* of depressive symptoms. The model proposes that chronic exposure to significant others who view and react negatively to a target increases the probability that the target will develop depressive symptoms. A good deal of evidence indicates that parental emotional and physical abuse increases the risk for depression and hopelessness (e.g., Kaufman, 1991; Kazdin, Moser, Colbus, & Bell, 1985). The social-cognitive model draws on attachment theory (Bowlby, 1980) and social-cognitive perspectives on the development of the self-concept (Cooley, 1902; Kenny & DePaulo, 1993; Leary, 1999; Mead, 1934; Shrauger & Schoeneman, 1979) in attempting to explain how parental emotional abuse would culminate in a depressive disorder. First, disrupted attachments with the significant other constitute a "loss" that increases the likelihood of a response pattern that resembles a depressive disorder (i.e., increased negative affect, shift in the valence of self-relevant cognition to a more negative direction, and dysfunctional interpersonal behaviors; Bowlby, 1980). Chronic activation of this response pattern, especially in childhood, is expected to predispose the target to depressive disorders in adulthood. Second, the *valence* of the other's appraisals and attributions will simultaneously alter the valence of the target's self-concept, affect, and behavior (Alloy et al., 2001; Kenny & DePaulo, 1993; Shrauger & Schoeneman, 1979). In support of his sociometer theory, Leary (1999) provided evidence that others' reactions exert a strong effect on self-esteem because self-esteem functions as a subjective monitor or gauge of the degree to which the individual is being valued, included, and accepted versus devalued, excluded, and rejected by other people. Amplifying the effects of perceived loss and lower self-esteem, depressogenic cognitive processes such as the development of negative associative networks will exacerbate negative self-relevant cognition, depressed mood, and depressive interpersonal displays.

A large body of research indicates that others' perceptions of a target can have profound effects on a target's behavior, affect, and cognitions, including the *self-concept* (Darley & Fazio, 1980; Miller & Turnbull, 1986; Rosenthal, 1994). For example, the valence of parents' perceptions of their children predicts the children's perceptions of their parents' appraisals and support *and* the valence of the children's self-perceptions (Felson, 1989; Sarason, Pierce, Bannerman, & Sarason, 1993). Dix (1993) offered evidence that children internalize their parents' perceptions of and attributions about their behaviors. Schafer and Keith (1985) have shown that the same processes are at work in married couples. Using a large sample of randomly selected married couples, they found that a spouse's appraisals influence the target spouse's self-concept via the target's perception of the spouse's appraisals.

The model's hypothesis is also consistent with a large amount of literature showing that parental rejection and criticism are linked to the subsequent development of depressive symptoms. Depressed adults are more likely to report that their parents were critical and rejecting (e.g., Gerlsma et al., 1990; Lizardi et al., 1995). Recent research on college students found that self-reported childhood emotional maltreatment (but not physical or sexual abuse) predicted future episodes of depression, levels of hopelessness, and suicidal ideation (Gibb, Alloy, Abramson, Rose, Whitehouse, Donovan, et al., 2001; Gibb, Alloy, Abramson, Rose, Whitehouse, & Hogan, 2001). A 10-year longitudinal study conducted by Lefkowitz and Tesiny (1984) on the effect of parental rejection on the development of depressive symptoms provided more compelling evidence. Parental rejection was operationalized as a composite of parents' ratings of the child on responsibility, forgetfulness, compliance, manners, and schoolwork. Lefkowitz and Tesiny's index of parental rejection is comparable to the social-cognitive construct of person schema. When parents evaluated their children negatively on a given item, they also indicated the extent to which they were annoyed by the children's behavior, thereby adding an affective component to the measure of parental rejection. Parental rejection prospectively predicted the children's level of depression 10 years later. However, because children's level of depression at baseline was not measured, the possibility that depression anteceded parental rejection cannot be ruled out.

According to the social-cognitive model, the most proximal cause of depression is perceived loss of support and negative appraisals. Negative parental behaviors, therefore, should adversely affect a child *only* if the child perceives those behaviors as indicating that the parent has withdrawn emotional support or negatively appraises them. Consistent with this hypothesis, a recent longitudinal study showed that maternal emotional support moderated the long-term association between spanking and problem behavior; that is, spanking was associated with an increase in problem behaviors over time only in the context of low emotional support by the mother (McLoyd & Smith, 2002).

Perceiving one's spouse as unsupportive and critical also appears to play a role in the development of depression. Barnett and Gotlib's (1988) review of etiological factors in depression identified marital discord as one of the few variables having support as an antecedent of depression. Using a longitudinal design, Schaefer and Burnett (1987) also reported that women's perceptions of their husbands' behavior toward them predicted subsequent psychological adjustment and mental health, even after controlling for baseline levels of psychological adjustment. Along these lines, it is worth noting that self-verification theory (Swann, de la Ronde, & Hixon, 1994) offers the counterintuitive hypothesis that low-self-esteem and depressed persons will be more maritally satisfied when their spouses' views of them are congruent with their own. According to self-verification theory, self-confirming evaluations will be sought, attended to, and believed because doing so promotes "perceptions of prediction and control by fostering intrapsychic and interpersonal coherence" (Giesler, Josephs, & Swann, 1996, p. 358). The social-cognitive model suggests otherwise. A study designed to test this hypothesis found that, consistent with the social-cognitive model, regardless of self-esteem and depression level, targets were more maritally satisfied when their partners viewed them positively and were less maritally satisfied when their partners viewed them negatively. Partner appraisal accounted for a relatively large amount of variance in target marital satisfaction, whereas the interaction effect predicted by self-verification theory did not approach significance (Sacco & Phares, 2001). Similar results from Murray et al. (1996) strengthen confidence in the reliability of this finding. In summary, a good deal of evidence suggests that interpersonal environments characterized by negative appraisals and reduced support foster the development of psychological distress and increase the likelihood of depressive reactions.

MATERNAL DEPRESSION

Mounting evidence indicates that the offspring of depressed mothers are at greater risk for social, academic, and psychological problems than are the children of nondepressed mothers (Billings & Moos, 1983; Hammen, Gordon, Burge, & Adrian, 1987; Kim-Cohen, Moffitt, Taylor, Pawlby, & Caspi, 2005; Weissman et al., 2004). Theory and research have increasingly focused on maternal cognitions and affect as mediators of parenting behaviors (Bugental & Johnston, 2000; Teti & Gelfand, 1997). The social-cognitive model offers one potentially useful conceptualization of interpersonal processes involving depressed mothers and their children. The model suggests that the depressed parent's *schema* of the child, *attributions* about the child's behaviors, and affective *reactions* to the child will be relatively negative. Each of these factors (schema, attributions, and affect) is expected to contribute independently and *mediate* the association between maternal depression and both parental relationship dissatisfaction and parental behaviors (e.g., criticism). In response to negative parental behaviors, the child is expected to perceive a loss of support and negative appraisals, which will culminate in lower self-esteem, negative affect, and dysfunctional interpersonal behaviors.

Evidence supports the model's conceptualization. Relative to nondepressed mothers, depressed mothers are more likely to perceive their children's behavior as negative and problematic (Boyle & Pickles, 1997; Brody & Forehand, 1986; Chilcoat & Breslau, 1997; Fergusson, Lynskey, & Horwood, 1993; Najman et al., 2000; Youngstrom, Izard, & Ackerman, 1999). Depressed mothers also pay greater attention to negative child characteristics and behaviors (e.g., Najman et al., 2000; Youngstrom et al., 1999), suggesting the possibility of a negative bias. They are also more likely to attribute their children's negative behavior to dispositional causal factors (e.g., internal, stable, global factors) and to see these behaviors as intentional and blameworthy (Bugental & Johnston, 2000; Conrad & Hammen, 1989; Dix, 1993; Geller & Johnston, 1995; Goodman & Gotlib, 1999; Teti & Gelfand, 1997; White & Barrowclough, 1998). Depressed mothers, not surprisingly, experience more negative affective reactions to their children (Cohn, Campbell, Matias, & Hopkins, 1990; Krech & Johnston, 1992).

As suggested by the model, maternal trait perceptions and maternal attributions predict negative affective reactions to the child and the mother's dissatisfaction with the relationship with her child (Sacco & Murray, 1997, 2001, 2003; Tenzer et al., in press). Moreover, the association between maternal depression and maternal relationship dissatisfaction is mediated by these social-cognitive and affective reactions (Sacco & Murray, 1997, 2001, 2003; Tenzer et al., in press). Finally, evidence suggests that these social-cognitive processes ultimately influence child adjustment. Goodman, Adamson, Riniti, and Cole (1994) found that mothers with a history of depression endorsed more critical attitudes toward their children, which, in turn, were associated with children's lower self-esteem and greater vulnerability to the development of a psychiatric disorder. Thus, evidence supports the model's conceptualization of the social-cognitive processes by which maternal depression negatively influences child adjustment.

TREATMENT IMPLICATIONS

To the extent that the model we have described is valid, it offers an integrated, systems-oriented perspective on the treatment of depression. First, therapists should make depressed (or depression-prone) individuals aware of their possible negative impact on others, and help them to modify potentially aversive social behaviors (e.g., social skills training). Second, the therapist should assess and address significant others' negative perceptions, attributions, and affective reactions to the depressed person during the depressive episode (e.g., attribution retraining, behavioral monitoring, anger management). Negative responses are likely to be stronger after longer-duration and repeated episodes of depression (Sacco et al., 1988). Third, the model suggests that others may retain a negative social-cognitive "set" that could bias interpretations of the formerly depressed person's responses, even after symptoms remit. Even hints of relapse may activate a well-developed negative schema of the depressed target. These biased interpretations and consequent interpersonal reactions could undermine recovery. Negatively biased automatic information processing may be corrected by making observers aware of their prejudice or motivating them to obtain accurate information (e.g., Beach, Whisman, & O'Leary, 1994; Neuberg, 1989). Fourth, therapists should attend to external stressors that produce negative affect in significant others (e.g., job stress), which can fuel negative social-cognitive and affective responses to the depressed patient (e.g., stress management). Fifth, the model clearly points to the need to develop adaptive relationship responses in both members of the dyad (e.g., communications training, behavioral marital therapy). Finally, therapy should assess and treat underlying social-cognitive diatheses in the depressed or depression-prone person that could bias social perceptions and heighten sensitivity to negative appraisals and rejection (e.g., cognitive therapy).

REFERENCES

Abramson, L. Y., Metalsky, G. I., & Alloy, L. B. (1989). Hopelessness depression: A theory-based subtype of depression. *Psychological Review, 96*, 358–372.

Abramson, L. Y., Seligman, M. E. P., & Teasdale, J. D. (1978). Learned helplessness in humans: Critique and reformulation. *Journal of Abnormal Psychology, 87*, 102–109.

Alloy, L. B., Abramson, L. Y., Tashman, N. A., Berrebbi, D. S., Hogan, M. E., Whitehouse, W. G., Crossfield, A. G., & Moroco, A. (2001). Developmental origins of cognitive vulnerability to depression: Parenting, cognitive, and inferential feedback styles of the parents of individuals at high and low cognitive risk for depression. *Cognitive Therapy and Research, 25*, 397–423.

Bargh, J. A., Chaiken, S., Raymond, P., & Hymes, C. (1996). The automatic evaluation effect: Unconditional automatic attitude activation with a pronunciation task. *Journal of Experimental Social Psychology, 32*, 104–128.

Barnett, P. A., & Gotlib, I. H. (1988). Psychosocial functioning and depression: Distinguishing among antecedents, concomitants, and consequences. *Psychological Bulletin, 104*, 97–126.

Beach, S. R. H., Whisman, M. A., & O'Leary, K. D. (1994). Marital therapy for depression: Theoretical foundation, current status, and future directions. *Behavior Therapy, 25*, 345–371.

Beck, A. T. (1967). *Depression: Clinical, experimental, and theoretical aspects.* New York: Harper & Row.

Benazon, N. R. (2000). Predicting negative spousal attitudes toward depressed persons: A test of Coyne's Interpersonal Model. *Journal of Abnormal Psychology, 109*, 550–554.

Berscheid, E. (1994). Interpersonal relationships. *Annual Review of Psychology, 45*, 79–129.

Billings, A. G., & Moos, R. H. (1983). Comparisons of children of depressed and nondepressed parents: A social-environmental perspective. *Journal of Abnormal Child Psychology, 11*, 463–486.

Billings, A. G., & Moos, R. H. (1985). Life stressors and social resources affect posttreatment outcomes among depressed patients. *Journal of Abnormal Psychology, 94*, 140–153.

Bowlby, J. (1980). By ethology out of psycho-analysis: An experiment in interbreeding. *Animal Behaviour, 28*, 649–656.

Boyle, M. H., & Pickles, A. R. (1997). Influence of maternal depressive symptoms on ratings of childhood behavior. *Journal of Abnormal Child Psychology, 25*, 399–412.

Bradbury, T. N., & Fincham, F. D. (1990). Attributions in marriage: Review and critique. *Psychological Bulletin, 107*, 3–33.

Bradbury, T. N., & Fincham, F. D. (1992). Attributions and behavior in marital interaction. *Journal of Personality and Social Psychology, 63*, 613–628.

Brewin, C. R., Andrews, B., & Gotlib, I. H. (1993). Psychopathology and early experience: A reappraisal of retrospective reports. *Psychological Bulletin, 113*, 82–98.

Brody, G. H., & Forehand, R. (1986). Maternal perceptions of child maladjustment as a function of the combined influence of child behavior and maternal depression. *Journal of Consulting and Clinical Psychology, 54*, 237–240.

Bugental, D. B., & Johnston, C. (2000). Parental and child cognitions in the context of the family. *Annual Review of Psychology, 51*, 315–344.

Burge, D., & Hammen, C. (1991). Maternal communication: Predictors of outcome at follow-up in a sample of children at high and low risk for depression. *Journal of Abnormal Psychology, 100*, 174–180.

Cane, D. B., & Gotlib, I. H. (1985). Implicit conceptualizations of depression: Implications for an interpersonal perspective. *Social Cognition, 3*, 341–368.

Cantor, N., & Kihlstrom, J. F. (1987). *Personality and social intelligence.* Englewood Cliffs, NJ: Prentice-Hall.

Carlston, D. E., & Skowronski, J. J. (1994). Savings in the relearning of trait information as evidence for spontaneous inference generation. *Journal of Personality and Social Psychology, 66*, 840–856.

Chambless, D. L., & Steketee, G. (1999). Expressed emotion and behavior therapy outcome: A prospective study with obsessive-compulsive and agoraphobic outpatients. *Journal of Consulting and Clinical Psychology, 67*, 658–665.

Chilcoat, H. D., & Breslau, N. (1997). Does psychiatric history bias mothers' reports? An application of a new analytic approach. *Journal of the American Academy of Child and Adolescent Psychiatry, 36*, 971–979.

Clark, M. S., Helgeson, V. S., Mickelson, K., & Pataki, S. P. (1994). Some cognitive structures and processes relevant to relationship functioning. In R. S. Wyer & T. K. Srull (Eds.), *Handbook of social cognition* (Vol. 2, pp. 189–238). Hillsdale, NJ: Lawrence Erlbaum Associates.

Clore, G. L., Schwarz, N., & Conway, M. (1994). Affective causes and consequences of social information processing. In R. S. Wyer & T. K. Srull (Eds.), *Cognitive social behavior* (pp. 73–108). New York: Elsevier/North-Holland.

Cohn, J. F., Campbell, S. B, Matias, R., & Hopkins, J. (1990). Face-to-face interactions of postpartum depressed and nondepressed mother–infant pairs at 2 months. *Developmental Psychology, 26*, 15–23.

Coiro, M. J., & Gottesman, I. I. (1996). The diathesis and/or stressor role of expressed emotion in affective illness. *Clinical Psychology: Science and Practice, 3*, 310–322.

Cole, J. D., & Kazarian, S. S. (1988). The Level of Expressed Emotion Scale: A new measure of expressed emotion. *Journal of Clinical Psychology, 44*, 392–397.

Conrad, M., & Hammen, C. (1989). Role of maternal depression in perceptions of child maladjustment. *Journal of Consulting and Clinical Psychology, 57*, 663–667.

Cooley, C. H. (1902). *Human nature and the social order.* New York: Scribner.

Coyne, J. C. (1976). Toward an interactional description of depression. *Psychiatry, 39*, 28–40.

Coyne, J. C., & Gotlib, I. H. (1983). The role of cognition in depression: A critical appraisal. *Psychological Bulletin, 94*, 472–505.

Crook, T., Raskin, A., & Eliot, J. (1981). Parent–child relationships and adult depression. *Child Development, 52*, 950–957.

Daley, S. E., & Hammen, C. (2002). Depressive symptoms and close relationships during the transition to adulthood: Perspectives from dysphoric women, their best friends, and their romantic partners. *Journal of Consulting and Clinical Psychology, 70*, 129–141.

Darley, J. M., & Fazio, R. H. (1980). Expectancy confirmation processes arising in the social interaction sequence. *American Psychologist, 35*, 867–881.

Davila, J. (2001). Paths to unhappiness: The overlapping courses of depression and romantic dysfunction. In S. R. H. Beach (Ed.), *Marital and family processes in depression: A scientific foundation for clinical practice* (pp. 71–87). Washington, DC: American Psychological Association.

Davila, J., & Bradbury, T. N. (1998). Psychopathology and the marital dyad. In L. L'Abate (Ed.), *Family psychopathology: The relational roots of dysfunctional behavior* (pp. 127–157). New York: Guilford.

Dix, T. (1991). The affective organization of parenting: Adaptive and maladaptive processes. *Psychological Bulletin, 110*, 3–25.

Dix, T. (1993). Attributing dispositions to children: An interactional analysis of attribution in socialization. *Personality and Social Psychology Bulletin, 19*, 633–643.

Dobson, K. S. (1989). Real and perceived interpersonal responses to subclinically anxious and depressed targets. *Cognitive Therapy and Research, 13*, 37–47.

Dolan, R. J. (2002). Emotion, cognition, and behavior. *Science, 298*, 1191–1194.

Dumas, J. E., & Serketich, W. J. (1994). Maternal depressive symptomatology and child maladjustment: A comparison of three process models. *Behavior Therapy, 25*, 161–181.

Erel, O., & Burman, B. (1995). Interrelatedness of marital relations and parent–child relations: A meta-analytic review. *Psychological Bulletin, 118*, 108–132.

Felson, R. B. (1989). Parents and reflected appraisal process: A longitudinal analysis. *Journal of Personality and Social Psychology, 56*, 965–971.

Fergusson, D. M., Lynskey, M. T., & Horwood, L. J. (1993). The effect of maternal depression on maternal ratings of child behavior. *Journal of Abnormal Child Psychology, 21*, 245–269.

Fincham, F. D., Beach, S. R., & Bradbury, T. N. (1989). Marital distress, depression, and attributions: Is the marital distress-attribution association an artifact of depression? *Journal of Consulting and Clinical Psychology, 57*, 768–771.

Fincham, F. D., Beach, S. R., & Nelson, G. (1987). Attribution processes in distressed and non-distressed couples: 3. Causal and responsibility attributions for spouse behavior. *Cognitive Therapy and Research, 11*, 71–86.

Fincham, F. D., & Bradbury, T. N. (1987). The impact of attributions in marriage: A longitudinal analysis. *Journal of Personality and Social Psychology, 52*, 739–748.

Fincham, F. D., & O'Leary, K. D. (1983). Causal inferences for spouse behavior in maritally distressed and non-distressed couples. *Journal of Social and Clinical Psychology, 1*, 42–57.

Fiske, S. T. (1995). Social cognition. In A. Tesser (Ed.), *Advanced social psychology* (pp. 149–193). New York: McGraw-Hill.

Fletcher, G. J. O., & Fincham, F. D. (1991). *Cognition in close relationships.* Hillsdale, NJ: Lawrence Erlbaum Associates.

Forgas, J. P. (1995). Mood and judgment: The affect infusion model (AIM). *Psychological Bulletin, 117*, 39–66.

Forrest, M. S., & Hokanson, J. E. (1975). Depression and autonomic arousal reduction accompanying self-punitive behavior. *Journal of Abnormal Psychology, 84*, 346–357.

Fuhrman, R. W., & Funder, D. C. (1995). Convergence between self and peer in the response-time processing of trait-relevant information. *Journal of Personality and Social Psychology, 69*, 961–974.

Geller, J., & Johnston, C. (1995). Depressed mood and child conduct problems: Relationships to mothers' attributions for their own and their children's experiences. *Child and Family Behavior Therapy, 17*, 19–34.

Gerlsma, C., Emmelkamp, P. M. G., & Arrindell, W. A. (1990). Anxiety, depression, and perception of early parenting: A meta-analysis. *Clinical Psychology Review, 10*, 251–277.

Gibb, B. E., Alloy, L. B., Abramson, L. Y., Rose, D. T., Whitehouse, W. G., Donovan, P., Hogan, M. E., Cronholm, J., & Tierney, S. (2001). History of childhood maltreatment, negative cognitive styles, and episodes of depression in adulthood. *Cognitive Therapy and Research, 25*, 425–446.

Gibb, B. E., Alloy, L. B., Abramson, L. Y., Rose, D. T., Whitehouse, W. G., & Hogan, M. E. (2001). Childhood maltreatment and college students' current suicidal ideation: A test of the hopelessness theory. *Suicide and Life-Threatening Behavior, 31*, 405–415.

Giesler, R. B., Josephs, R. A., & Swann, W. B. (1996). Self-verification in clinical depression: The desire for negative evaluation. *Journal of Abnormal Psychology, 105*, 358–368.

Gilbert, D. T., & Malone, P. S. (1995). The correspondence bias. *Psychological Bulletin, 117*, 21–38.

Gilbert, D. T., Pelham, B. W., & Krull, D. S. (1988). On cognitive dizziness: When person perceivers meet persons perceived. *Journal of Personality and Social Psychology, 54*, 733–740.

Goodman, S. H., Adamson, L. B., Riniti, J., & Cole, S. (1994). Mothers' expressed attitudes: Associations with maternal depression and children's self-esteem and psychopathology. *Journal of the American Academy of Child & Adolescent Psychiatry, 33*, 1265–1274.

Goodman, S. H., & Gotlib, I. H. (1999). Risk for psychopathology in the children of depressed mothers: A developmental model for understanding mechanisms of transmission. *Psychological Review, 106*, 458–490.

Gotlib, I. H., & Beach, S. R. H. (1995). A marital/family discord model of depression: Implications for therapeutic intervention. In N. S. Jacobson & A. S. Gurman (Eds.), *Clinical handbook of couple therapy* (pp. 411–436). New York: Guilford.

Gotlib, I. H., & Hammen, C. L. (1992). *Psychological aspects of depression.* New York: Wiley.

Gotlib, I. H., & Neubauer, D. L. (2000). Information-processing approaches to the study of cognitive biases in depression. In S. L. Johnson & A. M. Hayes (Eds.), *Stress, coping, and depression* (pp. 117–143). Mahwah, NJ: Lawrence Erlbaum Associates.

Hall, R. L., & Sacco, W. P. (1983, March). *The depression stereotype and its interpersonal impact.* Paper presented at the 29th annual meeting of the Southeastern Psychological Association, Atlanta.

Hammen, C. (2000). Interpersonal factors in an emerging developmental model of depression. In S. L. Johnson & A. M. Hayes (Eds.), *Stress, coping, and depression* (pp. 71–88). Mahwah, NJ: Lawrence Erlbaum Associates.

Hammen, C., & Brennan, P. A. (2002). Interpersonal dysfunction in depressed women: Impairments independent of depressive symptoms. *Journal of Affective Disorders, 72*, 145–156.

Hammen, C. L., Gordon, D., Burge, D., & Adrian, C. (1987). Maternal affective disorders, illness, and stress: Risk for children's psychopathology. *American Journal of Psychiatry, 144*, 736–741.

Hautzinger, M., Linden, M., & Hoffman, N. (1982). Distressed couples with and without a depressed partner: An analysis of their verbal interaction. *Journal of Behavior Therapy and Experimental Psychiatry, 13*, 307–314.

Holahan, C. J., Moos, R. H., Holahan, C. K., & Cronkite, R. C. (2000). Long-term posttreatment functioning among patients with unipolar depression: An integrative model. *Journal of Consulting and Clinical Psychology, 68*, 226–232.

Hooley, J. M., & Teasdale, J. D. (1989). Predictors of relapse in unipolar depressives: Expressed emotion, marital distress, and perceived criticism. *Journal of Abnormal Psychology, 98*, 229–235.

Horesh, N., & Fennig, S. (2000). Perception of spouses and relationships: A matched control study of patients with severe affective disorder in remission and their spouses. *Journal of Nervous and Mental Disease, 188*, 463–466.

Ito, T. A., Larsen, J. T., Smith, N. K., & Cacioppo, J. T. (1998). Negative information weighs more heavily on the brain: The negativity bias in evaluative categorizations. *Journal of Personality and Social Psychology, 75*, 887–900.

Jarvis, W. B. G., & Petty, R. E. (1996). The need to evaluate. *Journal of Personality and Social Psychology, 70*, 172–194.

Jenkins-Hall, K., & Sacco, W. P. (1991). Effect of client race and depression on the perceptions of white therapists. *Journal of Social and Clinical Psychology, 10*, 5–10.

Joiner, T. E. (1995). The price of soliciting and receiving negative feedback: Self-verification theory as a vulnerability to depression theory. *Journal of Abnormal Psychology, 104*, 364–372.

Joiner, T. E. (2000). Depression's vicious scree: Self-propagating and erosive processes in depression chronicity. *Clinical Psychology: Science and Practice, 7*, 203–218.

Joiner, T. E. (2001). Nodes of consilience between interpersonal-psychological theories of depression. In S. R. H. Beach (Ed.), *Marital and family processes in depression: A scientific foundation for clinical practice* (pp. 129–138). Washington, DC: American Psychological Association.

Joiner, T. E., & Coyne, J. C. (Eds.). (1999). *The interactional nature of depression: Advances in interpersonal approaches.* Washington, DC: American Psychological Association.

Joiner, T. E., & Metalsky, G. I. (1995). A prospective test of an integrative interpersonal theory of depression: A naturalistic study of college roommates. *Journal of Personality and Social Psychology, 69,* 778–788.

Joiner, T. E., Metalsky, G. I., Katz, J., & Beach, S. R. H. (1999). Depression and excessive reassurance-seeking. *Psychological Inquiry, 10,* 269–278.

Karney, B. R., & Bradbury, T. N. (2000). Attributions in marriage: State or trait? A growth curve analysis. *Journal of Personality and Social Psychology, 78,* 295–309.

Karney, B. R., Bradbury, T. N., Fincham, F. D., & Sullivan, K. T. (1994). The role of negative affectivity in the association between attributions and marital satisfaction. *Journal of Personality and Social Psychology, 66,* 413–424.

Katz, J., Beach, S. R. H., & Joiner, T. E. (1999). Contagious depression in dating couples. *Journal of Social and Clinical Psychology, 18,* 1–13.

Kaufman, J. (1991). Depressive disorders in maltreated children. *Journal of the American Academy of Child and Adolescent Psychiatry, 30,* 257–265.

Kazdin, A. E., Moser, J., Colbus, D., & Bell, R. (1985). Depressive symptoms among physically abused and psychiatrically disturbed children. *Journal of Abnormal Psychology, 94,* 298–307.

Kenny, D. A., & Acitelli, L. K. (2001). Accuracy and bias in the perception of the partner in a close relationship. *Journal of Personality and Social Psychology, 80,* 439–448.

Kenny, D. A., & DePaulo, B. M. (1993). Do people know how others view them? An empirical and theoretical account. *Psychological Bulletin, 114,* 145–161.

Kim-Cohen, J., Moffitt, T. E., Taylor, A., Pawlby, S. J., & Caspi, A. (2005) Maternal depression and children's antisocial behavior: Nature and nurture effects. *Archives of General Psychiatry, 62,* 173–181.

Krech, K. H., & Johnston, C. (1992). The relationship of depressed mood and life stress to maternal perceptions of child behavior. *Journal of Clinical Child Psychology, 21,* 115–122.

Lau, M. A., Gemar, M. C., & Segal, Z. V. (2000). Clarifying the role of interpersonal factors in depression chronicity from a cognitive perspective. *Clinical Psychology: Science and Practice, 7,* 228–231.

Leary, M. R. (1999). Making sense of self-esteem. *Current Directions in Psychological Science, 8,* 32–35.

Lefkowitz, M. M., & Tesiny, E. P. (1984). Rejection and depression: Prospective and contemporaneous analysis. *Developmental Psychology, 20,* 776–785.

Lizardi, H., Klein, D. N., Ouimette, P. C., Riso, L. P., Anderson, R. L., & Donaldson, S. K. (1995). Reports of the childhood home environment and early-onset dysthymia and episodic major depression. *Journal of Abnormal Psychology, 104,* 132–139.

Maass, A., Colombo, A., Colombo, A., & Sherman, S. J. (2001). Inferring traits from behaviors versus behaviors from traits: The induction-deduction asymmetry. *Journal of Personality and Social Psychology, 81,* 391–404.

McLeod, J. D., Kessler, R. C., & Landis, K. R. (1992). Speed of recovery from major depressive episodes in a community sample of married men and women. *Journal of Abnormal Psychology, 102,* 277–286.

McLoyd, V. C., & Smith, J. (2002). Physical discipline and behavior problems in African American, European American, and Hispanic children: Emotional support as a moderator. *Journal of Marriage and the Family, 64,* 40–53.

Mead, G. H. (1934). *Mind, self and society.* Chicago: University of Chicago Press.

Merikangas, K. R. (1984). Divorce and assortative mating among depressed patients. *American Journal of Psychiatry, 141,* 74–76.

Miller, D. T., & Turnbull, W. (1986). Expectancies and interpersonal processes. *Annual Review of Psychology, 37,* 233–256.

Miller, I. W., Keitner, G. I., Whisman, M. A., Ryan, C. E., Epstein, N. B., & Bishop, D. S. (1992). Depressed patients with dysfunctional families: Description and course of illness. *Journal of Abnormal Psychology, 101,* 637–646.

Miller, S. A. (1995). Parents' attributions for their children's behavior. *Child Development, 66,* 1557–1584.

Murray, D. W. (1998). The role of social cognition and affect in parent–child relationship satisfaction. *Dissertation Abstracts International, 58,* 4463.

Murray, D. W., & Sacco, W. P. (1998). Effect of child-relevant cognitions on mother's mood: The moderating effect of child-trait conceptions. *Cognitive Therapy and Research, 22,* 47–61.

Murray, S. L., Holmes, J. G., & Griffin, D. W. (1996). The benefits of positive illusions: Idealization and the construction of satisfaction in close relationships. *Journal of Personality and Social Psychology, 70,* 79–98.

Najman, J. M., Williams, G. M., Nikles, J., Spence, S., Bor, W., O'Callaghan, M., Le Brocque, R., & Andersen, M. J. (2000). Mothers' mental illness and child behavior problems: Cause-effect association or observation bias? *American Academy of Child and Adolescent Psychiatry, 39,* 592–602.

Neuberg, S. L. (1989). The goal of forming accurate impressions during social interactions: Attenuating the impact of negative expectancies. *Journal of Personality and Social Psychology, 56,* 374–386.

Nezlek, J. B., Hampton, C. P., & Shean, G. D. (2000). Clinical depression and day-to-day social interaction in a community sample. *Journal of Abnormal Psychology, 109,* 11–19.

Nicholson, K. J. (1997). *Cognitive, affective, and behavioral reactions to depressed vs. nondepressed targets during an interactive task.* Unpublished master's thesis, University of South Florida, Tampa.

Nicholson, K. J., & Sacco, W. P. (1999, August). *Interpersonal responses to depression: Negative social-cognition, affect, and non-genuine support.* Poster session presented at the annual meeting of the American Psychological Association, Boston.

Nolen-Hoeksema, S., Parker, L. E., & Larson, J. (1994). Ruminative coping with depressed mood following loss. *Journal of Personality and Social Psychology, 67,* 92–104.

O'Mahen, H. A., Beach, S. R. H., & Banawan, S. F. (2001). Depression in marriage. In J. Harvey & A. Wenzel (Eds.), *Close romantic relationships: Maintenance and enhancement* (pp. 299–319). Mahwah, NJ: Lawrence Erlbaum Associates.

Park, B. (1986). A method for studying the development of impressions of real people. *Journal of Personality and Social Psychology, 51,* 907–917.

Pratto, R., & John, O. P. (1991). Automatic vigilance: The attention-grabbing power of negative social information. *Journal of Personality and Social Psychology, 61,* 380–391.

Richters, J. E. (1992). Depressed mothers as informants about their children: A critical review of the evidence for distortion. *Psychological Bulletin, 112,* 485–499.

Roberts, J. E., & Monroe, S. M. (1992). Vulnerable self-esteem and depressive symptoms: Prospective findings comparing three alternative conceptualizations. *Journal of Personality and Social Psychology, 62,* 804–812.

Rosenthal, R. (1994). Interpersonal expectancy effects: A 30-year perspective. *Current Directions in Psychological Science, 6,* 176–179.

Rudolph, K. D., Hammen, C., & Burge, D. (1997). A cognitive-interpersonal approach to depressive symptoms in preadolescent children. *Journal of Abnormal Child Psychology, 25,* 33–45.

Sacco, W. P. (1999). A social-cognitive model of interpersonal processes in depression. In T. E. Joiner & J. C. Coyne (Eds.), *The interactional nature of depression: Advances in interpersonal approaches* (pp. 329–362). Washington, DC: American Psychological Association.

Sacco, W. P., & Beck, A. T. (1995). Cognitive theory and therapy. In E. E. Becker & W. R. Leber (Eds.), *Handbook of depression* (pp. 329–351). New York: Guilford.

Sacco, W. P., Dumont, C. P., & Dow, M. G. (1993). Attributional, perceptual, and affective responses to depressed and nondepressed marital partners. *Journal of Consulting and Clinical Psychology, 61,* 1076–1082.

Sacco, W. P., & Dunn, V. K. (1990). Effect of actor depression on observer attributions: Existence and impact of negative attributions toward the depressed. *Journal of Personality and Social Psychology, 59,* 517–524.

Sacco, W. P., & Hokanson, J. E. (1978). Expectations of success and anagram performance of depressives in a public and private setting. *Journal of Abnormal Psychology, 87,* 122–130.

Sacco, W. P., & Hokanson, J. E. (1982). Depression and self-reinforcement in a public and private setting. *Journal of Personality and Social Psychology, 42,* 377–385.

Sacco, W. P., Johnson, S. A., & Tenzer, S. A. (1993, August). *Parent perceptions, affective reactions, and depression in children.* Poster session presented at the annual meeting of the American Psychological Association, Toronto, Ontario, Canada.

Sacco, W. P., Milana, S., & Dunn, V. K. (1985). Effect of depression level and length of acquaintance on reactions of others to a request for help. *Journal of Personality and Social Psychology, 49,* 1728–1737.

Sacco, W. P., Milana, S., & Dunn, V. K. (1988). The effect of duration of depressive episode on the response of others. *Journal of Social and Clinical Psychology, 7,* 297–311.

Sacco, W. P., & Murray, D. (1997). Mother–child relationship satisfaction: The role of attributions and trait conceptions. *Journal of Social and Clinical Psychology, 16,* 24–42.

Sacco, W. P., & Murray, D. W. (2001, June). *Maternal depression and mother–child relationship satisfaction: A social-cognitive analysis.* Poster session presented at the annual meeting of the International Society for Research in Child and Adolescent Psychopathology, Vancouver, British Columbia, Canada.

Sacco, W. P., & Murray, D. W. (2003). Maternal dyadic relationship satisfaction as a function of hyperactivity and conduct problems: A social cognitive analysis. *Journal of Social and Clinical Psychology, 22,* 665–684.

Sacco, W. P., & Nicholson, K. J. (1999). A social-cognitive perspective on reassurance-seeking and depression. *Psychological Inquiry, 10,* 298–302.

Sacco, W. P., & Phares, V. (2001). Partner appraisal and marital satisfaction: The role of self-esteem and depression. *Journal of Marriage and the Family, 63,* 504–513.

Sarason, B. R., Pierce, G. R., Bannerman, A., & Sarason, I. G. (1993). Investigating the antecedents of perceived social support: Parents' views of and behavior toward their children. *Journal of Personality and Social Psychology, 66,* 1071–1085.

Schaefer, E. S., & Burnett, C. K. (1987). Stability and predictability of quality of women's marital relationships and demoralization. *Journal of Personality and Social Psychology, 53,* 1129–1136.

Schafer, R. B., & Keith, P. M. (1985). A causal model approach to the symbolic interactionist view of the self-concept. *Journal of Personality and Social Psychology, 48,* 963–969.

Scott, C. K., Fuhrman, R. W., & Wyer, R. S. (1991). Information processing in close relationships. In G. J. O. Fletcher & R. D. Fincham (Eds.), *Cognition in close relationships* (pp. 37–68). Hillsdale, NJ: Lawrence Erlbaum Associates.

Segal, Z. V., & Ingram, R. E. (1994). Mood priming and construct activation in tests of cognitive vulnerability to unipolar depression. *Clinical Psychology Review, 14,* 663–695.

Segrin, C. (1993). Interpersonal reactions to dysphoria: The role of relationship with partner and perceptions of rejection. *Journal of Social and Personal Relationships, 10,* 83–97.

Segrin, C., & Abramson, L. Y. (1994). Negative reactions to depressive behaviors: A communication theories analysis. *Journal of Abnormal Psychology, 103,* 655–668.

Segrin, C., & Dillard, J. P. (1992). The interactional theory of depression: A meta-analysis of research literature. *Journal of Social and Clinical Psychology, 11,* 43–70.

Senchak, M., & Leonard, K. E. (1993). The role of spouses' depression and anger in the attribution-marital satisfaction relation. *Cognitive Therapy and Research, 17,* 397–409.

Shrauger, J. S., & Schoeneman, T. J. (1979). Symbolic interactionist view of self-concept: Through the looking glass darkly. *Psychological Bulletin, 86,* 549–573.

Smith, E. R., & Zarate, M. A. (1992). Exemplar-based model of social judgment. *Psychological Review, 99,* 3–21.

Srull, T. K., & Wyer, R. A. (1989). Person, memory and judgment. *Psychological Review, 96,* 58–83.

Stader, S. R., & Hokanson, J. E. (1998). Psychosocial antecedents of depressive symptoms: An evaluation using daily experiences methodology. *Journal of Abnormal Psychology, 107,* 17–26.

Strack, S., & Coyne, J. C. (1983). Social confirmation of dysphoria: Shared and private reactions to depression. *Journal of Personality and Social Psychology, 44,* 798–806.

Swann, W. B., de la Ronde, C., & Hixon, J. G. (1994). Authenticity and positivity strivings in marriage and courtship. *Journal of Personality and Social Psychology, 66,* 857–869.

Swindle, R. W., Jr., Cronkite, R. C., & Moos, R. H. (1989). Life stressors, social resources, coping, and the 4-year course of unipolar depression. *Journal of Abnormal Psychology, 98,* 468–477.

Tenzer, S. A., Murray, D. W., Vaughan, C. A., & Sacco, W. P. (in press). Maternal depressive symptoms, relationship satisfaction, and verbal behavior: A social-cognitive analysis. *Journal of Social and Personal Relationships,*

Tenzer, S. A., & Sacco, W. P. (2002a, August). *Children's self-concept and maternal behavior: A social-cognitive analysis.* Poster session presented at the annual meeting of the American Psychological Association, Chicago.

Tenzer, S. A., & Sacco, W. P. (2002b, June). *Maternal social cognition mediates the association between relationship satisfaction and children's self-concept.* Poster session presented at the annual meeting of the American Psychological Society, New Orleans.

Tenzer, S. A., Sacco, W. P., & Vaughan, C. (2002, March). *Maternal appraisals and children's depression: Mediation by children's perceptions.* Poster session presented at the annual meeting of the Southeastern Psychological Association, Orlando.

Teti, D. M., & Gelfand, D. M. (1997). Maternal cognitions as mediators of child outcomes in the context of postpartum depression. In L. Murray & P. J. Cooper (Eds.), *Postpartum depression and child development* (pp. 136–164). New York: Guilford.

Ulrich-Jakubowski, D., Russell, D. W., & O'Hara, M. W. (1988). Marital adjustment difficulties: Cause of consequence of depressive symptomatology? *Journal of Social and Clinical Psychology, 7,* 312–318.

Van Overwalle, F., Drenth, T., & Marsman, G. (1999). Spontaneous trait inferences: Are they linked to the actor or to the action? *Personality and Social Psychology Bulletin, 25,* 450–462.

Vinokur, A., Schul, Y., & Caplan, R. D. (1987). Determinants of perceived social support: Interpersonal transactions, personal outlook, and transient affective states. *Journal of Personality and Social Psychology, 53,* 1137–1145.

Weissman, M. M., Feder, A., Pilowsky, D. J., Olfson, M., Fuentes, M., Blanco, C., Lantigua, R., Gameroff, M. J., & Shea, S. (2004). Depressed mothers coming to primary care: Maternal reports of problems with their children. *Journal of Affective Disorders, 78,* 93–100.

Whisman, M. A. (2001). The association between depression and marital dissatisfaction. In S. R. H. Beach (Ed.), *Marital and family processes in depression: A scientific foundation for clinical practice* (pp. 3–24). Washington, DC: American Psychological Association.

White, C., & Barrowclough, C. (1998). Depressed and non-depressed mothers with problematic preschoolers: Attributions for child behaviours. *British Journal of Clinical Psychology, 37,* 385–398.

Wyer, R. S., & Carlston, D. E. (1994). The cognitive representation of persons and events. In R. S. Wyer & T. K. Srull (Eds.), *Handbook of social cognition* (Vol. 1, pp. 41–98). Hillsdale, NJ: Lawrence Erlbaum Associates.

Wyer, R. S., & Srull, T. K. (Eds.). (1994). *Handbook of social cognition.* Hillsdale, NJ: Lawrence Erlbaum Associates.

Yarkin, K. L., Harvey, J. H., & Bloxom, B. M. (1981). Cognitive sets, attribution, and social interaction. *Journal of Personality and Social Psychology, 41,* 243–252.

Ybarra, O., & Stephan, W. G. (1996). Misanthropic person memory. *Journal of Personality and Social Psychology, 70,* 691–700.

Youngstrom, E., Izard, C., & Ackerman, B. (1999). Dysphoria-related bias in maternal ratings of children. *Journal of Consulting and Clinical Psychology, 67,* 905–916.

Chapter 7

Cognitive Therapy in the Treatment and Prevention of Depression[1]

Steven D. Hollon
Vanderbilt University

Depression is a complex disorder with both psychological and biological aspects. Animal models for inducing depression include separation-loss, learned helplessness (exposure to uncontrollable life events), and biochemical depletion, and each has found expression in etiological models of depression in humans (Hollon et al., 2002). Treatments for depression run the gamut from dynamic-interpersonal to cognitive behavioral to pharmacological interventions; all have shown some measure of success (Hollon, Thase, & Markowitz, 2002). Cognitive therapy has been among the most successful of these interventions—it has been shown to be at least as effective as alternative interventions in terms of acute response, and it appears to have an enduring effect not matched by medication treatment (Hollon & Shelton, 2001).

COGNITIVE THEORY AND THERAPY FOR DEPRESSION

These efforts have largely revolved around the articulation of a cognitive theory of psychopathology and an approach to therapy that derives from that model. A cognitive model of psychopathology is based on the notion

[1]Preparation of this manuscript was supported by grants MH60713 (R01) and MH01697 (K02) from the National Institute of Mental Health, Bethesda, MD.

that erroneous beliefs and maladaptive information processing can lead to emotional distress and problems in behavioral adaptation (Beck, 1976). With respect to depression, errors in thinking usually take the form of undue pessimism and lack of confidence in the self (Beck, 1991). Depressed individuals are troubled by negative automatic thoughts in specific situations (e.g., "I won't get that job even if I apply" or "She won't go out with me even if I ask her") that spring from more abstract underlying beliefs (e.g., "I'm incompetent" or "I'm unlovable") and are the source of such rules for living (underlying assumptions; e.g., "If I don't try I won't fail" or "If I don't get close to anyone I cannot be rejected"). These beliefs are part of a larger cognitive schema that also includes the operation of logical errors (information-processing heuristics) like all-or-none thinking or selective abstraction that serve to keep the depressed individual from recognizing the inaccuracy of his or her beliefs (Kovacs & Beck, 1978).

Cognitive therapy for depression is based on the notion that correcting these erroneous beliefs and maladaptive information-processing strategies can reduce distress and facilitate adaptive coping (Beck, 1970). The approach traditionally has focused on encouraging clients to use their own behaviors to test their beliefs; in essence, clients are taught to gather information and run experiments to test the accuracy of their negative beliefs (Beck, Rush, Shaw, & Emery, 1979). An emphasis was put on getting the client moving in early sessions, focusing on testing the accuracy of specific beliefs in specific situations during the middle stages of therapy, with attention on core beliefs and underlying assumptions coming only in the later stages. In recent years, the approach has incorporated a focus on core beliefs and underlying assumptions earlier in the course of treatment for more difficult patients, along with greater attention to childhood antecedents and the therapeutic relationship in addition to current life problems (referred to as the "three-legged stool"). This expansion of the original approach, called *schema-focused therapy*, evolved in response to efforts to treat more complicated patients with long-standing character disorders, the notion being that such patients had no healthy nondepressed schema to activate (Beck, Freeman, & Associates, 1990).

EFFICACY AND EFFECTIVENESS OF COGNITIVE THERAPY FOR DEPRESSION

Early Studies Suggested Superiority to Medications

In the mid 1970s, the antidepressant medications were considered the standard treatment for depression. They had been shown to be superior to pill-placebo in several hundred randomized controlled trials of acute treatment (Morris & Beck, 1974), and would soon be found to prevent relapse (relative to medication withdrawal) following successful treatment

(Prien & Kupfer, 1986). Psychotherapy had not been tested so extensively, but typically was less effective than medication and did little to enhance the medication's efficacy when provided in combination (Covi, Lipman, Derogatis, Smith, & Pattison, 1974; Daneman, 1961; Friedman, 1975; Klerman, DiMascio, Weissman, Prusoff, & Paykel, 1974).

Against this backdrop, the publication of an article by Rush and colleagues suggesting that cognitive therapy was more effective (and longer lasting) than medications created a quite a stir. In that study, depressed outpatients treated with 12 weeks of cognitive therapy showed greater improvement and were less likely to drop out of treatment than were patients treated with medications (Rush, Beck, Kovacs, & Hollon, 1977). Moreover, patients who responded to cognitive therapy were less likely to relapse or return to treatment over a subsequent 12-month naturalistic follow-up than were patients who responded to medications (Kovacs, Rush, Beck, & Hollon, 1981).

This article became one of the most frequently cited articles in psychology and helped launch the journal *Cognitive Therapy and Research*. It was soon joined by a second study from Edinburgh that seemed to confirm that cognitive therapy was more effective than medications, at least among patients in general practice (Blackburn, Bishop, Glen, Whalley, & Christie, 1981). Moreover, patients who responded to cognitive therapy were again less likely to relapse following treatment termination than were patients who responded to medications (Blackburn, Eunson, & Bishop, 1986).

Subsequent Studies Suggested Comparability

These early studies led some people to conclude that cognitive therapy might even be superior to medications in the treatment of depression (Dobson, 1989). However, there were problems with each that made drawing such a conclusion problematic (Meterissian & Bradwejn, 1989). In the study by Rush and colleagues (1977), drug doses were low and medication was withdrawn before the end of active treatment. This led us to overestimate differences favoring cognitive therapy over medications with respect to acute response, and to underestimate differences favoring cognitive therapy with respect to the prevention of relapse. In the case of the study by Blackburn and colleagues (1981), the advantage for cognitive therapy alone over drugs alone in the general practice sample occurred in the context of a response rate that was so low that it raised questions about the adequacy of the medication treatment. General practitioners have long been known to fail to prescribe adequate dosages of antidepressant medications; in that same trial, no such advantage was evident for cognitive therapy in a psychiatric setting where medication was provided by experienced research clinicians (Blackburn et al., 1981).

Several subsequent studies sought to compare cognitive therapy to medications in trials in which drug treatment was more adequately implemented. By this time, I had moved to the University of Minnesota and launched a controlled trial in which great care was exercised to ensure that medication treatment was adequately implemented. Medication treatment was delivered by experienced research psychiatrists with a history of involvement in other controlled trials. Average daily dosage levels were more than adequate (over 300 mg/day from Week 6 on), and several patients had their dosages raised above that level when indicated (to a high of 450 mg/day). Plasma levels were used to monitor compliance and absorption, and patients were continued at their maximally tolerated dose through the end of acute treatment.

As shown in Fig. 7.1, no advantage was observed for cognitive therapy over medications; rates of response were virtually identical between the two active modalities, although there was a modest advantage for combined treatment (Hollon et al., 1992). These results suggested that cognitive therapy was neither more nor less effective than medication treatment when each was adequately implemented. This finding was essentially replicated in a trial conducted at Washington University in St. Louis, a setting known for the rigor of its medication treatment (Murphy, Simons, Wetzel, & Lustman, 1984).

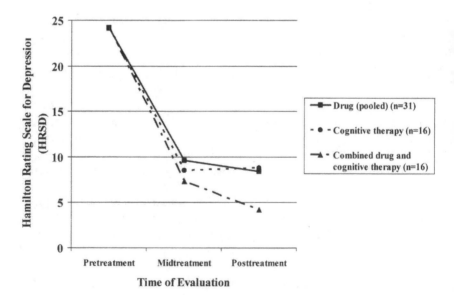

FIG. 7.1. Change in depression by condition among treatment completers. From Hollon et al. (1992), p. 778). Reprinted with permission, Copyright 1992. American Medical Association.

As in the earlier trials, there were also indications that cognitive therapy had an enduring effect that survived the end of treatment. As shown in Fig. 7.2, patients who responded to cognitive therapy were only about half as likely to relapse following treatment termination as were patients who responded to mediations (Evans et al., 1992). In fact, the magnitude of this preventive effect was as great as keeping patients on medications. Findings from the study by Murphy and colleagues (1984) largely paralleled those just reported; patients treated to remission with cognitive therapy were only about half as likely to relapse following treatment termination as were patients treated to remission with medications (Simons, Murphy, Levine, & Wetzel, 1986). Like the earlier studies already described, these findings suggest that cognitive therapy has an enduring effect that reduces subsequent risk, and that prior exposure to cognitive therapy is about as effective in that regard as is keeping patients on continuation medication.

Is Cognitive Therapy Effective for More Severely Depressed Patients?

Within a decade of the time it was first introduced, cognitive therapy had gained widespread acceptance as a treatment for depression and was being disseminated at a rapid rate. However, publication of the NIMH Treatment of Depression Collaborative Research Project (TDCRP) raised new questions about the relative efficacy of cognitive therapy, at least for more severely depressed outpatients (Elkin et al., 1989). In that trial, although no treatment differences were observed among less severely depressed outpatients, cognitive therapy was less effective than were either medica-

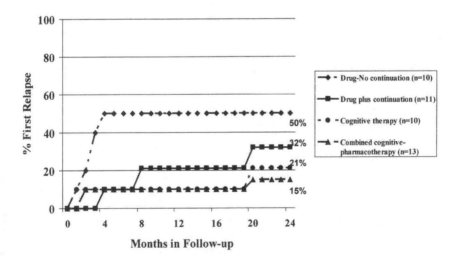

FIG. 7.2.   Relapse after successful treatment. From Evans et al. (1992, p. 805). Reprinted with permission, Copyright 1992. American Medical Association.

tions or interpersonal psychotherapy (IPT) among more severely depressed patients (Elkin et al., 1995). Moreover, there were only minimal indications of any enduring effect for cognitive therapy following treatment termination, although such differences as were apparent did favor that approach (Shea et al., 1992).

The TDCRP had a considerable impact on the field, in part because it was so large and was the first such trial of its kind to include a pill-placebo control. Adherents to a biological approach to depression have long been disinclined to believe that psychotherapy alone could be as effective as medications with more severely depressed patients, and the TDCRP appeared to confirm that belief (Klein, 1996). The notion that medications were necessary for more severely depressed patients became a cornerstone of treatment guidelines, especially those promulgated by organized psychiatry (American Psychiatric Association, 2000). However, the TDCRP was not without its problems, and there were differences between the sites that tracked their prior experience with the respective interventions that led some people to claim that cognitive therapy was less than adequately implemented at several of the sites (Jacobson & Hollon, 1996). DeRubeis and colleagues conducted a mega-analysis that focused on more severely depressed patients from the existing studies just described; as shown in Fig. 7.3, cognitive therapy was no less effective than were medications when data were aggregated across the available trials, and only the TDCRP appeared to show any advantage for medications (DeRubeis, Gelfand, Tang, & Simons, 1999).

These findings suggested that cognitive therapy is about as effective as medications when each is adequately implemented; however, no trial in the literature had as yet implemented both conditions adequately in the presence of a minimal treatment control. Against that backdrop, DeRubeis and I launched a two-site triple-blind placebo-controlled comparison of drugs and cognitive therapy in the treatment of more severely depressed outpatients that designed to explore the questions raised in these earlier trials (DeRubeis et al., 2005). In that study, 240 depressed outpatients, all meeting the same criteria used in the TDCRP to define severe depression, were randomly assigned to 16 weeks of acute treatment with either cognitive therapy, medication treatment (a double-sized condition), or a pill-placebo control. For ethical reasons, patients were kept on placebo for only 8 weeks; at that point the blind was broken and patients in that condition were provided with humanitarian treatment. At the end of acute treatment, responders to cognitive therapy were withdrawn from treatment and followed over the subsequent 2-year interval. Responders to medication treatment were randomly assigned to either continuation medication (for 1 year) or withdrawal onto pill-placebo (again triple-blind) and followed across that same interval, with all pills (drug or placebo) withdrawn for the duration of the second follow-up year.

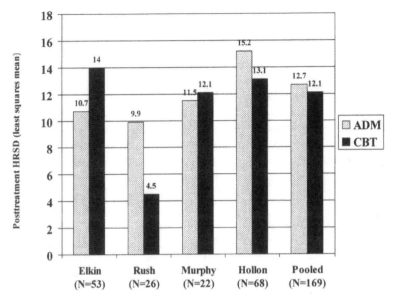

FIG. 7.3. Average response to cognitive behavior therapy versus antidepressant medications in severe depression. From DeRubeis et al. (1999, p. 1010). Reprinted with permission from the *American Journal of Psychiatry*, Copyright 1999. American Psychiatric Association.

Given the concerns raised about the previous trials, we went to considerable lengths to ensure that each modality was adequately implemented. Highly trained research psychiatrists were used at each of the sites, and met weekly to review patient progress. Paroxetine was used as the medication of choice, and doses were raised as rapidly as possible, usually reaching a maximally tolerated dose within the first 8 weeks (up to 50 mg/day). Patients who had shown a less than full response to paroxetine by Week 8 were augmented with either lithium or desipramine across the rest of the active treatment period. Those patients continued on medications after the end of acute treatment were kept at full dosage levels, and doses could be raised or augmentation initiated if such action was needed to ward off an impending relapse.

Similar efforts were made with respect to cognitive therapy. Our Pennsylvania site was the birthplace of cognitive therapy and the setting in which the original trial by Rush and colleagues was conducted. Both the Center for Cognitive Therapy and the Beck Institute are located in Philadelphia, and the respective institutions are home to a number of highly trained and experienced therapists who split their time between clinical research and training. If cognitive therapy for depression can be done well anywhere, it can be done well in Philadelphia. Therapists at our Vanderbilt site were somewhat less experienced with cognitive therapy and representative of what happens when that modality is exported to other settings. Potential therapists were selected from practitioners in the community who had some experience with the approach. They were given additional training, but it was clear from ratings of tapes sent back to the Beck Institute that they entered the trial with a lower level of competence that therapists at Penn. As a consequence, all three Vanderbilt therapists received additional training through the extramural program offered by the Beck Institute, and scores on competence ratings improved over the course of the trial (as did patient outcomes). Our sense is that much of the variability in patient outcomes in the literature reflects variability in therapist competence; it is not that cognitive therapy does not work when it is done well, it is just that it is harder to do well (at least with more difficult patients) than the early literature would lead one to believe.

Both active treatments outperformed the control condition in terms of acute response by midtreatment, with response rates of 40% for cognitive therapy and 49% for medication treatment versus 25% for the pill-placebo control. By the end of acute treatment (16 weeks), response rates were virtually identical between the two active modalities (58% versus 57%, respectively). Attrition was low in both conditions (15% and 16%, respectively); the majority of those who dropped out of cognitive therapy did not like the work involved, whereas most of those patients who dropped out of medication treatment did so because of problems with side effects. Overall, this pattern of findings suggests that cognitive therapy is about as effective as medications in the treatment of even more severely depressed outpatients (albeit somewhat slower in its actions), and that both treatments were essentially well received. The drug-placebo differences also indicate that the sample as a whole was drug responsive, and that medication treatment was adequately implemented.

There were differences between the sites in the pattern of response. In essence, patients at Penn did better in cognitive therapy than they did in medication treatment, and patients at Vanderbilt did better in medication treatment than they did in cognitive therapy. These differences between the sites could be attributed, in part, to differences in experience between the cognitive therapists; these differences shrank over the course of the trial as the Vanderbilt therapist received additional training. The differences also appeared to reflect a difference in augmentation strategy between the sites; the prescribing psychiatrists at Penn typically reduced the dose of paroxetine when they augmented with lithium or desipramine, whereas those at Vanderbilt did not. Although reducing the dosage of the core medication when adding an augmenting agent is standard practice in the field (to reduce the chances of complications), it appears to reduce the potency of the augmentation. It is of interest that response rates continued to increase among patients treated with medication from mid- to posttreatment at the Vanderbilt site, but not at the Penn site (they also increased in the two cognitive therapy conditions).

Patients who responded to cognitive therapy were essentially withdrawn from treatment at the end of 16 weeks and followed across a subsequent 2-year follow-up (Hollon et al., 2005). These patients could receive up to three booster sessions over that first year, but no more than one in any given month. From their perspective, cognitive therapy ended after 16 weeks and they were on their own to use the skills they had learned in that earlier treatment. Patients who responded to medications were randomly assigned to either continuation medication (for the first year of the 2-year follow-up) or withdrawn onto pill-placebo. As was the case for patients assigned to pill-placebo during acute treatment, placebo withdrawal was accomplished triple-blind; that is, neither the patient nor the therapist nor the independent evaluator knew whether the pills provided contained active medication.

Most critically, patients who responded to cognitive therapy were less likely to relapse following treatment termination than were treatment responders withdrawn from medication (31% versus 76%), and were no more likely than were treatment responders continued on medications (47%). This is wholly consistent with the earlier studies already described that suggested that cognitive therapy has an enduring effect that protects patients against subsequent relapse, and that this effect is at least as great as the effect produced by keeping patients on medications. Differences between continuation medication and medication withdrawal were consistent with what is typically found in the literature and fully significant when noncompliance was taken into account. Moreover, patients who showed only partial response or who had earlier ages of onset or more prior episodes were at greater risk of relapse if they were not protected by either prior exposure to cognitive therapy or ongoing continuation medication. This suggests that not all patients may require the protection afforded by exposure to cognitive therapy or ongoing medication, but those who do can have their risk reduced to that of low-risk patients.

Cognitive therapy was more costly to provide initially than was medication treatment, but may be more cost effective over the long run. It cost about $2,000 per patient to provide a course of cognitive therapy during the current study (20 sessions at $100 per session), whereas medication treatment only cost about $1,000 (12 sessions at $75 per session and $125 per month for medications). However, by the eighth month of the follow-up, the cost of keeping patients on continuation medications had passed those associated with prior cognitive therapy. Current practice in psychiatry is moving toward keeping recurrent or chronic patients on medications indefinitely; given that cognitive therapy appears to have an enduring effect, it may prove to be considerably less expensive than medication treatment over the long run.

At the end of the first 12 months of continuation, patients were withdrawn from any ongoing medication and followed (along with patients previously treated with cognitive therapy) over 12 additional months of naturalistic follow-up. These patients could be considered to have recovered from their initial episodes by virtue of the fact that they had gone more than 6 months without relapse following initial remission (Frank et al., 1991). Half of the patients withdrawn from medications experienced a recurrence (onset of a new episode) over the subsequent year, compared to only 25% of the patients with prior exposure to cognitive therapy. This suggests that cognitive therapy's enduring effect may well extend to the prevention of recurrence.

Cognitive Therapy and the Prevention of Recurrence

This last indication, although intriguing, is far from conclusive. The sample size is too small to inspire real confidence, and only a fraction of the patients initially assigned stayed free from relapse long enough to meet criteria for recovery. This leaves open the possibility that the differences observed could have been a consequence of differential retention and not a true treatment effect. If too high a proportion of patients are lost along the way, then it is possible that initial treatment acted like a differential sieve, screening high-risk patients out of one modality while retaining them in another (Klein, 1996). To forestall such an possibility, what is needed is a study that maximizes the number of patients who meet criteria for full recovery and does so by minimizing the differences between prior treatment conditions.

That is precisely the study that we are currently trying to implement. In our current trial (still ongoing), depressed patients are first treated to remission (1 month with minimal symptoms) and then recovery (6 months without relapse) with medications alone or combined treatment including cognitive therapy. At that point, all recovered patients are withdrawn from cognitive therapy and randomly assigned to either maintenance medication or medication withdrawal, and then are followed over the next 3 years with respect to recurrence. The project is a three-site study, adding Rush Medical Center in Chicago to our ongoing collaboration between Penn and Vanderbilt.

Our goal is to bring as many patients as possible to full recovery; therefore, medication treatment is designed to be both flexible and aggressive. Patients typically are started on a dual serotonin-norephinepherine reuptake inhibitor (SNRI) like venlafaxine and augmented (in the case of partial response) or switched to another medication (if unable to tolerate or in the event of subsequent nonresponse). Patients are given up to 18 months to meet criteria for remission, which allows sufficient time to try each patient on at least three different medication classes, including the older tricyclic antidepressants (TCAs) and monoamine oxidase inhibitors (MAOIs). Levels are raised aggressively to the maximum tolerated dose, and augmenting and ancillary medications are allowed if they are likely to boost response or help deal with side effects.

Similarly, our choice of combined treatment over cognitive therapy alone was driven by a desire to minimize differences between the conditions other than the actual contrast of interest. Because we were interested in seeing if cognitive therapy's enduring effect extended to the prevention of recurrence, and because prior studies suggested that such an effect is robust regardless of whether cognitive therapy is accompanied by medications, choosing combined treatment served to minimize differences between the conditions related solely to medication taking. Moreover, by taking patients off of all pills in the medication withdrawal condition (rather than withdrawing them onto pill-placebos), we increased the external validity of the findings, because that is what would happen in actual clinical practice.

The study is still ongoing and it would be premature to talk about findings, but attrition is low (about 15%) and the vast majority of the patients appear to be meeting criteria for remission (some on their second or third medication). If current rates hold, we should be able to get 75%–80% of the patients originally assigned into full recovery and eligible for the second randomization (and subsequent medication withdrawal). Such a rate would be considerably higher than most previous studies, which typically got only about half of the patients initially assigned into their maintenance phase (e.g., Frank et al., 1990).

Cognitive therapy's enduring effect appears to be robust whether cognitive therapy is provided alone or in combination with medications (Evans et al., 1992) or after patients are first brought to remission with medications (Paykel et al., 1999). Similarly, well-being therapy, an extension of cognitive therapy that incorporates attention to positive activities and self-perceptions, has been shown to reduce risk for recurrence when added to continuation medication treatment (Fava, Rafanelli, Grandi, Conti, & Belluardo, 1998). Mindfulness-based cognitive therapy (which incorporates training in meditation) has been shown to reduce risk for relapse/recurrence when provided to patients first treated to remission with medications or psychotherapy, and may be particularly helpful for patients with a history of three or more episodes (Ma & Teasdale, 2004; Teasdale et al., 2000). Finally, there are indications that cognitive behavioral interventions can be used to reduce risk for depression in children and adolescents (early and late) at risk but not currently in episode (Clarke et al., 2001; Jaycox, Reivich, Gillham, & Seligman, 1994; Seligman, Schulman, DeRubeis, & Hollon, 1999). These are very exciting findings that speak directly to the possibility of prevention.

In summary, there are converging lines of evidence that cognitive therapy is about as effective as drugs in the treatment of depression (regardless of severity), and that it has an enduring effect that appears to reduce risk. Moreover, this enduring effect appears to be robust regardless of whether cognitive therapy is provided with or without medications (and if so when) and whether it incorporates additional techniques or foci that are not part of the standard approach. We next turn to a consideration of just how cognitive therapy exerts its effects.

TESTING COGNITIVE THEORY: ACTIVE INGREDIENTS AND MECHANISMS OF CHANGE

The first question of interest is whether cognitive therapy works (when it works) by virtue of the particular strategies specified by theory. All cognitive therapists are trained to help their patients explore the accuracy of their own beliefs and their links to affect and behavior. It seems reasonable to ask whether those strategies and techniques really contribute to the process of change; that is, are they active ingredients driving therapeutic change? The notion that theoretically specified ingredients play a causative role in change is not universally supported—some people have argued that nonspecific relationship factors found in all human interactions are actually the true agents of change.

In fact, the quality of the working alliance has been found to be predictive of response in numerous studies across a number of different treatments, including cognitive therapy (Gaston, Marmar, Gallagher, & Thompson, 1991; Krupnick et al., 1994). The problem with the bulk of this research is that it has failed to control for temporal antecedence; that is, simply correlating measures of process with measures of change does not tell us whether good alliance precedes subsequent change or whether positive change leads to the perception of good alliance.

DeRubeis and colleagues have addressed this issue in a pair of studies, the latter drawing on data from the Minnesota study already described (DeRubeis & Feeley, 1990; Feeley, DeRubeis, & Gelfand, 1999). In each, measures of therapy process were taken across the course of treatment and related to both prior and subsequent change in depression. What they found was that early implementation of specific cognitive behavioral strategies predicted subsequent change in depression, whereas early change in depression predicted subsequent quality of alliance. In brief, therapists who engaged in strategies specified by theory produced greater changes in their patients, and patients who got better came to like their therapists more. This suggests that it may not be necessary to form a relationship before beginning the work of therapy; rather, relationships develop in the course of doing productive and theoretically specified work directed at reducing existing distress.

DeRubeis and colleagues have also found important indications of active ingredients in the course of change in treatment. Although plots of treatment outcome in most studies show group means that decrease in a smooth and negatively decelerated fashion, change for individual patients is often anything but gradual. In examining the course of individual change from the TDCRP and the Minnesota studies cited earlier, Tang and DeRubeis (1999) found that nearly half of the patients in cognitive therapy showed "sudden gains" of at least a standard deviation in depression scores from one session to the next. Further examination revealed that these sudden gains were not just random fluctuations; in most instances they were maintained and accounted for about half of the change over across the course of therapy. Moreover, patients who experienced sudden gains were more likely to show a full response to treatment and to maintain it longer than were patients who showed a more gradual pattern of change. Finally, an examination of the preceding sessions showed a much higher incidence of cognitive change in the sessions just prior to the sudden gains than in other sessions. This improved treatment response in patients who show sudden gains has been replicated, but further research has also found that these sudden gains occur at about the same frequency in pharmacotherapy and pill-placebo treatment (Vittengl, Clark, & Jarrett, 2005). These results indicate that further research on the mechanisms of change in both psychotherapy and pharmacotherapy are crucial.

This leads logically to the question of whether cognitive therapy works by virtue of changing beliefs and information processing. In most studies, medication treatment will produce as much change in most measures of cognition as does cognitive therapy (Imber et al., 1990; Simons, Garfield, & Murphy, 1984). However, the relevant question is not whether change in cognition is specific to cognitive therapy, but rather whether the pattern of change over time is consistent with causal agency (Hollon, DeRubeis, & Evans, 1987). In the Minnesota study already described, early change in cognition predicted later change in depression in cognitive therapy but not in medication treatment (DeRubeis et al., 1990). This is exactly the pattern that would be expected if cognitive change was a mechanism of change in depression in cognitive therapy but a consequence in medication treatment.

One class of cognition tends to show nonspecific change. Whereas stream-of-consciousness beliefs are likely to show nonspecific change over time (people become less negative as they become less depressed), more stable patterns of underlying information processing show a different pattern of change. As shown in Fig. 7.4 (based on the Minnesota study), attribution style tended to change more slowly than did measures of surface cognition (following change in depression rather than leading it), and showed greater change in cognitive therapy than it did in medication treatment (despite comparable changes in depression). Moreover, difference in attribution style at the end of treatment was one of the better predictors of subsequent risk for relapse following treatment termination

(Hollon, DeRubeis, & Evans, 1996). Research has additionally shown that cognitive therapy can also reduce the occurrence of negative cognitions during relapse of depression. Following 6 months of active treatment by pharmacotherapy alone or in combination with cognitive therapy or family therapy, patients were assessed monthly for 1 year. Patients who received cognitive therapy showed a lessened increase in negative cognitions during depressive symptom relapse than did patients who did not receive cognitive therapy (Beevers & Miller, 2005). This suggests that the way in which an individual processes information about negative life events may play a role in how he or she responds to those events. It further suggests that cognitive therapy may exert its preventative effect (in part) through changing the way in which people process information about those negative life events.

In that regard, it is of interest that Teasdale and colleagues have found that cognitive therapy tends to make people less extreme in their judgments, and that this reduction in extremity was predictive of subsequent reductions in risk (Teasdale et al., 2001). In our own recent placebo-controlled comparison among more severely depressed patients, explanatory style again showed greater change in cognitive therapy than it did in medication treatment, and again predicted risk for relapse in that latter condition. However, unlike our previous Minnesota trial, a small number of patients in cognitive therapy became unduly positive in their explanatory style (something we did not see following medication treatment). These

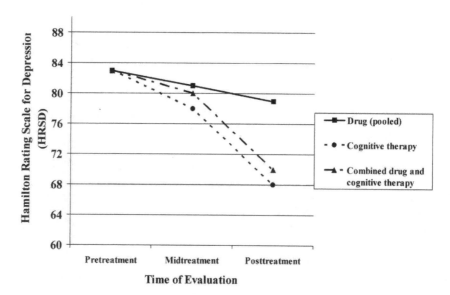

FIG. 7.4.   Changes in attributional style as a function of differential treatment. From Hollon et al. (1996), p. 309. Reprinted with permission, Copyright 1996. Guilford Press.

patients were as likely to relapse as were patients with more negative explanatory style, just as was noted by Teasdale and colleagues. This suggests that it is accuracy in thinking that is key, and not just becoming more positive or optimistic.

On the whole, these findings indicate that helping patients learn to examine the accuracy of their own beliefs represents an active ingredient in cognitive therapy for depression, and that success in this regard represents an important mechanism of change. Gains are often sudden but may require much preparatory work, and accuracy appears to be more beneficial over the long run than is any simple optimism that is not grounded in empirical realities. Although process studies on the active ingredients and mechanisms of change are less numerous and conclusive than are outcome studies pointing to its immediate and enduring effects, they are promising nonetheless, and point the way to important tests of the underlying model on which the approach is based.

CONCLUSION

It appears that cognitive therapy is about as effective as medications (even for more severely depressed patients) and that it has an enduring effect that reduces subsequent risk. This enduring effect is perhaps its most important feature; there is strong and consistent evidence that teaching people how to examine the accuracy of their own beliefs can reduce their subsequent risk for depression, whether they have a history of prior depression or are just approaching the age of risk. Given that depression tends to be a chronic recurrent disorder and that medications only suppress the expression of symptoms (they do little to change the underlying course of the disorder), this is a very major advance. Work on the processes and mechanisms that underlie these effects is less well developed but appears to suggest that teaching people how to examine the accuracy of their beliefs may be key to the approach.

REFERENCES

American Psychiatric Association. (2000). Practice guideline for the treatment of patients with major depressive disorder (revision). *American Journal of Psychiatry, 157*(Suppl. 4), 1–45.

Beck, A. T. (1970). Cognitive therapy: Nature and relation to behavior therapy. *Behavior Therapy, 1,* 184–200.

Beck, A. T. (1976). *Cognitive therapy and the emotional disorders.* New York: International Universities Press.

Beck, A. T. (1991). Cognitive therapy: A 30-year retrospective. *American Psychologist, 46,* 368–375.

Beck, A. T., Freeman, A., & Associates. (1990). *Cognitive therapy of personality disorders.* New York: Guilford.

Beck, A. T., Rush, A. J., Shaw, B. F., & Emery, G. (1979). *Cognitive therapy of depression.* New York: Guilford.

Beevers, C. G., & Miller, I. W. (2005). Unlinking negative cognition and symptoms of depression: Evidence of a specific treatment effect for cognitive therapy. *Journal of Consulting and Clinical Psychology, 73*, 68–77.

Blackburn, I. M., Bishop, S., Glen, A. I. M., Whalley, L. J., & Christie, J. E. (1981). The efficacy of cognitive therapy in depression: A treatment trial using cognitive therapy and pharmacotherapy, each alone and in combination. *British Journal of Psychiatry, 139*, 181–189.

Blackburn, I. M., Eunson, K. M., & Bishop, S. (1986). A two-year naturalistic follow-up of depressed patients treated with cognitive therapy, pharmacotherapy and a combination of both. *Journal of Affective Disorders, 10*, 67–75.

Clarke, G. N., Hornbrook, M. C., Lynch, F., Polen, M., Gale, J., Beardslee, W. R., O'Conner, E., & Seeley, J. (2001). Offspring of depressed parents in a HMO: A randomized trial of a group cognitive intervention for preventing adolescent depressive disorder. *Archives of General Psychiatry, 58*, 1127–1134.

Covi, L., Lipman, R. S., Derogatis, L. R., Smith, J. E., & Pattison, J. H. (1974). Drugs and group psychotherapy in neurotic depression. *American Journal of Psychiatry, 131*, 191–197.

Daneman, E. A. (1961). Imipramine in office management of depressive reactions (a double-blind study). *Diseases of the Nervous System, 22*, 213–217.

DeRubeis, R. J., Evans, M. D., Hollon, S. D., Garvey, M. J., Grove, W. M., & Tuason, V. B. (1990). How does cognitive therapy work? Cognitive change and symptom change in cognitive therapy and pharmacotherapy for depression. *Journal of Consulting and Clinical Psychology, 58*, 862–869.

DeRubeis, R. J., & Feeley, M. (1990). Determinants of change in cognitive therapy for depression. *Cognitive Therapy and Research, 14*, 469–482.

DeRubeis, R. J., Gelfand, L. A., Tang, T. Z., & Simons, A. D. (1999). Medications versus cognitive behavioral therapy for severely depressed outpatients: Mega-analysis of four randomized comparisons. *American Journal of Psychiatry, 156*, 1007–1013.

DeRubeis, R. J., Hollon, S. D., Amsterdam, J. D., Shelton, R. C., Young, P. R., Salomon, R. M., O'Reardon, J. P., Lovett, M. L., Gladis, M. M., Brown, L. L., & Gallop, R. (2005). Cognitive therapy vs. medications in the treatment of moderate to severe depression. *Archives of General Psychiatry, 62*, 409–416.

Dobson, K. (1989). A meta-analysis of the efficacy of cognitive therapy for depression. *Journal of Consulting and Clinical Psychology, 57*, 414–419.

Elkin, I., Gibbons, R. D., Shea, M. T., Sotsky, S. M., Watkins, J. T., Pilkonis, P. A., & Hedeker, D. (1995). Initial severity and differential treatment outcome in the National Institute of Mental Health Treatment of Depression Collaborative Research Program. *Journal of Consulting and Clinical Psychology, 63*, 841–847.

Elkin, I., Shea, M. T., Watkins, J. T., Imber, S. D., Sotsky, S. M., Collins, J. F., Glass, D. R., Pilkonis, P. A., Leer, W. R., Docherty, J. P., Fiester, S. J., & Parloff, M. B. (1989). NIMH Treatment of Depression Collaborative Research Program: I. General effectiveness of treatments. *Archives of General Psychiatry, 46*, 971–982.

Evans, M. D., Hollon, S. D., DeRubeis, R. J., Piasecki, J. M., Garvey, M. J., Grove, W. M., & Tuason, V. B. (1992). Differential relapse following cognitive therapy, pharmacotherapy, and combined cognitive-pharmacotherapy for depression. *Archives of General Psychiatry, 49*, 802–808.

Fava, G. A., Rafanelli, C., Grandi, S., Conti, S., & Belluardo, P. (1998). Prevention of recurrent depression with cognitive behavioral therapy: Preliminary findings. *Archives of General Psychiatry, 55*, 816–820.

Feeley, M., DeRubeis, R. J., & Gelfand, L. A. (1999). The temporal relation of adherence and alliance to symptom change in cognitive therapy for depression. *Journal of Consulting and Clinical Psychology, 67,* 578–582.

Frank, E., Kupfer, D. J., Perel, J. M., Cornes, C., Jarrett, D. B., Mallinger, A. G., Thase, M. E., McEachran, M. S., & Grochocinski, V. J. (1990). Three-year outcomes for maintenance therapies in recurrent depression. *Archives of General Psychiatry, 47,* 1093–1099.

Frank, E., Prien, R. F., Jarrett, R. B., Keller, M. B., Kupfer, D. J., Lavori, P. W., Rush, A. J., & Weissman, M. M. (1991). Conceptualization and rationale for consensus definitions of terms in major depressive disorder: Remission, recovery, relapse, and recurrence. *Archives of General Psychiatry, 48,* 851–855.

Friedman, A. S. (1975). Interaction of drug therapy with marital therapy in depressive patients. *Archives of General Psychiatry, 32,* 619–637.

Gaston, L., Marmar, C., Gallagher, D., & Thompson, L. (1991). Alliance prediction of outcome beyond in-treatment symptomatic change as psychotherapy processes. *Psychotherapy Research, 1,* 104–112.

Hollon, S. D., DeRubeis, R. J., & Evans, M. D. (1987). Causal mediation of change in treatment for depression: Discriminating between nonspecificity and noncausality. *Psychological Bulletin, 102,* 139–149.

Hollon, S. D., DeRubeis, R. J., & Evans, M. D. (1996). Cognitive therapy in the treatment and prevention of depression. In P. M. Salkovskis (Ed.), *Frontiers of cognitive therapy* (pp. 293–317). New York: Guilford.

Hollon, S. D., DeRubeis, R. J., Evans, M. D., Wiemer, M. J., Garvey, M. J., Grove, W. M., & Tuason, V. B. (1992). Cognitive therapy, pharmacotherapy and combined cognitive-pharmacotherapy in the treatment of depression. *Archives of General Psychiatry, 49,* 774–781.

Hollon, S. D., DeRubeis, R. J., Shelton, R. C., Amsterdam, J. D., Salomon, R. M., O'Reardon, J. P., Lovett, M. L., Young, P. R., Haman, K. L., Freeman, B. B., & Gallop, R. (2005). Prevention of relapse following cognitive therapy versus medications in moderate to severe depression. *Archives of General Psychiatry, 62,* 417–422.

Hollon, S. D., Muñoz, R. F., Barlow, D. H., Beardslee, W. R., Bell, C. C., Bernal, G., Clarke, G. N., Franciosi, L. P., Kazdin, A. E., Kohn, L., Linehan, M. M., Markowitz, J. C., Miklowitz, D. J., Persons, J. B., Niederehe, G., & Sommers, D. (2002). Psychosocial intervention development for the prevention and treatment of depression: Promoting innovation and increasing access. *Biological Psychiatry, 52,* 610–630.

Hollon, S. D., & Shelton, R. C. (2001). Treatment guidelines for major depressive disorder. *Behavior Therapy, 32,* 235–258.

Hollon, S. D., Thase, M. E., & Markowitz, J. C. (2002). Treatment and prevention of depression. *Psychology in the Public Interest, 3,* 39–77.

Imber, S. D., Pilkonis, P. A., Sotsky, S. M., Elkin, I., Watkins, J. T., Collins, J. F., Shea, M. T., Leber, W. R., & Glass, D. R. (1990). Mode-specific effects among three treatments for depression. *Journal of Consulting and Clinical Psychology, 58,* 352–359.

Jacobson, N. S., & Hollon, S. D. (1996). Prospects for future comparisons between drugs and psychotherapy: Lessons from the CBT-versus-pharmacotherapy exchange. *Journal of Consulting and Clinical Psychology, 64,* 104–108.

Jaycox, L. H., Reivich, K. J., Gillham, J., & Seligman, M. E. P. (1994). Prevention of depressive symptoms in school children. *Behaviour Research and Therapy, 32,* 801–816.

Klein, D. F. (1996). Preventing hung juries about therapy studies. *Journal of Consulting and Clinical Psychology, 64,* 74–80.

Klerman, G. L., DiMascio, A., Weissman, M., Prusoff, B., & Paykel, E. S. (1974). Treatment of depression by drugs and psychotherapy. *American Journal of Psychiatry, 131*, 186–191.

Kovacs, M., & Beck, A. T. (1978). Maladaptive cognitive structures in depression. *American Journal of Psychiatry, 135*, 525–533.

Kovacs, M., Rush, A. T., Beck, A. T., & Hollon, S. D. (1981). Depressed outpatients treated with cognitive therapy or pharmacotherapy: A one-year follow-up. *Archives of General Psychiatry, 38*, 33–39.

Krupnick, J., Collins, J., Pilkonis, P. A., Elkin, I., Simmens, S., Sotsky, S. M., & Watkins, J. T. (1994). Therapeutic alliance and clinical outcome in the NIMH Treatment of Depression Collaborative Research Program: Preliminary findings. *Psychotherapy, 31*, 28–35.

Ma, S. H., & Teasdale, J. D. (2004). Mindfulness-based cognitive therapy for depression: Replication and exploration of differential relapse prevention effects. *Journal of Consulting and Clinical Psychology, 72*, 31–40.

Meterissian, G. B., & Bradwejn, J. (1989). Comparative studies on the efficacy of psychotherapy, pharmacotherapy, and their combination in depression: Was adequate pharmacotherapy provided? *Journal of Clinical Psychopharmacology, 9*, 334–339.

Morris, J. B., & Beck, A. T. (1974). The efficacy of the anti-depressant drugs: A review of research (1958–1972). *Archives of General Psychiatry, 30*, 667–674.

Murphy, G. E., Simons, A. D., Wetzel, R. D., & Lustman, P. J. (1984). Cognitive therapy and pharmacotherapy, singly and together, in the treatment of depression. *Archives of General Psychiatry, 41*, 33–41.

Paykel, E. S., Scott, J., Teasdale, J. D., Johnson, A. L., Garland, A., Moore, R., Jenaway, A., Cornwall, P. L., Hayhurst, H., Abbott, R., & Pope, M. (1999). Prevention of relapse in residual depression by cognitive therapy. *Archives of General Psychiatry, 56*, 829–835.

Prien, R. F., & Kupfer, D. J. (1986). Continuation drug therapy for major depressive episodes: How long should it be maintained? *American Journal of Psychiatry, 143*, 18–23.

Rush, A. J., Beck, A. T., Kovacs, M., & Hollon, S. D. (1977). Comparative efficacy of cognitive therapy and pharmacotherapy in the treatment of depressed outpatients. *Cognitive Therapy and Research, 1*, 17–37.

Seligman, M. E. P., Schulman, P., DeRubeis, R. J., & Hollon, S. D. (1999). The prevention of depression and anxiety. *Prevention & Treatment, 2*. Retrieved December 21, 1999 from http://journals.apa.org/prevention/volume2/pre0020008a.html

Shea, M. T., Elkin, I., Imber, S. D., Sotsky, S. M., Watkins, J. T., Collins, J. F., Pilkonis, P. A., Beckham, E., Glass, D. R., Dolan, R. T., & Parloff, M. B. (1992). Course of depressive symptoms over follow-up: Findings from the National Institute of Mental Health Treatment of Depression Collaborative Research Program. *Archives of General Psychiatry, 49*, 782–787.

Simons, A. D., Garfield, S. L., & Murphy, G. E. (1984). The process of change in cognitive therapy and pharmacotherapy in depression: Changes in mood and cognition. *Archives of General Psychiatry, 41*, 45–51.

Simons, A. D., Murphy, G. E., Levine, J. L., & Wetzel, R. D. (1986). Cognitive therapy and pharmacotherapy for depression: Sustained improvement over one year. *Archives of General Psychiatry, 43*, 43–48.

Tang, T. Z., & DeRubeis, R. J. (1999). Sudden gains and critical sessions in cognitive-behavioral therapy for depression. *Journal of Consulting and Clinical Psychology, 67*, 894–904.

Teasdale, J. D., Scott, J., Moore, R. G., Hayhurst, H., Pope, M., & Paykel, E. S. (2001). How does cognitive therapy prevent relapse in residual depression: Evidence from a controlled trial. *Journal of Consulting and Clinical Psychology, 69,* 347–357.

Teasdale, J. D., Segal, Z. V., Williams, J. M. G., Ridgeway, V. A., Soulsby, J. M., & Lau, M. A. (2000). Prevention of relapse/recurrence in major depression by mindfulness-based cognitive therapy. *Journal of Consulting and Clinical Psychology, 68,* 615–623.

Vittengl, J. R., Clark, L. A., & Jarrett, R. B. (2005). Validity of sudden gains in acute phase treatment of depression. *Journal of Consulting and Clinical Psychology, 73,* 173–182.

Chapter 8

A Polarity-Specific Model
of Bipolar Disorder[1]

Sheri L. Johnson
University of Miami

Ray Winters
University of Miami

Björn Meyer
University of Roehampton

Despite strong genetic contributions to bipolar disorder (Vehmanen, Kaprio, & Loennquivst, 1995), several studies have shown that the social environment could be important to the course of the disorder. For example, longitudinal studies using interview-based measures of life events showed that people with bipolar disorder who experienced a negative life event had more than four times the risk of relapse compared to individuals without a life event (Ellicott, Hammen, Gitlin, Brown, & Jamison, 1990). Other research has demonstrated a strong role for family levels of expressed emotion in predicting bipolar relapse (Miklowitz, Goldstein, & Neuchterlein, 1987; Miklowitz, Simoneau, Sachs-Ericsson, Warner, & Sudath, 1996; Priebe, Wildgrube, & Muller-Oerlinghausen, 1989). In short, early studies suggested a potentially strong role for the social environment in this biologically based disorder, but many questions remained unanswered (Johnson & Roberts, 1995).

[1]The authors would like to thank Charles Carver, Steven K. Sutton, Ian Gotlib, and Paul Blaney for their helpful comments on this work. This research was supported by a grant from the National Alliance for Schizophrenia and Depression and by grant # 35590 from the National Institute of Mental Health.

The first author began by replicating and extending findings that the social environment did influence bipolar disorder. Over time, our team became more interested in the specific symptoms and processes that were most affected. Initial analyses suggested that many social environmental effects were relatively specific to bipolar depression and operated less robustly for mania. In this context, we began to ask which aspects of the social environment most affected mania. Current findings suggest that the social environment also has a powerful influence on manic symptoms, but that it is important to take into account the nature of the underlying biological diathesis. Specifically, environmental and psychological disruptions that influence behavioral activation predict increased mania. In contrast, behavioral activation variables are less robust predictors of bipolar depression. In consequence, a polarity-specific model of bipolar disorder has emerged.

In the next section, we review the design of our studies, then discuss our findings, with particular attention to predictors, which appear to be polarity specific. We present a model of how mania may be driven by elevations in the behavioral activation system (BAS), then discuss implications of the neurobiology of the BAS for understanding cognitive mechanisms involved in the genesis of manic episodes.

INITIAL RESEARCH

In 1991, the first author began to examine the role of the social environment in the course of bipolar disorder. In this first study, people were recruited during a hospitalization. Standardized symptom severity assessments (the Modified Hamilton Rating Scale for Depression and the Bech-Rafaelsen Mania Rating Scale) were conducted monthly for 1 year. The second study, funded by NIMH, investigated life events and social support using a similar design, but following individuals over a 2-year period. The second study included expanded assessment of potential mediators and moderators of life events, including the Rosenberg Self-Esteem Scale, the Interpersonal Support Evaluation List, the NEO-Five Factor Personality Inventory—Short Form, the Dysfunctional Attitudes Scale, the Behavioral Activation and Behavioral Inhibition Scales, and the Pittsburgh Sleep Quality Index.

Assessing Life Events

A relatively unique feature of these studies was the means of assessing life events. Life events were assessed every 6 months by an interviewer who was unaware of symptom status, using the Life Events and Difficulties Schedule (LEDS; Brown & Harris, 1978b). This interview-based measure was developed to address several of the theoretical and methodological issues involved in the study of life stressors and psychopathology.

First among these issues, many individuals with depression or psychiatric disorders are biased to perceive their stressors as overwhelming. One common solution to this problem has been to use objective ratings of the severity of stressors. For example, some objective rating systems assign standardized weights for each general class of event, such as pregnancy or crimes. Unfortunately, the events within any one class can vary substantially. Within the LEDS, the interviewer gathers contextual details, which are then used in rating the severity of each event. For example, an unwanted pregnancy for a 13-year-old girl is likely to be assigned much greater severity than would a long-awaited pregnancy of a woman with a well-established partnership and strong resources for parenting. Hence, an interviewer presents each event and its context to a team of raters. Raters then evaluate the severity of the event, anchoring their judgments using a dictionary that contains over 10,000 examples of life event ratings.

Second, the symptoms of psychiatric disorders themselves often create stressful circumstances. For example, oversleeping, a symptom of depression, can create occupational troubles, and irritability can create marital conflict. Consequently, elevated rates of life events could easily reflect disruptions caused by prodromal symptoms. To control for this, the interviewer gathers details on how each event unfolded and then raters consensually determine whether symptomatic behavior or judgment could have caused the event. Only events rated independent of symptoms are used in primary analyses.

A third problem relates to a person's ability to accurately date life events. There is empirical evidence that people are biased to shift the timing of events to account for the onset of psychiatric symptoms (Brown & Harris, 1978a). This "telescoping" phenomenon is combated in the LEDS through the use of calendars, anchors, and verification of dates against public or private records (Shum, 1998).

Although labor intensive, the LEDS achieves stronger reliability and validity than do self-report measures of life events (Gorman, 1993; McQuaid et al., 1992). In a series of cross-cultural, prospective studies, severe life events have been shown to predict depressive and other psychiatric episodes (Brown & Harris, 1989).

Pattern of Findings

Initial results, which examined effects without differentiating polarity of episode, demonstrated a strong impact of the social environment on the timing of recovery and relapse in bipolar disorder. Among individuals already experiencing an episode, independent, severe life events were associated with a threefold increase in the time to recovery; the median time to recovery among individuals with such a life event was more than 1 year (Johnson & Miller, 1997). Life events also operated as a trigger for relapse

(Johnson et al., 1997). Effects of life events were not explained by noncompliance in the face of major stressors (Johnson, Winett, & Mellman, 1998). Somewhat surprisingly, medication did not buffer the effects of life events. For individuals who were not taking adequate medications, the median time to relapse after a severe, independent life event was 12 days (Johnson & Miller, 1996), yet strong life events effects were apparent even with adequate medication.

We also examined social support using the Interpersonal Support Evaluation List. Social support provided some protection from the effects of life events. Among individuals with daily family contact, social support was a robust buffer of the impact of life events (Winett, Johnson, & Miller, 1996). In sum, the conclusion from our own and other findings on bipolar disorder is that the environment appears to have a powerful influence on the course of this serious disorder.

Our next step was to examine how the environment affected more specific outcomes and symptom patterns. In particular, a major question has been whether the predictors of bipolar depression and mania differ. Evidence from biological studies suggested important differences in bipolar depression and mania. For example, three studies, using varied methodology, indicated that genetic concordance is higher for mania than for depression (Simpson & DePaulo, 1998). Additionally, lithium and other mood stabilizers have greater efficacy for mania than for depression (Hlasta et al., 1997).

In attempting to assess mania and depression separately, we quickly stumbled on a methodological issue. In our early work, we had focused almost exclusively on episodes, using survival analyses to assess which individuals were more likely to experience episodes, and how quickly episodes started and ended. Our emphasis on episodes was congruent with most of the psychosocial research in this field. However, when we began to contemplate polarity-specific patterns, preliminary analyses suggested that many episodes that began with mania shifted into depression, and that the total duration of these "manic" episodes then reflected largely depressive periods. Similarly, many people experienced at least some mix of symptoms of depression and mania, and the nature of the mix seemed to have particular repercussions for how seriously the episode influenced functioning. Given this, we shifted the nature of our analyses, from examining episodes to a new approach of examining depressive and manic symptom severity separately and as continua. One advantage in this shift from a dichotomy to a continuum was an increase in statistical power (Cohen, 1983).

Distinguishing Depression from Mania

Our analyses suggested that a range of psychosocial variables predicted changes in bipolar depression over a 4- to 6-month period, including negative life events, social support (Johnson, Winett, Meyer, Greenhouse, & Miller, 1999), neuroticism (Lozano & Johnson, 2001), self-esteem (Meyer, Johnson, & Winters, 2001), negative cognitive styles (Johnson & Fingerhut, 2004), and interactions of marital status and gender (Looby & Johnson, in preparation). Each of these domains appeared to have a robust impact—for example, accounting for 25% of the variance in depression changes after accounting for initial depression levels. In short, the psychosocial variables that predicted bipolar depression appear remarkably similar to those that predict unipolar depression.

In contrast, none of these variables predicted changes in mania within our datasets. Indeed, each of these variables correlated at a magnitude of less than .20 with follow-up mania scores. The inability of these variables to predict mania was surprising, given the robust impact of stress and social support on a broad range of psychiatric and biological processes. We should note that others have found that negative events and cognition did predict increases in hypomanic symptoms among undergraduates (Reilly-Harrington, Alloy, Fresco, & Whitehouse, 1999). However, our findings were congruent with other psychosocial findings that began to emerge at approximately the same time. For example, the two most carefully researched psychotherapies for bipolar disorder—family therapy and interpersonal psychotherapy—appear to be more powerful in reducing depressive symptoms than manic symptoms (Frank, 1999; Miklowitz, Simoneau, & Richards, 1997).

Mania appears to be one of the few psychiatric disorders in which life events and lack of social support do not trigger symptoms. One puzzle, then, was whether psychosocial variables could help explain the genesis of manic episodes. In thinking about this question, we returned to an earlier review paper (Johnson & Roberts, 1995), in which we had argued that mania, as a more biologically driven phenomenon, would be predicted by psychosocial variables that could be tied to the underlying diathesis.

Support for this premise was provided by findings that life events that disrupted sleep were more frequent in the 6 weeks before episodes of mania than in the period preceding depression (Malkoff-Schwartz et al., 1998). Sleep disruption, then, appears to be a more powerful trigger for manic than depressive onset, and psychosocial features that were coupled with the biological vulnerability of sleep disruption seemed to be more powerful for predicting mania. In short, several strands of research suggest that bipolar depression and mania are predicted by differing vulnerability factors and triggers.

A previous review (Johnson & Roberts, 1995) had highlighted a model involving the behavioral activation system for its unique ability to integrate biological and social aspects of vulnerability within bipolar disorder. We now turn to that model and our research bearing on it.

BAS AND MANIA

Several investigators have proposed that bipolar symptoms are tied to the functioning of the behavioral facilitation system/behavioral activation system (BAS; Depue, Collins, & Luciana, 1996; Depue & Iacono, 1989; Gray, 1994).[2] This system regulates appetitive motivation and promotes goal-directed behavior. To facilitate goal-directed behavior, it regulates narrower systems such as positive affect (Watson & Tellegen, 1985), incentive–reward motivation, sociability/social potency, desire for excitement, and motor activity/arousal (Depue, Krauss, & Spoont, 1987).

The behaviors regulated by the BAS, described earlier, correspond closely to the manic symptoms of mood change, inflated self-esteem, decreased need for sleep, increased talkativeness, flight of ideas, increased goal-directed activity, and excessive involvement in pleasurable activities. Based on this overlap, Depue hypothesized that mania may be the outcome of excessively high BAS activity (Depue & Iacono, 1989; Depue & Zald, 1993).

Several variables influence BAS activity. BAS activity level is affected by the presence of incentive stimuli—that is, environmental stimuli that typically serve as cues for goal-directed behavior. Also, Depue and others have suggested that there are individual differences in both mean (trait) BAS activity and variability around the mean level. Bipolar individuals, as a group, are hypothesized to experience high variability in BAS activity levels (Depue & Zald, 1993; Spoont, 1992; Winters, Scott, & Beevers, 2000). The extent of variability in BAS activity is thought to predict course of bipolar disorder (Depue & Zald, 1993). Individuals with high BAS variability are expected to be more vulnerable to mood symptoms after life events (Depue et al., 1987; Depue & Iacono, 1989).

Before our research, studies of bipolar disorder bearing on this hypothesis focused only on the regulatory implications of the model. In one study, cyclothymic participants, relative to control participants, were found to take significantly longer to return to baseline cortisol levels following a laboratory math-challenge stressor (Depue, Kleinman, Davis, Hutchinson, & Krauss, 1985). In another study, cyclothymic participants took three times longer than did control participants to return to pre-event mood and behavioral levels following a daily stressor (Goplerud & Depue, 1985). Other studies have documented the importance of lower-level mood variability as a predictor of outcome within bipolar disorder. For example, people who exhibit the greatest baseline variability in mood appear to be most vulnerable to life events: among people with bipolar disorder, less stable symp-

---

[2]This system has been referred to as the behavioral approach system, or simply BAS (Gray, 1979); the behavioral activation system, also referred to as BAS (Fowles, 1980); and the behavioral facilitation system, or BFS (Depue & Zald, 1993). We have chosen to use the phrase *behavioral activation system*.

toms predicted relapse after an earthquake (Aronson & Shukla, 1987). In short, intriguing evidence had begun to emerge for the importance of mood dysregulation as a predictor of vulnerability to mania.

In contrast to this, broader aspects of the model had received very limited empirical attention. Relatively little research had been conducted addressing some fairly simple and direct questions about this model, such as: Do individuals with higher BAS levels have increased vulnerability to mania? Do BAS levels fluctuate along with manic symptoms? Do goal-relevant life events predict mania? These questions have been a focus of our work. They are addressed in the following section.

Our Research on BAS and Mania

Much of our research on BAS functioning and bipolar disorder has used the BIS/BAS scales, a 24-item self-report measure (Carver & White, 1994). BAS scales assess the tendency to experience strong positive affect or behavioral approach when cues of incentive or goal-oriented situations are present. Three subscales capture aspects of presumed BAS functioning: Fun-seeking (e.g., "I will often do things for no other reason than that they might be fun"), Drive (e.g., "If I see a chance to get something I want, I move on it right away"), and Reward Responsiveness (e.g., "When good things happen to me, it affects me strongly"). The BIS scale assesses the tendency to experience negative affect or behavioral inhibition when cues of threat are present.

The BIS/BAS scales have good internal consistency and factor analytic support. Although these scales demonstrate expected relations to related scales (extraversion, trait anxiety, etc.), they are more predictive of affective responses to incentives and threat than are related personality scales (Carver & White, 1994). A major community study provides normative data (Jorm et al., 1999), and the BAS scales have been shown to predict left anterior brain activity (Sutton & Davidson, 1997). Self-reported BAS levels are correlated with sensitivity to cues of reward in a conditioning task, but not to cues of punishment (Zinbarg & Mohlman, 1998).

We have examined the relations between BIS/BAS scales and symptom patterns. The first of these studies examined 63 undergraduates at risk for hypomania as measured by the General Behavior Inventory. Robust correlations were obtained between the BAS scale and the self-report Internal State Survey (ISS) mania scale (Meyer, Johnson & Carver, 1999). Specifically, among at-risk students, BAS correlated .48 with mania. In contrast, among students not at risk, the correlation between BAS and mania was only .20.

We then conducted a longitudinal study to assess whether BAS levels would predict the onset of manic episodes among people with Bipolar I disorder. We found that higher BAS Reward Responsiveness, measured during a period of recovery, predicted increases in manic symptoms over the next 6 months. Although BAS Fun-seeking seemed to fluctuate with symptoms, reward responsiveness was a stable, traitlike characteristic that appeared to operate as a vulnerability characteristic. Reward responsiveness appears to be the subscale that is most congruent with conceptualizations of the BAS system within bipolar disorder.

These findings utilized Carver and White's (1994) Behavioral Activation scale. The first author and colleagues also found convergent evidence with items from the achievement-striving facet of the NEO Five Factor Personality Inventory. These items, measured at a 6-month follow-up, accounted for a significant proportion of the variance in manic symptoms over the next 4 months, after controlling for baseline mania: Among bipolar individuals, high goal investment and newly established goals were predictive of increases in mania (Lozano & Johnson, 2001). Additionally, among a sample of 464 college students, hypomania was associated with positive expectancies about attaining upcoming goals (Meyer, Beevers, & Johnson, 2004). Related research has been conducted by Coryell and his colleagues (1989), drawing on the reports of high socioeconomic status among individuals with bipolar disorder. They investigated achievement among family members of individuals with bipolar disorder. Family members of bipolar probands did demonstrate higher levels of achievement than did family members of nonbipolar probands. These findings indicate that dysregulation in the setting and pursuit of goals in bipolar individuals may trigger manic episodes (see Johnson, 2005, for a review).

In sum, self-reported BAS is associated with manic symptoms in both undergraduate and clinical populations; variability in self-reported BAS is associated with manic shifts, and higher goal investment and achievement striving are indicators of impending manic symptoms. None of these BAS-relevant variables predicted bipolar depression. The links between these variables and mania, however, strengthened our belief that the BAS model might inform as to which aspects of the environment would be likely to trigger manic symptoms.

To examine the implications of the BAS model for environmental triggers of mania, we also investigated life events that have relevance for behavioral activation. In a separate sample of 41 people, we selected the life event with the highest degree of goal attainment (as measured using the Brown and Harris Goal Attainment scale) and examined whether these events were followed by increases in manic symptoms. Controlling for manic symptoms in the month before an event occurred, the partial correlation between the intensity of the goal attainment event and increase in manic symptoms over the next 2 months was significant (partial $r = -.37$, one-tailed $p = .01$). More general positive events did not predict mania, as had been found in previous research on positive life events (Reilly-Harrington et al., 1999). Individuals who experienced goal-relevant life events were at increased risk for mania. This suggests that environmental features tied to behavioral activation are important triggers for mania (Johnson, Sandrow, et al., 2000).

Further Mechanisms

Is higher self-reported BAS just a symptom of mania? No. Each of the findings described previously holds even after controlling for baseline symptom levels.

Is BAS activity merely a correlate of some more fundamental aspect of vulnerability to bipolar disorder? In this regard, we have begun to examine how BAS is related to other risk factors for bipolar disorder. One of the most consistently documented risk factors for mania has been sleep deprivation. It is well established that sleep deprivation temporarily relieves depression (see Wu & Bunney, 1990, for a review). It is also acknowledged that monitoring social rhythms, including keeping a normal sleep cycle, is an important part of psychotherapy for bipolar disorder (Jones, Sellwood, & McGovern, 2005). Sleep deprivation also precedes increases in manic symptoms (Wehr, 1991). Following sleep deprivation, approximately 10% of bipolar individuals with depression switch into hypomanic or manic episodes (Colombo, Benedetti, Barbini, Campori, & Smeraldi, 1999). Two case reports demonstrated that prolonging sleep decreases bipolar symptoms (Wehr et al., 1998; Wirz-Justice, Quinto, Cajochen, Werth, & Hock, 1999). Recent preliminary findings show that forced 14-hour periods of darkness daily can drastically reduce symptoms of mania (Barbini et al., 2005). Thus, sleep deprivation appears to be one of the ways in which events in the person's environment could trigger manic symptoms (Ehlers, Frank, & Kupfer, 1988; Wehr, Sack, & Rosenthal, 1987).

Given this, we were interested in models of how sleep deprivation could influence BAS levels. Animal research had suggested that sleep deprivation might increase activation (Everson, Bergmann, & Rechtschaffen, 1989; Rechtschaffen, Bergmann, Everson, Kushida, & Gilliland, 1989). In our bipolar sample, we found that self-reported sleep loss and BAS levels appear to be separate pathways to manic symptoms; sleep deprivation is only modestly correlated with BAS self-report scores, and both variables independently predicted onset of increased manic symptoms (Johnson, Meyer, & Winett, 1999). Nonetheless, given strong links between sleep and behavioral activation in animal studies, we aver that further research is necessary to test this aspect of the model.

Summary of BAS and Mania Findings

We believe that knowledge about the BAS system contributes substantially to our understanding how individuals with bipolar disorder become manic. The system has implications for understanding the environmental triggers and the process of how mania unfolds, providing important windows for intervention. Our current model for understanding triggers of bipolar episodes is displayed in Fig. 8.1.

In view of the evidence that BAS engagement is a direct and important trigger of manic symptoms, we have begun to examine other implications of this model. One aspect that has been particularly intriguing for us concerns the implications of the neurobiological research on BAS. Most of this research has been conducted outside of the domain of bipolar disorder. We discuss this research briefly, as a means of pointing toward new directions. Understanding these neurobiological components of BAS suggests cognitive mechanisms that may fuel the onset of hypomania.

NEUROBIOLOGICAL SUBSTRATES OF BAS AND MANIA

The neurobiological substrates of the BAS have been well studied (see Winters et al., 2000, for a review). There is substantial evidence that the neurobiological structure of BAS is dopamine (DA)-secreting neurons of the ventral tegmental area (VTA). VTA DA neurons enhance appetitive motivational strength by increasing the effective incentive value assigned to environmental stimuli that serve as cues for goal-directed activity.

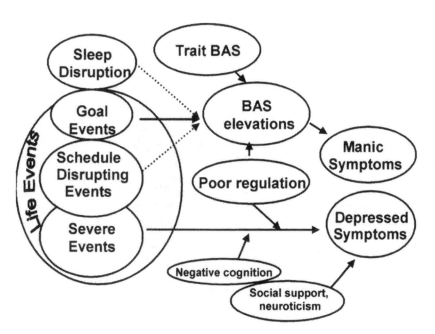

FIG. 8.1.   A polarity-specific model of bipolar disorder.

Several types of research have provided support for this theory. In single-cell recording studies, ventral tegmental dopamine (VTA DA) neurons respond to incentive stimuli, but rarely to stimuli that signal punishment (Mirenowicz & Schultz, 1996). The extremely motivating paradigm of intracranial self-stimulation of the medial forebrain bundle results in an increase in DA secretion and signal flow in the nucleus accumbens (e.g., Nakahara, Ozaki, Miura, Miura, & Nagatsu, 1989). Further, D_1 and D_2 agonists enhance a range of goal-directed behaviors, including affective aggression, social behaviors, sexual activity, and goal-directed behaviors involving learning. Conversely, DA antagonists (which reduce the activity of VTA DA neurons) impair the same behaviors (see reviews by Depue & Collins, 1999; Le Moal & Simon, 1991).

Findings from several types of research on bipolar disorder provide support for the importance of the same dopaminergic neural pathways and mechanisms in the genesis of manic symptoms. For example, in one study, administration of the dopamine precursor, L-DOPA, evoked manic episodes in 11 of 12 bipolar patients (Buki & Goodnick, 1998). Amphetamine and cocaine use increase dopamine levels and precipitate manic episodes among bipolar individuals (Antelman et al., 1998; Gatley et al., 1999). Conversely, dopamine antagonists reverse natural and drug-induced manic states (Swerdlow & Koob, 1987). Most major biological treatments for bipolar disorder—including lithium, carbamezapine, tricyclic antidepressants, and monoamine oxidase inhibitors—influence dopaminergic systems (Goodwin & Jamison, 1990). Other major pharmacotherapies influence serotonin, which would then regulate dopamine through negative feedback (Depue & Zald, 1993). Suhara et al. (1992) found that bipolar individuals demonstrate decreased dopamine binding within the prefrontal cortex compared to healthy controls. At a subsyndromal level, central dopamine agonist-induced reactivity, specifically D_2 reactivity, correlates highly with trait positive affect and achievement orientation, but not with other personality dimensions (Depue & Collins, 1999; Depue, Luciana, Arbisi, Collins, & Leon, 1994).

Alternative neurotransmitter models of mania have also been proposed. Early studies described noradrenergic activation as relevant to mania, but most of these studies failed to control for concomitant functional increases in dopamine (Swerdlow & Koob, 1987). Other neurotransmitters and cellular mechanisms are likely to be important; for example, Protein Kinase C and GABA (Petty, Kramer, & Davis, 1998; Soares & Mallinger, 1997; Wang, Markowitz, Levinson, Undie, & Friedman, 1999). Nonetheless, a role for dopamine in the genesis of mania receives empirical support. Beyond more general theories of neurotransmitter activity, several models of the specific neuronal pathways involved in manic symptoms emphasized the importance of VTA DA neurons (Depue & Zald, 1993; Hestenes, 1992; Swerdlow & Koob, 1987). In sum, many of the current neurobiological models of BAS and of bipolar disorder emphasize the involvement of the same brain structures.

These models provide ideas about the mechanisms underlying the dysregulation of mood and behavioral engagement observed among bipolar individuals. One view with substantial empirical support is that deficits in serotonin functioning contribute to dysregulation in bipolar individuals (Depue & Zald, 1993; Spoont, 1992). Serotonin neurons decrease dopamine secretion by exerting presynaptic inhibition on VTA DA neurons that synapse at the nucleus accumbens (Hetey, Kudrin, Shemanow, Reyevsky, & Oelssner, 1985). The nucleus accumbens interfaces between the limbic system, which processes affective information, and the basal ganglia, which are involved in the generation of motor activity (e.g., Robbins & Everitt, 1992; Swerdlow & Koob, 1987). As such, the nucleus accumbens is a particularly important modulator of emotional behavior.

The interaction between DA-secreting and serotonin-secreting neurons at the nucleus accumbens is extremely important to the regulation of motivated behavior, because it allows the brain to adjust motivational intensity as environmental circumstances warrant. There are situations in which it is adaptive to keep constant the effective incentive value of a stimulus (and thereby have a constant incentive motivational state), such as those that require a steady level of motivation in pursuit of a goal. In contrast, other situations require that the incentive value be adjusted upward or downward, for example, increasing incentive value when a deadline approaches and decreasing it after reaching a goal. These adjustments in incentive value and appetitive motivational strength require that BAS be able to amplify the incentive value of stimuli and that the serotonin system be able to antagonize this activity so as to decrease the magnitude of amplification when appropriate. Deficits in the regulation of BAS through the serotonin mechanism at the nucleus accumbens would lead to motivational and mood states that would be maladaptive in situations involving goal-directed behaviors. For example, affective and behavioral responses to incentive stimuli or to being thwarted in pursuit of a goal (i.e., frustration) may be inappropriately strong.

COGNITIVE IMPLICATIONS OF BAS FUNCTIONING

One of the intriguing aspects of the brain regions theorized to be involved in bipolar disorder is that they suggest windows into understanding the cognitive changes associated with mania. That is, these brain structures affect cognition; understanding their role gives us clues into how cognition may shift during the early phases of mania.

More specifically, in bipolar individuals, the delay in signals to the nucleus accumbens from serotonin neurons would allow BAS-mediated increases in stimulus incentive value and appetitive motivation to go unchecked for extended periods of time. The deficit in this regulatory mechanism would allow for more intense and sustained reactivity to cues of reward among bipolar individuals compared to others. Accordingly, hypomanic individuals are expected to demonstrate longer and more intense attention to incentive stimuli. This hypothesis fits with the cognitive-behavioral "portfolio theory," which draws on the clinical phenomenology of bipolar disorder. Portfolio theory hypothesizes that a positive shift in the perceived ability to achieve reinforcement will correlate with manic symptoms, and that this facet of cognition will predict course (Leahy, 1999).

With this idea in mind, studies have tested whether people with bipolar disorder show an attentional bias for positive stimuli (cf. Lyon, Startup, & Bentall, 1999). However, studies to date have an important drawback. Specifically, the positive word sets used (e.g., *calm, sunshine*) do not provide clear cues of incentive (e.g., *win, money, love*). We have recently begun a pilot study of attentional bias for incentive stimuli among individuals with bipolar disorder compared to normal controls.

Beyond increased attention to incentive stimuli, the high DA activity in regions of the nucleus accumbens during hypomania would be expected to influence selective attention (Weiner, 1990; Weiner & Feldon, 1997), such that attention would shift among stimuli more rapidly. These neurobiologically driven shifts in cognition may help explain the hypomanic experience of flight of ideas and distractibility.

Another aspect of cognition, memory recall, may also be altered by the positive mood state associated with hypomania. Previous research has shown that mood-congruent recall is more robust for positive affect than for negative affect (Blaney, 1986; Eich, Macauley, & Lam, 1997; Weingartner, Miller, & Murphy, 1977). Positive moods may enhance recall of positive memories. Increased accessibility of positive memories, particularly those involving previous successes, could elevate self-esteem and confidence. Behaviorally, these cognitive shifts may increase the likelihood that the bipolar individual will engage in new goals, thereby enhancing positive affect even further. In short, at a cognitive, motivational, and behavioral level, recursive loops may maximize the goal-setting behavior and positive affect that spiral into mania.

In sum, the brain regions involved in hypomania are likely to manifest in cognitive shifts. These cognitive shifts may influence behavioral choices such that bipolar individuals create an increasingly overstimulating environment for themselves as hypomania unfolds. In this manner, biology, cognition, and behavior are likely to interact in a highly reciprocal manner.

CONCLUSION

Overall, our findings to date suggest two general conclusions and themes for future research. First, psychosocial models drawn from unipolar research appear readily applicable to understanding the course of bipolar depression. Negative life events, neuroticism, maladaptive cognitions, and poor social support all contribute to the prediction of the course of bipolar depression. They are not as relevant for the course of mania. Second, the BAS model for understanding mania has thus far received support. Self-reported BAS, goal-attainment life events, achievement striving, and goal-relevant cognition predict the course of mania. We are just beginning to examine the implications of this model for understanding information processing, and we believe that the neurobiology of the BAS may help provide a model for how cognition contributes to the spiral into manic symptoms.

The distinct quality of triggers for manic and depressive symptoms has led us to develop what we call a "polarity-specific model of bipolar disorder." We believe that the environment is an important consideration in understanding how both depressive and manic episodes begin. We add the caveat, however, that quite distinct aspects of the environment appear involved in depression versus mania. Understanding the nature of these environmental dimensions provides a window for integrating the psychological, cognitive, and biological processes involved in the genesis of episodes.

REFERENCES

Antelman, S. M., Caggiula, A. R., Kucinski, B. J., Fowler, H., Gershon, S., Edwards, D. J., Austin, M. C., Stiller, R., Kiss, S., & Kocan, D. (1998). The effects of lithium on a potential cycling model of bipolar disorder. *Progress in Neuro-Psychopharmacology and Biological Psychiatry, 22*, 495–510.

Aronson, T. A., & Shukla, S. (1987). Life events and relapse in bipolar disorder: The impact of a catastrophic event. *Acta Psychiatrica Scandinavica, 75*, 571–576.

Barbini, B., Bendetti, F., Colombo, C., Dotoli, D., Bernasconi, A., Cigala-Fulgosi, M., Florita, M., & Smeraldi, E. (2005). Dark therapy for mania: A pilot study. *Bipolar Disorders, 7*, 98–101.

Blaney, P. (1986). Affect and memory: A review. *Psychological Bulletin, 99*, 229–246.

Brown, G. W., & Harris, T. O. (1978a). *Social origins of depression: A study of psychiatric disorder in women.* New York: Free Press.

Brown, G. W., & Harris, T. O. (1978b). *The Bedford College life events and difficulty schedule: Directory of contextual threat of events.* London: Bedford College, University of London.

Brown, G. W., & Harris, T. O. (1989). *Life events and illness.* New York: Guilford.

Buki, V. M. V., & Goodnick, P. (1998). Catecholamines. In P. J. Goodnick (Ed.), *Mania: Clinical and research perspectives* (pp. 119–134). Washington, DC: American Psychiatric Press.

Carver, C. S., & White, T. (1994). Behavioral inhibition, behavioral activation, and affective responses to impending reward and punishment: The BIS/BAS Scales. *Journal of Personality and Social Psychology, 67*, 319–333.

Cohen, J. (1983). The cost of dichotomization. *Applied Psychological Measurement, 7*, 249–253.

Colombo, C., Benedetti, F., Barbini, B., Campori, E., & Smeralid, E. (1999). Rate of switch from depression into mania after therapeutic sleep deprivation in bipolar depression. *Psychiatry Research, 86*, 267–270.

Coryell, W., Endicott, J., Keller, M., Andreasen, N., Grove, W., Hirschfeld, R. M. A., & Scheftner, W. (1989). Bipolar affective disorder and high achievement: A familial association. *American Journal of Psychiatry, 146*, 983–988.

Depue, R. A., & Collins, P. F. (1999). Neurobiology of the structure of personality: Dopamine, facilitation of incentive motivation, and extraversion. *Behavioral and Brain Sciences, 22*, 491–569.

Depue, R. A., Collins, P. F., & Luciana, M. (1996). A model of neurobiology—environment interaction in developmental psychopathology. In M. F. Lenzenweger & J. J. Haugaard (Eds.), *Frontiers of developmental psychopathology* (pp. 44–76). New York: Oxford University Press.

Depue, R. A., & Iacono, W. G. (1989). Neurobehavioral aspects of affective disorders. *Annual Review of Psychology, 40*, 457–492.

Depue, R. A., Kleinman, R. M., Davis, P., Hutchinson, M., & Krauss, S. (1985). The behavioral high-risk paradigm and bipolar affective disorder: VIII. Serum free cortisol in nonpatient cyclothymic subjects selected by the General Behavior Inventory. *American Journal of Psychiatry, 142*, 175–181.

Depue, R. A., Krauss, S. P., & Spoont, M. R. (1987). A two-dimensional threshold model of seasonal bipolar affective disorder. In D. Magnuson & A. Ohman (Eds.), *Psychopathology: An interactional perspective* (pp. 95–123). San Diego: Academic Press.

Depue, R. A., Luciana, M., Arbisi, P., Collins, P., & Leon, A. (1994). Dopamine and the structure of personality: Relation of agonist-induced dopamine activity to positive emotionality. *Journal of Personality and Social Psychology, 67*, 485–498.

Depue, R. A., & Zald, D. H. (1993). Biological and environmental processes in nonpsychotic psychopathology: A neurobiological perspective. In C. G. Costello (Ed.), *Basic issues in psychopathology* (pp. 127–237). New York: Guilford.

Ehlers, C. L., Frank, E., & Kupfer, D. J. (1988). Social zeitgebers and biological rhythms. *Archives of General Psychiatry, 45*, 948–952.

Eich, E., Macauley, D., & Lam, R. W. (1997). Mania, depression, and mood-dependent memory. *Cognition and Emotion, 11*, 607–618.

Ellicott, A., Hammen, C., Gitlin, M., Brown, G., & Jamison, K. (1990). Life events and the course of bipolar disorder. *American Journal of Psychiatry, 147*, 1194–1198.

Everson, C. A., Bergmann, B. M., & Rechtschaffen, A. (1989). Sleep deprivation in the rat: III. Total sleep deprivation. *Sleep, 12*, 13–21.

Fowles, D. C. (1980). The three arousal model: Implications of Gray's two-factor learning theory for heart rate, electrodermal activity, and psychopathology. *Psychophysiology, 17*, 87–104.

Frank, E. (1999, July). *Interpersonal psychotherapy.* Presentation at the Third Annual International Conference on Bipolar Disorder, Pittsburgh.

Gatley, S. J., Volkow, N. D., Gifford, A. N., Fowler, J. S., Dewey, S. L., Ding, Y. S., & Logan, J. (1999). Dopamine-transporter occupancy after intravenous doses of cocaine and methylphenidate in mice and humans. *Psychopharmacology, 146*, 93–100.

Goodwin, F. K., & Jamison, K. R. (1990). *Manic depressive illness.* New York: Oxford University Press.

Goplerud, E., & Depue, R. A. (1985). Behavioral response to naturally occurring stress in cyclothymia and dysthymia. *Journal of Abnormal Psychology, 94*, 128–139.

Gorman, D. M. (1993). A review of studies comparing checklist and interview methods of data collection in life event research. *Behavioral Medicine, 19*, 66–73.

Gray, J. A. (1979). Anxiety and the brain: Not by neurochemistry alone. *Psychological Medicine, 9*, 605–609.

Gray, J. A. (1994). Framework for a taxonomy of psychiatric disorder. In H. M. Van Goozen, N. E. Van De Poll, & J. A. Sergeant (Eds.), *Emotions: Essays on emotion theory* (pp. 29–59). Hillsdale, NJ: Lawrence Erlbaum Associates.

Hestenes, D. (1992). A neural network theory of manic-depressive illness. In D. S. Levine & S. J. Leven (Eds.), *Motivation, emotion, and goal direction in neural networks* (pp. 209–257). Hillsdale, NJ: Lawrence Erlbaum Associates.

Hetey, L., Kudrin, F. S., Shemanow, A. Y., Reyevsky, K. S., & Oelssner, W. (1985) Presynaptic dopamine and serotonin receptors modulating tyrosine hydroxylase activity in synaptosomes of the nucleus accumbens of rats. *European Journal of Pharmacology, 113*, 1–10.

Hlastala, S. A., Frank, E., Mallinger, A., Thase, M. E., Ritenour, A., & Kupfer, D. J. (1997). Bipolar depression: An underestimated treatment challenge. *Depression and Anxiety, 5*, 73–83.

Johnson, S. L. (2005). Mania and dysregulation in goal pursuit: A review. *Clinical Psychology Review, 25*, 241–262.

Johnson, S. L., & Fingerhut, R. (2004). Negative cognitive styles predict the course of bipolar depression, not mania. *Journal of Cognitive Psychotherapy, 18*, 149–162.

Johnson, S. L., Fingerhut, R., Miller III, I., Keitner, G., Ryan, C., & Solomon, D. (1997, October). *Do minor life events impact the course of bipolar disorder?* Poster presentation at the 12 annual meeting of the Society for Research on Psychopathology, Palm Springs, CA.

Johnson, S. L., Meyer, B., & Winett, C. (1999). A polarity-specific model of psychosocial factors and the course of bipolar disorder. In *Bipolar disorders, volume 1, supplement 1, abstract book for the Third International Conference on Bipolar Disorder* (p. 37). Pittsburgh: Stanley Center.

Johnson, S. L., & Miller, I. (1996, September). *Life events, medication compliance and relapse in bipolar disorder.* Poster presentation at the 11th annual meeting of the Society for Research on Psychopathology, Atlanta.

Johnson, S. L., & Miller, I. (1997). Negative life events and recovery from episodes of bipolar disorder. *Journal of Abnormal Psychology, 106*, 449–457.

Johnson, S. L., & Roberts, J. R. (1995). Life events and bipolar disorder: Implications from biological theories. *Psychological Bulletin, 117*, 434–449.

Johnson, S. L., Sandrow, D., Meyer, B., Winters, R., Miller, I., Solomon, D., & Keitner, G. (2000). Increases in manic symptoms after life events involving goal-attainment. *Journal of Abnormal Psychology, 109*, 721–727.

Johnson, S. L., Winett, C. A., & Mellman, T. (1998, November). *The relation between life events, sleep, and symptom severity in bipolar disorder.* Poster presentation at the 13th annual meeting of the Society for Research in Psychopathology, Cambridge, MA.

Johnson, S. L., Winett, C., Meyer, B., Greenhouse, W., & Miller, I. (1999). Social support and the course of bipolar disorder. *Journal of Abnormal Psychology, 108*, 558–566.

Jones, S. H., Sellwood, W., & McGovern, J. (2005). Psychological therapies for bipolar disorder: The role of model-driven approaches to therapy integration. *Bipolar Disorders, 7*, 22–32.

Jorm, A. F., Christensen, H., Henderson, A. S., Jacomb, P. A., Korten, A. E., & Rodgers, B. (1999). Using the BIS/BAS scales to measure behavioural inhibition and behavioural activation: Factor structure, validity and norms in a large community sample. *Personality and Individual Differences, 26*, 49–58.

Leahy, R. L. (1999). Decision-making and mania. *Journal of Cognitive Psychotherapy, 13*, 83–105.

Le Moal, M., & Simon, H. (1991). Mesocorticolimbic dopaminergic network: Functional and regulatory roles. *Physiological Reviews, 71*, 155–234.

Looby, S., & Johnson, S. (in preparation). Marital status and the gender difference in bipolar depression.

Lozano, B., & Johnson, S. (2001). Can personality traits predict increases in manic and depressive symptoms? *Journal of Affective Disorders, 63*, 103–111.

Lyon, H. M., Startup, M., & Bentall, R. P. (1999). Social cognition and the manic defense: Attributions, selective attention, and self-schema in bipolar affective disorder. *Journal of Abnormal Psychology, 108*, 273–282.

Malkoff-Schwartz, S., Frank, E., Anderson, B., Sherrill, J. T., Siegel, L., Patterson, D., & Kupfer, D. J. (1998). Stressful life events and social rhythm disruption in the onset of manic and depressive bipolar episodes. *Archives of General Psychiatry, 55*, 702–707.

McQuaid, J. R., Monroe, S. M., Roberts, J. R., Johnson, S. L., Garamoni, G., Kupfer, D. J., & Frank, E. (1992). Toward the standardization of life stress assessments: Definitional discrepancies and inconsistencies in methods. *Stress Medicine, 8*, 47–56.

Meyer, B., Beevers, C. G., & Johnson, S. L. (2004). Goal appraisals and vulnerability to bipolar disorder: A personal projects analysis. *Cognitive Therapy and Research, 28*, 173–182.

Meyer, B., Johnson, S., & Carver, C. (1999). Exploring behavioral activation and inhibition sensitivities among college students at-risk for mood disorders. *Journal of Psychopathology and Behavioral Assessment, 21*, 275–292.

Meyer, B., Johnson, S. L., & Winters, R. (2001). Responsiveness to threat and incentive in bipolar disorder: Relations of the BIS/BAS scales with symptoms. *Journal of Psychopathology and Behavioral Assessment, 23*, 133–143.

Miklowitz, D. J., Goldstein, M. J., & Neuchterlein, K. H. (1987). The family and the course of recent onset mania. In K. Hahlweg & M. J. Goldstein (Eds.), *Understanding of major mental disorder: The contribution of family interaction research* (pp. 195–211). New York: Family Process Press.

Miklowitz, D. J., Simoneau, T. L., & Richards, J. A. (1997). *Family-focused psychoeducation in the outpatient treatment of bipolar disorder.* Paper presented at the 31st annual meeting of the Association for the Advancement of Behavior Therapy, Miami.

Miklowitz, D. J., Simoneau, T. L., Sachs-Ericsson, N., Warner, R., & Suddath, R. (1996). Family risk indicators in the course of bipolar affective disorder. In C. Mundt, M. J. Goldstein, K. Hahlweg, & P. Fiedler (Eds.), *Interpersonal factors in the origin and course of affective disorder* (pp. 204–217). London: Gaskell.

Mirenowicz, J., & Schultz, W. (1996). Preferential activation of midbrain dopamine neurons by appetitive rather than aversive stimuli. *Nature, 379*, 449–451.

Nakahara, D., Ozaki, N., Miura, Y., Miura, H., & Nagatsu, T. (1989). Increased dopamine and serotonin metabolism in rat nucleus accumbens produced by intracranial self-stimulation of medial forebrain bundle as measured by in vivo microdialysis. *Brain Research, 495*, 178–181.

Petty, F., Kramer, G. L., & Davis, L. L. (1998). Gamma-aminobutyric acid. In P. J. Goodnick (Ed.), *Mania: Clinical and research perspectives* (pp. 157–169). Washington, DC: American Psychiatric Press.

Priebe, S., Wildgrube, C., & Muller-Oerlinghausen, B. (1989). Lithium prophylaxis and expressed emotion. *British Journal of Psychiatry, 154*, 396–399.

Rechtschaffen, A., Bergmann, B. M., Everson, C. A., Kushida, C. A., & Gilliland, M. A. (1989). Sleep deprivation in the rat: X. Interaction and discussion of findings. *Sleep, 12*, 68–87.

Reilly-Harrington, N., Alloy, L. B., Fresco, D. M., & Whitehouse, W. G. (1999). Cognitive styles and life events interact to predict of bipolar and unipolar symptomatology. *Journal of Abnormal Psychology, 108*, 567–578.

Robbins, T., & Everitt, B. (1992) Functions of dopamine in the dorsal and ventral striatum. *Seminars in Neuroscience, 4*, 119–143.

Shum, M. S. (1998). The role of temporal landmarks in autobiographical memory processes. *Psychological Bulletin, 124*, 423–443.

Simpson, S. G., & DePaulo, J. R. (1998). Genetics. In P. J. Goodnick (Ed.), *Mania: Clinical and research perspectives* (pp. 81–100). Washington, DC: American Psychiatric Press.

Soares, J. C., & Mallinger, A. G. (1997). Intracellular phosphatidylinositol pathway abnormalities in bipolar disorder patients. *Psychopharmacology Bulletin, 33*, 685–691.

Spoont, M. (1992). Modulatory role of serotonin in neural information processing: Implications for human psychopathology. *Psychological Bulletin, 112*, 330–350.

Suhara, T., Nakayama, K., Inoue, O., Fukuda, H., Shimizu, M., Mori, A., & Tateno, Y. (1992). D1 dopamine receptor binding in mood disorders measured by positron emission tomography. *Psychopharmacology, 106*, 14–18.

Sutton, S. K., & Davidson, R. J. (1997). Prefrontal brain asymmetry: A biological substrate of the behavioral approach and inhibition systems. *Psychological Science, 8*, 204–210.

Swerdlow, N. R., & Koob, G. F. (1987). Dopamine, schizophrenia, mania, and depression: Toward a unified hypothesis of cortico-striato-pallido-thalamic function. *Behavioral & Brain Sciences, 10*, 197–245.

Vehmanen, L., Kaprio, J., & Loennqvist, J. (1995). Twin studies of bipolar disorder. *Psychiatria Fennica, 26*, 107–116.

Wang, H. Y., Markowitz, P., Levinson, D., Undie, A. S., & Friedman, E. (1999). Increased membrane-associated protein kinase C activity and translocation in blood platelets from bipolar affective disorder patients. *Journal of Psychiatric Research, 33*, 171–179.

Watson, D., & Tellegen, A. (1985). Toward a consensual structure of mood. *Psychological Bulletin, 98*, 219–235.

Wehr, T. A. (1991). Effects of wakefulness and sleep on depression and mania. In J. Monplaisir & R. Godbout (Eds.), *Sleep and biological rhythms* (pp. 42–86). London: Oxford University Press.

Wehr, T. A., Sack, D. A., & Rosenthal, N. E. (1987). Sleep reduction as a final common pathway in the genesis of mania. *American Journal of Psychiatry, 144*, 201–204.

Wehr, T. A., Turner, E. H., Shimada, J. M., Lowe, C. H., Barker, C., & Leibenluft, E. (1998). Treatment of a rapidly cycling bipolar patient by using extended bed rest and darkness to stabilize the timing and duration of sleep. *Biological Psychiatry, 43*, 822–828.

Weiner, I. (1990). Neural substrates of latent inhibition: The switching model. *Psychological Bulletin, 108*, 442–461.

Weiner, I., & Feldon, J. (1997). The switching model of latent inhibition: An update of neural substrates. *Behavioural Brain Research, 88*, 11–25.

Weingartner, H., Miller, H., & Murphy, D. L. (1977). Mood-state-dependent retrieval of verbal associations. *Journal of Abnormal Psychology, 86*, 276–284.

Winett, C., Johnson, S. L., & Miller, I. (1996, September). *Life events, social support and recovery in bipolar disorder*. Poster presentation at the 11th annual meeting of the Society for Research on Psychopathology, Atlanta.

Winters, R., Scott, W., & Beevers, C. (2000). Affective distress as a central and organizing symptom in depression: Neurobiological mechanisms. In S. L. Johnson, A. M. Hayes, T. Field, N. Schneiderman, & P. McCabe, (Eds.), *Stress, coping, and depression* (pp. 117–219). Mahwah, NJ: Lawrence Erlbaum Associates.

Wirz-Justice, A., Quinto, C., Cajochen, C., Werth, E., & Hock, C. (1999). A rapid-cycling bipolar patient treated with long nights, bedrest, and light. *Biological Psychiatry, 45,* 1075–1077.

Wu, J. C., & Bunney, W. E. (1990). The biological basis of an antidepressant response to sleep deprivation and relapse: Review and hypothesis. *American Journal of Psychiatry, 147,* 14–21.

Zinbarg, R. E., & Mohlman, J. (1998). Individual differences in the acquisition of affectively valenced associations. *Journal of Personality & Social Psychology, 74,* 1024–1040.

Author Index

Subject Index